Country of Exiles

ALSO BY WILLIAM LEACH

*Land of Desire: Merchants, Power, and the Rise
of a New American Culture*

*True Love and Perfect Union: The Feminist Reform
of Sex and Society*

Country of Exiles

THE

DESTRUCTION

OF

PLACE

IN

AMERICAN

LIFE

William Leach

PANTHEON BOOKS   NEW YORK

Library of Congress Cataloging-in-Publication Data
Leach, William, 1944—
    Country of exiles : the destruction of place in American life / William Leach.
        p.   cm.
    Includes index.
    ISBN 0-679-44219-7
    1. United States—Civilization—1970– 2. United States—Social conditions—1980– 3. United States—Economic conditions—1981– 4. National characteristics, American. 5. Place (Philosophy)
I. Title.
E169.12.L39   1999
973.92—dc21   98-29599
                                                                     CIP

Random House Web Address: www.randomhouse.com

Book design by Fritz Metsch

Printed in the United States of America

First Edition

9 8 7 6 5 4 3 2 1

In Memory of Christopher Lasch

Who and what were these strangers who, it seemed, did not know the meaning of rest and respite, knew neither measure nor limits? . . . What was the restlessness which continually drove them on, like some curse, to new works and enterprises of which no one could see the end?

—IVO ANDRIC,
The Bridge over the Drina

Contents

Preface

Years ago I told an historian friend of mine that I thought historians had an obligation to write about the present, especially when that present seemed to mark a radical departure from the past. Given their knowledge of the past, who would understand better what was going on in the present? Well, I took my own naive advice and realized very quickly how far more attractive—and safer—it was to dwell on the past, rather than on the present. This book has been the hardest one I have ever written. I wrote it out of a need that could not be suppressed. It is a testimony to what I think has happened to America in the past twenty years.

Acknowledgments

Many people in business, university, and government have helped me with this study, including, in no particular order, Jim Pinkelman, Christopher Jocks, Christopher Arellano, Bill Withuhn, Bruce Lambert, Mark Prisloe, Mary Young, Henry Moon, Donald Lotz, Dimitri Rallis, David Melmar, Terry Kranz, Craig Lundsdorf, Elaine Quiver, John Mohawk, Ed Lee, Scott E. Bennett, Robert Arnold, Michael Tubridy, Steven Staiger, Charles Elias, Mark Juergensmeyer, Joshua Freeman, David Noble, Paul Donnelly, Margo Anderson, Myron Weiner, Robert Bonnette, Daniel Stein, Larry Weiers, Barry Bluestone, and Paul F. Richardson. I thank Jameson Doig and Gerhardt Muller for reading chapter 1 on highways and gateways; both scholars protected me from many errors of fact and interpretation. Mary Furner, Ann Fabian, Charles Blackmar, Nell Lasch, Peter Dimock, and Peter Agree looked at the entire manuscript, bringing to bear on it much skill and wisdom and saving me from much embarrassment, for which I thank them. I owe thanks to Georges Borchardt, Jeannette Hopkins, Ed Cohen, and Grace McVeigh.

Not all the people above agreed with what I say in this book, but I appreciated their help nonetheless.

My editor, Dan Frank, has just the right blend of patience and brains; he deserves my thanks and my respect. And once again, I am grateful to Elizabeth Blackmar, who suffered constant rewrites, all the while telling me that this book justified the trouble: without her, it would not have been written.

Country of Exiles

Introduction:
Veblen in Silicon Valley

In 1920 Thorstein Veblen, America's most acerbic economist, traveled across the United States, from Manhattan to northern California, and returned to a spot that meant a great deal to him—an isolated cabin on a ridge in a mountain range, bordered by the town of Pescadero and the Pacific Ocean on the west and the Santa Clara Valley on the east. The place was not too far from Stanford University, where Veblen had taught just before World War I. He had built the cabin himself, out of wood left from an old chicken coop owned by the family of Leland Stanford. He had carried it up the mountain in a horse-drawn wagon, along the muddiest of winding routes shrouded in fog.

In the few years he taught at Stanford, Veblen often took refuge in this hideaway. He recovered there (according to a friend, R. L. Duffus, in a later reminiscence of Veblen) a bond with the earth and even with the Norwegian-immigrant village in Minnesota where he moved as a boy with his family, after living in Wisconsin.[1] If the cabin existed today it would be entangled in the progeny of Silicon Valley, with its colossal homes and nearly 200,000 software millionaires, most enriched by the stock market boom on Wall Street. The university, too, has been surrounded by such suburbs as Atherton and Los Altos Hills, where billionaire venture capitalists have erected their gated palaces, their private golf courses, and their own airports, a denouement that even Veblen, champion of engineers but nemesis of bankers, might have found Veblenian.[2]

In Veblen's day the whole region was mostly rural. His cabin stood on a crest that had, according to Duffus, "an untamed quality," "a survival of something that hadn't surrendered to the presence of men."[3] Framed by second-growth redwoods, it was high enough up for Veblen to see a vista of rolling forested hills as well as the emerald-blue Pacific itself; Veblen so loved this dwelling that he acquired legal possession of it and of the land on which it stood. But when he visited from Manhattan in 1920, he learned that a careless real estate agent had sold the cabin as part of a larger sale of the adjacent property. This knowledge, which later proved mistaken (the property had in fact been *saved* from sale by one of his friends), infuriated Veblen. To him the sale stood for much that was wrong in American society and, above all, in American business enterprise. Veblen despised how many businessmen seemed bent on transforming everything, and land above all, into vendible commodities, how they tended to measure everything from labor to art by its market value, and how they pushed even the most rooted thing into a floating state so that it might be recirculated.

In a rage, Veblen picked up a hatchet and hacked at the shack, smashing every window and terrifying the companions who had made the trip with him. A friend later remarked that he went "at the matter with a dull intensity that was like madness, the intensity of a physically lazy person roused to sudden activity. If there was dispute over ownership, he wanted to make sure that the place would be uninhabitable." He had made the original cabin with his own hands. "He belonged there," Duffus recalled. "He belonged on that mountain. . . . I am not sure he ever belonged in any city."[4]

Veblen nailed a sign to the battered cabin, saying "this property belongs to Thorstein Veblen," then drove back down the mountain with his friends in a strained silence, until one friend had the courage to ask him what the title of his next book might be. "Absentee Ownership," Veblen responded. (The book took three years to write and would memorialize his act of destruction.) By absentee owners, he meant those real estate brokers, investment bankers, and transnational industrialists who owned property at a distance but never worked it, never were "on the ground" (as he put it) to tend it, except as a source of revenue; these men hired others to manage their properties while they did business elsewhere, always alert to new opportunities. Veblen also meant by absentee owners "the American people," whom, by the 1920s, he thought, longed to be "absentee owners" themselves, getting "something for nothing." Finally, Veblen meant himself, for he too owned property at a distance and—what may have galled him most—had failed to protect it. He had hoped that by some kind of magic it would have been saved so that he might someday live there. Veblen had been absent, living clear across the country, in New York City, so far from a place he wanted to keep that he had let it slip away (or so he thought).[5]

This story shows how much Veblen, an exile or outsider practically all his life, experienced the significance of place, how much he wanted to claim a place as his own. Duffus remembered how stirred Veblen became when he spoke of Norway, how "lands [there] had been in the same peasant family for a thousand years." At the end of the twentieth century many

Americans feel this same longing, this same need for continuity and stability, and for confident attachment to a place to be from.

But many Americans also feel something of the same rage that overtook Veblen, as well as his longing for place. Like him, they feel betrayed. Like him, they can imagine the ground slipping away. They can fantasize forces and institutions acting ceaselessly, indifferent to their welfare, hammering stability into instability, the fixed into the flexible, the rooted into the rootless.

In the last two decades, we have returned to a world that Veblen might have recognized but on a scale, perhaps, that he could not have imagined. The place-indifferent bankers and money managers, whom Veblen feared, have asserted themselves on a global canvas. So, too, a system of transportation has appeared, featuring a dizzying profusion of highways, gateways, and vehicles—all helping to create a worldwide economic interdependence while challenging the integrity of local places. A vast landscape of the temporary has arisen, peopled with thousands of floating executives and countless numbers of part-time and temporary workers, all unable or unwilling to make long-term connections to their communities. A service economy, whose key industries are tourism and gambling, has grown up to threaten the settled character of towns, cities, and regions. A system of great research universities also belongs to this universe, fostering transnational mobility and a disposition to think and live beyond America.

This book, which I offer more as an informed reflection than as a scholarly history, examines the impact of these changes on the American sense of place. It deals with the weakening of place as a centering presence in the lives of ordinary people. It is animated by the premise that the well-being of most Americans rests on a healthy connectedness to place, and that a wearing away of such a relationship is dangerous.

I do not equate place with community because in recent years community has come to mean practically any group of people joined together by almost any shared characteristic (corporate, academic, racial, ethnic, sexual, and so forth). Community has been transformed into a transparent condition, barely related to concrete geographical places with histories. I also want to distinguish my approach to place from the one espoused by such nature writers as poet Gary Snyder. Snyder considers land or nature as critical to the meaning of place, at the cost of disregarding culture, history, and tradition, or the country as a part of any notion of place. Land and nature are very important, but Snyder writes of the "non-nationalistic idea of community, in which commitment to pure place is paramount" and in which no one can be excluded. There is, I believe, no such thing as a "pure place," and someone, at one time or another, is always excluded.[6] Finally, I do not think of place as property because the transformation of land into property has done as much to destroy a sense of place as to empower and engage it.

Place, of course, may contain or signify all these things—community, nature, property—in some measure, but its meaning is bound to a geographical reality both historical and profoundly lasting. I mean by place in part what landscape writer J. B. Jackson has said of it. Place "is something we ourselves create in the course of time"; it involves the "same timetable" we all share, "the same work hours, the same religious observances, the same habits and customs."[7] At its best, it is the collective outgrowth of our control over our own lives and destinies.

Place has a layered quality for those people who feel it. For most it has taken the form of the country, of the provincial or regional areas of the country (and these provincial areas can exist in cities as well as in rural towns), and of specific home-towns and neighborhoods, each with its own history, its own store of common memories and traditions, its smells and sounds that never wholly disappear from memory. All of these, too, at their best, have been joined together by a common tissue, providing people with a manifold sense of connection and achievement.

Today this tissue is stretched and torn. Although we have extended life chronologically through medical invention and intervention, we have also impoverished the cultural-psychic richness of the world around us. We live longer but emptier, without those nurturing habitats or places which remind us where we came from and, therefore, who we are. Despite the aging of the population and rising levels of debt (both of which should have the effect of slowing people down or making them think twice about "getting out" or "moving on"), many people seem more at sea than they have ever been.

In many ways, of course, this is an old story. From the late colonial period on, Americans have been advocates and captives of the need to move, to get out of town, to end up far from the spot where they began. At the same time, a contending pattern was taking shape, one that encouraged Americans to settle down, domesticate themselves, and forge a coherent identity. The first pattern we might call centrifugal, because it thrust outward and cared little for boundaries and centers; the second we might call centripetal, because it favored centers and boundaries and cultivated a sense of place. Until recent times, the two patterns have worked together, reaching some kind of equilibrium or tension, to create America. After the 1970s, however, this balancing act—itself not always just or fair—has been put in jeopardy, with the centrifugal trend taking over and spilling into every area of life.

SPECTRE OF PLACELESSNESS

From the 1790s on, indifference to place has been a hallmark of American life. "An American changes his residence ceaselessly," Alexis de Tocqueville wrote in 1835. Twenty years later, Nathaniel Hawthorne observed that "no people on earth have such vagabond habits as ours."[8] Whole populations swarmed across the continent, enticed by fantasies of paradise; by hopes of freedom and individual liberation; by great reserves of mostly unoccupied public lands; by government policies (subsidies to railroads, homestead laws, eviction of Indians from their homelands) that made it easy for people to move; by the treatment of land as property to sell and speculate on rather than as community to live in; and, most of all, by prospects of unlimited wealth.

In the 1840s and fifties these goads and pressures caused the biggest internal migration of people up to that time in American history. Some pioneering men from the Old South, impelled by an ebullient demand for cotton, migrated with their slaves (numbering in the hundreds of thousands) as far west as the Texas plain and Arkansas; together, slave and master, one coerced, the other willing, settled a wilderness that bears their imprints to this day.[9] Other migrants traveled in family groups much further west, but often only the men left; at the end of the 1840s, men (again, in the hundreds of thousands, some, too, with their slaves) took part in the great California Gold Rush, journeying by land on foot or in wagons, and by sea in ships as far down as Panama, then up again along the Pacific Coast to the foothills of the Sierras, east of San Francisco, not very far from what would become Silicon Valley.[10] Nothing better than this search for gold expressed the febrile spirit of American life at midcentury, making men rich, but in the process, separating them from their wives, families, and friends, and frequently crippling the communities they left behind.[11]

Such was the American way. Unlike most Europeans, who rarely moved far from where they were born (unless, of course, they were forced by economic change to migrate to cities or to emigrate, a pattern I will discuss below), Americans often decided to migrate whenever prospects elsewhere looked brighter. The very size of the country, of course, with its untapped resources, dictated much of this mobility. But after 1850, as the country grew more urbanized and seemed to invite more settlement, Americans still displayed the same propensity to move, to get out.[12]

At the same time, moreover, that people were going from place to place *within* the United States in the 1840s and fifties, they were also moving *into* it in unprecedented numbers, looking for work and land. Dislocated by economic turmoil and political chaos, nearly 2.75 million Irish and Germans sailed to America between 1845 and 1855, usually on rickety packet ships under savage conditions. It was the greatest single wave of newcomers relative to the size of the population in American history.[13]

After 1885, this migratory stream swelled as the country moved out of a phase of settling and pioneering into an era of unshackled industrial growth. Immigration achieved record levels, accelerated by the invention of safer high-powered steamships, by the absence or removal of any significant legal or political restrictions (aside from Chinese exclusion) and by the demands of the American economy.[14] By 1900 mass migration concentrated largely in the cities of the northeast, causing "a geographic displacement of native northeastern workers to the west."[15] At the same time, immigration touched not only the cities but towns and villages everywhere. By 1920, North Dakota had a greater proportion of immigrants in its population than New York did, Minnesota more than New Jersey, and Utah more than Pennsylvania.[16] This influx brought a great variety of peoples, at once enriching and threatening the existing culture. For millions of native-born Americans with "roots in farms and small towns," it aroused by 1910 what historian John Higham called "a mounting sense of danger—even dispossession."[17]

But it was not immigration that decentered America so much as American industrial and financial capitalism, which formed the critical impetus behind this migratory flow. By the turn of the century, American industry was immersed in a global capitalist system even more interrelated than it is today. Despite the bias toward protectionism that marked the economies of most developed nations, minimal controls existed over international financial business and capital flows. Information, too, traveled easily from country to country. Only two countries—Russia and Turkey—required passports.[18]

In this open climate, American manufacturers championed immigration because competitive success depended upon a reliable, flexible pool of cheap labor to tend the new continuously operating factory machines, to dig the new tunnels, and to erect the new skyscrapers.[19] At the turn of the century, industry had such a pool, which contained both immigrants and native-born Americans, most largely unorganized and unprotected. And despite an upsurge in craft union strength between 1898 and 1905, which by the 1910s had succeeded in getting the eight-hour day for many workers, labor unions had to contend with business's top-down imposition of manage-

ment controls and scientific efficiency, with its rigid clock-
driven work patterns. Such changes much diminished the
power of labor to shape the production process.[20] From the
1870s to World War I, moreover, federal and state troops were
regularly called up to crush labor dissidence.[21] Factories or
farms employed (and exploited) large numbers of women and
children; casual work, the kind of work we now call temporary and which was least able to foster stability and settlement,
was pervasive and typical.

The new economy, however, relied on more than labor
pools. It also produced a class of global capitalists who spent
years outside the United States in quest of fortune. Among
them was Herbert Hoover. Before he entered government service and was elected president (in 1928), Hoover had been
abroad longer than any other man to hold that office before or
since. For nearly twenty-five years, after his graduation from
Stanford University with a degree in engineering, he was out
of the country, one of thousands of nomadic American mining engineers whose expertise was sought after by businesses
and governments.[22] Hoover managed a coal mine in China, a
copper mine in Burma, a gold mine in Siberia, and a zinc mine
in Australia. In Australia he set up the Zinc Corporation, one
of the world's first multinationals. He then worked for sixteen
years in London as a financier, underwriting stock flotations
and assisting other wealthy businessmen in the creation of
giant corporations.[23]

Industrial capitalism at the turn of the century yielded one
more significant centrifugal outcome: it laid the foundation for
what Americans would come to know as "mass consumer
society." This society promised to give all people (not just the
select few) material well-being and luxury; it gave birth, after
1880, to all those institutions we have come to associate with
mass consumption—department stores, chain stores, mail-

order houses, and a flood of available credit.[24] But American business did more than strive to inspire a desire for goods and to create a new institutional landscape to sustain it; it also changed the way Americans looked at and understood place. Consumer capitalism, in other words, was not just shopping. Intrinsic to it was the cult of the new, the need to overturn the past and begin again, and to disregard all kinds of attachments in the interest of getting the "new and improved," whether goods, jobs, entertainment, or places.

A cardinal feature was the desire to improvise or simulate place, to make up or invent places that people had only dreamed of but never thought possible to inhabit. This desire was shared by many Americans who had left the past behind and were therefore free to imagine any place they wished, to mix medieval with modern, Paris fashion with the Taj Mahal. Only Americans displayed such a high degree of passion for themed theatrical environments—in amusement parks, on the theatrical stage, in movie palaces and on the screen, and even in department stores around the country after 1895—that invoked anywhere while at the same time being unimpressed by real places. No attitude was more subversive to taking seriously a sense of place, or the world people actually lived and died in.

Many people at the time worried about the makeshift comings and goings of Americans, prominent among them the Harvard philosopher Josiah Royce. Like Veblen, Royce led a transient life. He ended up in a place (Massachusetts) far away from where he was born (California). His own parents had been "pioneers of 1849," stricken by the gold fever, daring to traverse the Sierras.[25] He wrote many books, including a history of California; whereas most historians of the day remembered the gold rush as an heroic episode, Royce condemned it for its "semi-barbarism."[26] In 1902, while at Harvard, he observed the many "sojourners and newcomers" in America, not only those from other countries but the many from within the country, on the move, traveling from one place to another, never in one community long enough to acquire a love for it. "Such classes," he wrote, "even in modern New England, are too large. The stranger, the sojourner, the newcomer, is an inevitable factor in the life of most American communities."[27] Royce was pained to confess his own newcomer status to his lecture audiences: "I myself, as a native of California, now resident of New England, belong to such a class."[28] He lamented the ease with which many people ended relations with their hometowns and their country, even with their families, as they struggled to pursue or protect their own personal interests.[29] "We as a nation," he wrote in 1908, "have been forgetting loyalty."[30] All kinds of commitments "have lost their meaning for many people, simply because people have confounded loyalty with mere bondage to tradition, or with mere surrender of individual rights and preferences."[31] In America today, "nobody is at home."[32]

COUNTERVAILING TRENDS

There is another side to this history, a countervailing side that offset the nearly anarchical trend of the country's economy and culture. Even as the nation seemed to spin about, it was also crystalizing as an historical entity, with clear geographical boundaries and a powerful sense of national identity. The very thing that tended to weaken local communities also helped to strengthen the national identity, as people abandoned their older neighborhoods or regions, mixing with other newcomers in new places, ignoring or forgetting the differences among them. Royce also observed this pattern in California, where

"Americans from the North and South" mingled and "came to understand one another as Americans."[33] At the same time, the courage that often inspired people to move also led them to stay put and build new cities and communities, as well as a nation.

This countervailing side of place-making has not gotten its historical due, although some historians have begun to pay more attention to those who "stayed behind" and "put down roots" than to those who "moved on."[34] From the mid-1800s on, just as the country seemed in constant turmoil, there were those who refused to migrate. One of these was Henry Thoreau, who, after years of living in Concord, Massachusetts, made this 1858 entry in his journal: "Think," he observed,

of the consummate folly of attempting to go away from *here!* When the constant endeavor should be to get nearer and nearer *here.* Here are all the friends I ever had or shall have, and as friendly as ever. . . . How many things can you go away from? They see the comet from the northwest coast just as plainly as we do, and the same stars through its tail. . . . *Here,* of course, is all that you love, all that you expect, all that you are. . . . What more do you want? Bear it away then! Foolish people imagine that what they imagine is somewhere else.[35]

Another countervailing feature of this earlier time was the tremendous sense of *Americanness* felt by many people, by those who remained behind as well as by those who sweated their way to California and Oregon, or, later on, migrated to the teeming cities in the East and Midwest. This sense of Americanness distinguished all those who had fled the Old World to build a new one, on their own, practically from scratch (the Indians notwithstanding, and African slaves always the tragic exceptions, although blacks, when emancipation came, often freely embraced an American identity). Americans did not simply inherit the world they lived in but created it themselves and often under great duress. It was this sense of making something new, and of *choosing* to do so as free individuals "without bootlicking," that bound diverse—and often very mobile—individuals together into a people.[36] It was this sense, too, that greatly mollified or checked what divided them (and I mean here religious, ethnic, and class differences), and that laid the bulwark for a lasting patriotism, a patriotism that often surprised (and annoyed) foreigners when they encountered it. "The American," wrote Tocqueville, "taking part in everything that is done in his country, feels a duty to defend anything criticized there, for it is not only his country that is being attacked, but himself. . . . Nothing is more annoying in the ordinary intercourse of life than this irritable patriotism of Americans."[37]

American patriotism was often distorted by nationalist fervor, which twisted pride into aggression; and it could be (and was) repeatedly exploited or degraded to serve the interests of selfish business groups or imperialist, sanctimonious politicians.[38] But it was nevertheless real and deep (even if it did not always take the healthy or benign regional form Royce described) and it would be rekindled again and again over the years—after the Civil War, later in the twentieth century during the world wars, and also in the midst of the Great Depression. It gave life to a powerful single narrative that, however much it might have obscured and even denied underlying inequities, held the country together.

This tremendous sense of American identity brought with it an experience of the country as a civic entity, as a commonweal, as one whole *public* (as opposed to private) realm with historic boundaries that called for stewardship and protection.

It was in the interest of this public realm that the government created after 1890 the national forests and park reserves, withholding well over 100 million acres of land from private circulation (no other country had dared to carry reform that far). These reserves were set aside primarily to ensure the supply of water and wood, but many Americans also agreed with George Perkins Marsh, pioneer preservationist, that "the wise use of nature's bounty [provides] man with permanent, fixed values in a changing world." "It is time," Marsh said in his landmark book, *Man and Nature,* "for some abatement in the restless love of change which characterizes us, and makes us almost a nomad rather than sedentary people."[39]

Public well-being was served by the passage of the childlabor laws and by the anti-trust laws (however little they did finally to prevent oligopoly). It was also served—if with much harshness—in the treatment of the Indians at the end of the century, a treatment that did not tolerate any measure of tribal autonomy and that attempted to *force* assimilation.[40] A broader public interest also lay behind immigration policy, which demanded assimilation, and when that seemed to fail, outright restriction in the 1920s. To the sadness and fury of many, this restriction cut off the vast stream of migrants from Europe but it fostered assimilation by "depriving the ethnic minorities of constant, large-scale reinforcements."[41]

In all these ways, from the creation of forest reserves to immigration restriction, the federal government imposed limits, defining the public realm, even as the public realm appeared to many to be unraveling.

By 1965 more Americans felt like Americans, not as German-Americans or Italian-Americans or American Indian, than ever before in our history. Even racial discrimination and hierarchy, despite all the bitterness caused by them, seemed beatable as an obstacle to the making of a convincing, widely shared American identity. As a result of constant intermixings of ethnic groups, probably a majority of whites (as well as a majority of blacks, though for partly tragic reasons) had no knowledge of their non-American ancestors. Nor did they give a damn. The pain suffered for so many years over religiously and ethnically mixed marriages seemed, for most people, a thing of the past. Some Americans were a jumble of as many as twelve or more groups, so who could know, in any case, exactly "where they came from."[42]

"For every Greek or Hungarian," wrote journalist Peter Schrag, Jewish emigré from Vienna, in 1969, "there are a dozen American-Americans who are past ethnic consciousness."[43] Traveling around the country in the early sixties, novelist John Steinbeck learned that "for all our interwoven breeds drawn from every part of the world, we are a nation, a new breed. . . . It is a fact that Americans from all sections and of all racial extractions are more alike than the Welsh are like the English. . . . The American identity is an exact and provable thing."[44] Such a state of things did not mean that all Americans had become alike (many differences would remain, often far deeper and more divisive than any shaped by ethnicity or race). What it did mean was that Americans had discovered themselves in a common past. This situation, in its own right an extraordinary historical achievement, was so much the case by 1970 that, according to historian Arthur Mann, most white college students had so lost the idea of "ethnicity" as to "have a hard time getting hold of the concept." "The melting pot did happen."[45] Black or white, most people saw themselves as coming not from some foreign land but from the states, cities, and regions within the country.[46]

Other matters as well engendered a greater sense of place. Between 1930 and 1970, partly as a result of immigration restrictions, the labor movement achieved some of its greatest successes, the standard of living rose for all Americans, and disparities of wealth and wages were greatly diminished.[47] Workers, both skilled and unskilled, were protected and able to settle down without fear.[48] Furthermore, the exploitation of children and adolescents for the most part declined, as millions of them were taken out of the labor market and sent to school. Many American women—above all, white American women—stayed at home to rear their children. Without question, many of these women—isolated, often lonely, shut out from wider experience, or simply ill equipped to bring up children—suffered under these conditions; the culture was wrong to have imposed on them burdens they were unable to bear. Others, however, from the 1920s into the late 1960s, remained as anchors of their communities, continuous and stable presences in the lives of their families and neighborhoods.

Perhaps the most significant aspect, finally, of this countervailing pattern was the existence of groups of men and women who had a strong sense of place. These people heard the message of "go out and get yours" but did what they could to stay put. At one end of this scale were many corporate managers who, even after World War II, showed loyalty to their workers and their communities, managers whose very identities were bound to the places where they prospered.[49] At the other end of the scale were the many inward-looking religious communities, such as the Amish or Mennonites in Pennsylvania, Iowa, and Illinois, who epitomized ties to place. Indian tribes also belonged to this group; even in the face of countless efforts to terminate their cultures, many tribes stood the test of time, holding fast to their traditions to become faithful custodians of the land.[50]

In the middle of these two extremes of community-oriented corporation and local tribe stood the largest of these place-oriented groups: the working-class men and women of

America's cities and towns. Among them were evangelical Protestants, black and white, as well as working-class and lower-middle-class Catholics who organized their lives not around "the culture of capitalism" or the "culture of acquisitiveness and personal gain" but around their churches and religious beliefs, their families, their schools and holiday fairs, their sports teams and scout groups, as well as their television sets and movie houses.[51]

It would be foolish, of course, to try to make this age look any better than it was or to idealize these working people. Many were beleaguered by debt, by conflicts over money, by unpredictable, awful episodes of unemployment, and by a commercial dream-life over which they had little control, except to turn their backs on it. Discrimination existed, bias of all kinds existed, often so grating as to force people to leave their hometowns, as many Southern blacks did for much of this century, going North or elsewhere for more freedom and decent work. Consumerism, or that truly American prejudice of constant production and spending, and constant improvisation, had assuredly taken its toll in shaping the way Americans organized their time or spent their money. At the same time, many people, however much they may have behaved according to established patterns of consumption or shared some of the age's prejudices, lived decently, paid their taxes, took care of each other and their children, and stayed, for the most part, where they were, sometimes protecting their communities and forging bonds of faith and trust.

A NEW DAY FOR DRIFTERS

Today, this achievement—the centripetal pull that always seemed to check the centrifugal side of the American experience—no longer has the strength it once had. As early as the late sixties, in fact, many Americans worried over the corrosion of the social fabric and the emergence of disconnectedness as characteristic of American society. Peter Schrag, in his *Out of Place in America,* observed in 1970 that Americans were living in a society where the "bulldozers of modernization invade the neighborhood like tanks." "We are refugees in our own country," he said.[52] In 1972, two writers—Vance Packard, the noted free-lance journalist, and George W. Pierson, historian at Yale University—both published books on mobility as the most pronounced feature of American society. Pierson, in *The Moving American,* observed that "ours has been the mobile society par excellence. . . . We don't seem anchored to place. Our families are scattered about. . . . No locality need claim us long."[53] Packard's *A Nation of Strangers* described the "loneliness" that marked a society constantly on the move, a theme also picked up by Ralph Keyes in *We the Lonely People* (1973) and Suzanne Gordon in *Lonely in America* (1975). Sociologist Peter Berger wrote in his 1973 book *The Homeless Mind* that "American society represents a climax to the movement toward mobility." "A high proportion of people in America," he said, "plan their lives against the geographical backdrop of a continent." At the same time, Berger thought that this very freedom had caused what he called "a deepening condition of homelessness."[54]

The irony, of course, was that the 1970s was the decade in which mobility rates had decisively *dropped,* not risen; yet Americans nevertheless felt increasingly decentered. Mobility in and of itself, in other words, was no measure of feelings of placelessness. One could feel centered—feel at home in the world—and yet still move, still travel great distances, still leave home and never come back.[55] What these books were telling us was not that mobility was inherently bad but that the conditions behind it—such as the weakening of the family, misguided wars, political scandal (to name a few mentioned in these books)—were eroding an older, more optimistic sense of place. And they were pointing to trends that would only worsen, when the migratory behavior of Americans actually did begin to contribute to the transformation of the country.

After 1980 the centrifugal side of American life began to return in earnest. As never before, Americans—especially educated professionals whose services commanded a national market—were free to go wherever they wished in the country, a freedom promoted by employers who enticed them with job offers; by biological technologies to manage their fertility; by such governmental programs as social security and federal housing loans, both portable (not place-specific) and thereby helping to give people the confidence to move; by family-care providers (i.e., nannies and servants); by no-fault divorce laws, allowing couples to cancel their marriages without placing blame on one another; by telephones and computers which seemed to overcome distance; and even by the growth of police forces to pick up the burden of "protecting" communities left behind or ignored by residents too busy to care.[56] Not all of these factors were commensurable, nor did they always invite mobility, but their cumulative effect was to discredit anything that might inhibit movement. In any case, whatever the cause, internal migration rose again, reaching post–World War II levels when 20 percent of the people were in motion.[57]

Mass immigration after 1970 also approximated turn-of-the-century levels, as a result of a 1965 law that ended all quotas, and of a 1990 law, backed by a coalition of business groups, liberals, and ethnic lobbyists, that greatly raised the numerical cap for all immigrants and created a new gallery of visa categories to meet the demands of business. When the original 1965 law passed, no one anticipated the volume of immigration that ensued, but in time it was "revolutionary," to quote historian Louis Winnick, averaging well over one million people a year and in some states surpassing the record levels set in the 1910s.[58]

This immigration also differed from the old, and not only because migrants were arriving from parts of the world unfamiliar to most Americans. It differed because of the *context* in which people came. The America of the post-1975 era was not the America of the nineteenth century, when an industrializing country employed migrants in factories and mines and when much of the continent was still unoccupied. Post-1970s America was a developed country with a population of more than 250 million people, most with skills equal (or potentially equal) to the demands of the economy.[59]

The modern context differed in yet another way: it tended to assist immigrants in a multitude of ways. In the past, immigrants confronted many obstacles, from aching loneliness and despair to sickness and extreme poverty (which they often had to face alone). After 1970, however, newcomers entered a world that offered many advantages—a system of government-transfer payments, entrenched ethnic lobbies and pro-immigrant groups (from the Ford Foundation to a countrywide army of immigration lawyers), a transportation system that made it easy for many to come and go (thus reducing the "trauma" that once afflicted nearly all earlier migrants), affirmative action, an array of schools, colleges, and universities that welcomed them, and so forth— which previous immigrant generations never enjoyed.[60]

From one point of view, this flow of people into the country has had a positive impact. As they had in the past, many immigrants brought with them an aversion to moral corruption, a passion for their new country, and energy and inventiveness. Sanford Ungar, dean of communications at American University, observes in his book *Fresh Blood* that "immigrants bring us new foods and original ways to look at

old problems." "They are the valedictorians of today," writes
Ungar, "the concert pianists and rocket scientists of tomorrow." They have restored life to old neighborhoods abandoned
by earlier migrants; without them, cities such as New York and
Los Angeles would have continued their decline.[61]

From another angle, however, the new arrivals have had
an equally centrifugal impact. Many spoke languages and
practiced religions (Hinduism, Islam, Buddhism) unknown to
most Americans. More than 70 percent of all Asians and more
than 45 percent of all Hispanics who now reside in the United
States arrived here after 1970, with the vast majority coming after the late 1970s. Almost overnight they transformed
neighborhoods into foreign enclaves, set off from the rest of
America.[62] They helped disrupt shared cultural memory, undermining community unity and adding to pressures that have
induced millions of native-born Americans, white and black,
to leave cities for the suburbs and small towns.[63] Their existence, moreover, contributed to the income and wealth gaps
in this country by, above all, helping to keep down the wages
of both skilled and unskilled workers.[64]

The presence of so many new migrants also tended to aggra-
vate racial-ethnic tensions, especially at a time when so many
Americans actually opposed assimilation, supported group differences, and were tolerant of dual citizenship (which many
migrants themselves have demanded).[65] In 1904 Abraham
Cahan, editor of the Jewish *Forward* on New York's Lower East
Side, exhorted his immigrant readers "to be Americans," not
foreigners. "We shall love America and help to build America,"
Cahan insisted. "We shall accomplish in the New World a hundred times more than we could in the Old."[66] In 1996, Bill
Clinton, on a visit to Ireland, spoke glowingly of "my people,"
by which he meant the Irish, not the Americans—a measure of
how far we have come. Two years later, the editors of the *New*

York Times celebrated in New York City a "new phenomenon"—the emergence of a "transnational immigrant culture," which helps "many people maintain lifelong relationships with their ancestral lands."[67]

Migration, then, both internal and from abroad, returned in force after 1980, but I want to make clear that it was *not* the decisive fact that has helped make the country more decentered. The migrants themselves, in other words, were "not to blame."[68] Population movements should not be seen as governing causes but as *related* to other more fundamental changes that have occurred since the late 1970s. These changes constitute the central subjects of this book—the return of the global economy with its cohort of transnational businessmen and businesswomen; the spread of a landscape of the temporary populated by skilled and unskilled people alike, willing or compelled to go anywhere to find work; and the expansion of a service economy (above all of tourism and gambling) that has replaced manufacturing as the primary employer of unskilled workers.

To get a sense, moreover, of what has been happening to America over the past fifteen years, one need only look at some unlikely places in the country, which have only recently evolved into major centers of historical change.

I am thinking here of three centers in particular—marine port terminals, research universities, and Indian reservations. Since 1970 the great port terminals on either coast, from the Port of Long Beach/Los Angeles in California to the Port of Elizabeth/Newark in New Jersey, have become sprawling gateways of international trade, each enormous, nearly autonomous, and crucial to the movement of a vast diversity of cargo. Research universities, too, from Stanford to MIT, have grown bigger. Today they approach city-states in scope, with billion-dollar budgets, close ties with transnational businesses, and even their own foreign policies. Most surprising of all have been many Indian reservations, enriched by the boom in casino gambling. From the Viejas in California to the Pequots in Connecticut, these tribes have acquired nearly sovereign power, each able to change, irrevocably, the character of their surrounding neighborhoods.

Such ports, universities, and reservations have much in common and, perhaps, few analogues in America. They form a new breed of semi-sovereign political institution, complementing the greater power of the transnational corporations and the federal government.

Finally, a new cosmopolitan mentality has taken shape over the last fifteen or so years, which, perhaps more than anything else has challenged traditional perspectives on place. In the chapters that follow, I approach America as a place or as human geography with a history. But looking at the country as a place is not an easy undertaking, since so many Americans throughout history have preferred to see the country not as a place but as an idea and as a process.[69] They have argued that Americans were a people not because they shared a common place, past, or language, but because they shared a set of abstract universal principles or ideas generated by the eighteenth-century Enlightenment and articulated in the country's founding documents. This argument, of course, often fudged the difference between the Constitution, a decisively provincial and place-making document because it built the foundation for the nation, and the Declaration of Independence, which appealed to the universal experience of all peoples to justify a revolution.[70] At the same time, given the newness of the country and the radical nature of the split from the British, it made sense for Americans to emphasize the universal side over the place-building side as the critical cohesive force in American life.

In our time, however, long after the early rationale for it

had disappeared, the notion of the country as a philosophical (rather than historical) entity has still overshadowed any claim to the contrary. Robert Dole, in a farewell speech he delivered to the Senate in May 1996, before embarking on his failed bid for the presidency, described "America as much more than a place on the map, it's an idea." "America is an idea," said Newt Gingrich, in his 1995 *To Renew America,* "the most idea-based civilization in history." Therefore, "anyone can be an American." "America is a set of ideas and if you believe in those ideas, you are an American," said Gary Bauer, president of the Family Research Council, in Washington, D.C., in 1997.[71]

Many Americans, then, insisted upon describing America as an idea. But they have taken the further step of claiming that the country has always been "an idea in the making," an idea always being "reinvented," an ideological promise yet unfulfilled, on the verge, never quite there. "We're sort of constantly in the act of becoming," said President Bill Clinton in a 1997 interview with the *Wall Street Journal.*[72] Michael Walzer, political thinker at Princeton University, has asserted that America is a "radically unfinished society," a "continually negotiated and contingent" culture.[73] "If America is about nothing else," Lewis Lapham, editor of *Harper's* magazine, said in a 1992 essay "Who and What Is an American?", "it is about the invention of self. Because we have little use for history, and because we refuse the comforts of a society established on the blueprint of class privilege, we find ourselves set adrift at birth in an existential void, inheriting nothing except the obligation to construct a plausible self." "Who else is the American hero if not a wandering pilgrim who goes forth on a perpetual quest?"[74]

Not surprisingly, current immigrants have embraced this view. Thus Janet Wolf, professor of English at the University of Rochester and a recent British migrant, declared in her book *Resident Alien* that she was drawn to America because it was "a

site for a potential self," rather than a country with a past.[75]
Bharati Mukherjee, Indian-born novelist, said in 1997 that "I
am an American for whom 'America' is the stage for the
drama of self-transformation."[76]

There is much truth, of course, in all of this. Ever since
there was an America, it was an idea and a process, above all for
those who have wanted to begin again or dreamed of starting
over. But this can be carried too far.

In the current jargon, the country is never done, never
there, never truly together, a setting suited best to those able
to adapt painlessly to life's shifting demands. In this context,
no practical difference exists between those who colonized
and settled here and those who immigrated here, between
those born here and those en route, between hotels and historical monuments. As Newt Gingrich says, "anyone can be an
American." Or, as Michael Walzer insists, "anyone can come
here." In this context, fresh blood is always preferable to old
blood, getting out always superior to remaining, new models
always better than last year's washed-up specimens, because all
these resonate with the idea of becoming, of what it means—
for some people anyway—to be an American. In this context,
moreover, the conception of a place lodged in time and space,
in which people share many of the same things, remember the
same things, has no meaning. If America is an idea, then any
place can be America. Such generalizing obscures the way
countries are concrete places, have people in them, have histories of conflict and sacrifice in them, and have been literally
sustained by "historical memories real and imaginary," to
quote philosopher Isaiah Berlin.[77]

The countervailing trends that so marked the country
before 1970 seem to have lost much of their potency. Placelessness, therefore, presents a greater challenge to the country
than ever, far more so than it did at the turn of the last century,

which for all of its chaos and change, was still a world of boundaries—in moral life, in politics, in the relations among men, women, and children, in national cultures and geographies. In our time, it is no longer a question of settling countries or continents but of standing ground against the placeless and learning how to marshal the power of centering against the landscape of the temporary.

Josiah Royce warned in 1907 that unless Americans acquired or cultivated a stronger sense of "provincial loyalty" as well as a livelier tie to their country (as opposed to the "nation" which, distinct from the country, projected abstract, insensitive institutional power), then they would have only themselves to blame when the national state intervened to take over those tasks the people could not do for themselves. The absence of provincial ideals, he said (and by this he did not mean "sectionalism"), opened the way for governmental meddling and management of all kinds. Without such ideals, "further centralization of power can only increase the estrangement of our national spirit from its own life." "History shows that if you want a great people to be strong, you must depend upon provincial loyalties to mediate between the people and the nation."[78]

Since Royce's day, many Americans have often felt the need to promote a sense of place. Novelist Wallace Stegner has written that "our migratoriness has hindered us from becoming a people of communities and traditions, especially in the West. It has robbed us of the gods who make places holy." Critic Wendell Berry has observed that "our present 'leaders'—the people of wealth and power—do not know what it means to take a place seriously: to think it worthy, for its own sake, of love and study and careful work. They cannot take a place seriously because they must be ready at any moment, by the terms of power and wealth in the modern world, to destroy any place."[79]

Boundary and space, place and freedom—these things do not contradict each other but go together. People need to feel a bond to a concrete reality larger than the self, a reality that gives deeper meaning to existence.[80] They need to be stewards of the concrete places (not the world place or planet) in which they live, because to lose that stewardship is to lose faith in oneself and in one's own society. Historically this concrete reality has taken the form of the country, the province, and the hometown because these have carried much particular meaning—from individual hopes and ideals to the very smell of the earth itself, the very curve or fullness of a particular landscape—that have enriched the lives of most ordinary people and helped them reach and think beyond themselves. People require a firm sense of place so they can dare to take risks. A society whose common store of memories has been beaten down or shattered is open to further disruption; for such a society cannot defend or protect itself from the stronger incursions of those who know what they want and how to get it.

Years ago, Thorstein Veblen, after hacking away at his cabin, descended from his mountaintop to write *Absentee Ownership,* an account of those people who viewed their properties only in money terms or as the means to profit and wealth. In the past twenty-five years, many Americans are still absentee in the sense Veblen meant, investing in a shadow world of concentrated wealth from which they hope to reap untold riches. But they are absent in other ways as well, absent from their children's lives, absent from their communities and country, willing more than ever to delegate to others—by choice or by necessity—those responsibilities they once carried out themselves. The reasons for this are complex, but let me begin with highways and gateways, place-makers and destroyers.

One

Intermodal Highways and Gateways, Visible and Invisible

In the summer of 1995, I visited the towns in Arkansas where Bill Clinton was born and grew up. To get to Hope from Hot Springs, I had to drive many miles down Interstate 30, a long, wide, four-lane highway that stretched to Dallas and beyond. Somewhere near Friendship, Arkansas, the highway grew jammed with trucks on all four lanes; the foothills of pine timber on either side of the road, so unrelieved in their thick greenness, took a back seat to a spectacle of movement. At one point, on a bridge over the Ouachita River, near Arkadelphia, I pulled over to the side of the road to stretch my legs and to look at a river I would likely never see again. A mist hovered over the black water. In that moment, I felt a terrible rush of sucking air. The bridge shook, as truck after loaded truck barreled through.

This road was inhospitable to anything but trucks. It was a passageway for trucks with goods on their way to Texas, and deeper into Mexico. On this day, the vehicles might have been more than forty-eight feet long (ten years earlier, such lengths were rare), many in double-trailer combinations. The cargo was equally impressive, ranging from pesticides and logs to automobiles and watermelons. In 1980, the total intercity freight moved by truck in the United States was about 2 billion tons. In 1995, when I visited Hope, the figure had risen to 3.4 billion. By 1997 nearly 4 billion tons of raw materials and goods were being carried by trucks to domestic markets.[1]

The tonnage, the trucks, the road—all these revealed the new sweep of American trade. Since the 1950s, the American economy has reconnected with the international economy of the late nineteenth century. In those pre-1914 days, when few controls held back the movement of money, goods, and people, "only a madman would have doubted that the international economic system was the axis of the material existence of the race," as economic historian Karl Polanyi observed over fifty years ago.[2] Yet that system did almost grind to a halt after World War I, as governments struggled to manage markets and as ideologies divided nations. Such post-twenties conditions, which many people took for granted and understood as irrevocable, lasted until around 1970, when the international economic order finally regained its ascendancy.

As never before, business has pierced through both national and international frontiers, a sign of which has been a new world of transport, with its highways on land, sea, and in the air, its gateways of entry and exit, and its almost bewildering diversity of vehicles. This world of movement has been conceived by enterprising businessmen in trucking, rail, and shipping; by technological innovations and government policies; and by the greatest corporate merger mania in American history. An intermodal system of mobility has been erected to link up many modes of transport into a "seamless whole." It has ushered into life centers of commerce (such as the great ports of Long Beach/Los Angeles in California and Newark/Elizabeth in New Jersey, to say nothing of the spectacular marine terminals in Texas, Virginia, southern Louisiana, and Oregon). And it has helped both to re-create the nature of place and to undermine it as well.

HIGHWAYS AND GATEWAYS: LAND, AIR, AND SEA

Throughout history, many Americans have longed to "eliminate all barriers between goods and people," to quote Herbert Hoover.[3] The dream of defeating time and space through transport and communication, in fact, has had more followers in America than in any other country. This is ironic, for even as Americans have seen roads and gateways as avenues of freedom, they have also arranged them into a system meant to discipline that freedom—a trap as well as an escape.[4]

The history of U.S. transport began in the early nineteenth century with the first turnpikes and canals, followed by the railroads, which bound the economy and country into a single unified market and which many Americans viewed as the principal source of economic as well as civic and moral improvement (a view still alive today).[5] By mid-century, the first steam ships carried great numbers of people and goods across oceans with unheard-of speed and safety.

After 1920, cars, trucks, and airplanes were added to this empire of movement. At the same time, Americans much extended a distinct set of parallel roads—one national, the other local. Some time ago, the landscape writer J. B. Jackson distinguished between these two road systems. The national one he called "centrifugal," or "palace," because it reflected the interest of ruling elites, surged outward, and ignored boundaries. The local system, on the other hand, was "centripetal," or "vernacular," formed for ordinary people and to draw them into their neighborhoods; it was "the bane of long-range travelers and of a government wanting to expedite military or commercial traffic."[6] In the 1950s, with the passage of the Interstate Highway Act, the federal government opted radically in behalf of the palace roads, betting on the success of an arterial network of paved interstate highways, and converting national road-building into a Faustian enterprise, the greatest public-works project in history.[7]

In the 1980s and nineties, every aspect of the national system took new form, visible and invisible. It took invisible form with the first electronic computer highways in the mid-1980s. By 1993, fifty million Americans were using computers at work, on average three times as many workers as in Japan, twice as many as in Germany.[8] Computers allowed business to monitor and track the flow of goods, money, labor.[9] Electronically transmitted, data of all kinds, as well as capital, overshot frontiers and created the illusion that borders did not exist.

The expansion of the visible paths of movement, with their railroads, airplanes, trucks, and ships, was even more dramatic. After years of decline, freight railroads returned in force, covering one-third more revenue-tonnage-miles in 1995 than in the 1980s, and 50 percent more than in the 1950s.[10] By the mid-nineties there were 5,500 air carriers in operation (nearly double the sum in 1980) and more than 18,000 airports (public and private), a figure the rest of the world's nations put together could hardly match.[11] "All around the country," complained an industry critic in 1998, "there are too many airports."[12]

By the nineties, the United States had twenty-four million miles of paved roads, half of which had been added since 1965 and all of which equaled the combined miles of all the paved roads in Canada, Germany, the United Kingdom, Japan, France, Poland, Brazil, Hungary, Mexico, Italy, and China.[13]

Along these roads, moreover, moved a river of registered trucks (from single-unit vehicles to giant combinations), which carried more than 80 percent of American domestic freight and whose numbers had risen fourfold between 1970 and 1995, from 14.2 million to nearly 58 million.[14] Between 1990 and 1997 alone, the number of trucks on city and town roads increased by 50 percent, clogging the streets from San Diego to tiny Woodstock, Vermont.[15] Fifteen thousand trucks a day, flowing in from the New Jersey Turnpike and its corridor roads, converged at Port Elizabeth/Newark in New Jersey alone, to pick up or dispatch their goods.[16]

Think of all those moving billboards, ever more garish and childlike in their colors, and ever longer too. In 1984 only 1 percent of trailers were over forty-eight feet in length; fifteen years later, fifty-three-footers had become the national standard. Despite the imposition of a federal freeze on truck lengths in 1991, many states found ways to bring longer trucks, even triple trailer combines, to the roads.[17] Single, privately owned rigs, costing upwards of $150,000, had room enough for kitchens, exercise machines, and full-size bed closets.[18]

Elsewhere in the world, many governments—France and Germany included—have banned the use of triple trailers, limited the size of doubles, and restricted overall the size of individual vehicles; in the United States, regulations have been much less onerous.[19]

The increase in the number of trucks has caused, in turn, an increase in the number of truckers, with six-hundred-thousand new drivers on the road between 1990 and 1997. A giant army of more than three million people—mostly white men but one-fifth minority and the largest percentage of women ever (5.3 percent)—drove heavy-duty trucks by day and night, mostly alone and harried by deadlines, and sometimes confused about what part of the country they were in. The demand for new drivers skyrocketed by 1998 and companies recruited gay truckers as well as women, tailoring truckstops to suit their needs. Even the federal government pledged $1 million to help train "dislocated" unemployed Americans to drive the big trucks.[20] What occupant of a passenger car has not felt the buffeting of the eighteen-wheelers, the giant tractor-trailer rigs and turnpike-doubles, as they rip across the landscape?

Along with the trucks were the ships, coming from all points on the compass, across the Pacific from Asia, through the Gulf of Mexico, and across the Atlantic. By the mid-1990s American oceanborne commerce had reached nearly $520 billion, a stunning increase from the $45 billion in 1970.[21] The Pacific Asian trade, which before 1975 passed mostly through the Panama Canal to Gulf and eastern ports, now went straight to California, packing the big western marine terminals with everything from Chinese plastics to Peruvian seafood.[22] The Suez Canal, after years of fading use, also returned (if unsteadily) as a major avenue for goods from South Asia, energizing in some degree such eastern port cities as Baltimore and Norfolk.[23]

Most of this trade was not carried by U.S. ships; by the 1980s, American-owned carriers accounted for less than 14 percent of international ocean commerce, a steep fall from the days of World War II, when American shipping led the world. Yet however much nationalists might have regretted it, the decline in commercial seapower had no effect, one way or the other, on the growth of American international trade, which had risen nearly 100 percent since 1970.[24] Since the late 1980s, a new generation of mammoth container-vessels were on the seas, most owned by Asian and European companies. Like the tractor semitrailers, they were far bigger than the ships of the recent past. They carried twenty-foot and even forty-foot-long containers shaped like boxcars, standardized to hold practically any kind of commodity, from cars to boots. Uniform and dull, the newest ships were too big to navigate the Panama Canal.[25]

In 1996 Maersk, the Danish-owned carrier, together with partner Sea-Land, an American firm and the top container line in the world, launched the largest containership of them all, the *Regina Maersk*. Driven by the world's largest diesel engine, it was half a mile long, with capacity to carry 6,000 twenty-foot containers arranged in five tiers, above and below the deck, aft and stern. Fully automated and computerized, it had only a skeletal crew of thirteen who met only at meals and otherwise communicated by walkie-talkie. To traverse the deck by day was like being in a monster hotel at night with no one around.[26] In July of 1998, the *Regina Maersk* sailed for the first time into the New York harbor but only with difficulty since that harbor, like every other harbor on the East Coast, was too shallow to accommodate it. Its presence excited intense interest, and even a congressional hearing dwelled on the challenge it posed to American shipping. By all accounts, *Regina Maersk* was the wave of the future and unless New York and other ports increased the depth of their harbors, Maersk, the third most powerful containership line, threatened to take its business elsewhere.[27]

Super-containerships have changed the seascape. They have brought to life huge ports, the deeply dredged gateways where the different highways of the world (rail, road, ocean, and, to some degree, air) intersect to form the key axes of international trade. Among these ports is the Port of Long Beach in southern California, which, along with its nearby neighbor, the Port of Los Angeles, forms one continuous harbor in the San Pedro Bay and constitutes the busiest port complex in the United States.[28] Emerging over the past fifteen years, Long Beach has become in every way, physically, politically, and economically, a monument to the international circulation of goods.

In physical terms, the Port of Long Beach has undergone constant change since its beginnings as a single little dock in 1912. To look down on it from its highest point (the Harbor Square administration building) is to see a vast commercial choreography—the many piers with their berths that hold the incoming and outgoing ships; the crane gantries, as tall as twenty-story skyscrapers, hoisting cargo off and on the ships; the sloping, raised highways leading into and around the piers; the two long rail lines starting at the docks and then reaching far back into downtown Los Angeles; the giant container yards; and the trucks, the thousands of trucks in their lollypop colors (red, green, blue, yellow, even maroon, purple, and pink), pouring onto the port ramps and through the port gates, lining up by the hundreds, ready for the day's business.[29]

The Port of Long Beach, however, is also fascinating for its political character. Although authorized "into existence" by the State of California, it has, for years, inhabited the shadow world of public authorities, a world largely beyond the scrutiny and control of the American public, or any other body, for that matter.[30] Governed by a board of five commissioners (plus a president) appointed by the city, the Long Beach Port Authority functions as a big landlord, renting properties (berths and terminals) to the world's ocean carriers. It has the power to finance, build, and manage capital projects; to issue tax-exempt bonds; and to contract with local, state, and federal governments, as well as with foreign governments. It controls all salaries, appointments, contracts, and budgets.[31] Its authority, to be sure, is hardly total, though one trade analyst at the port saw fit in 1997 to boast that "we are accountable to no one."[32] Environmental and state laws, for one thing, confine development along the shore, often to the great frustration of the port management. Nevertheless, like the one hundred other similar marine or port terminals in the country (including the Port Authority of New York and New Jersey, prototype of all such ports), the Port of Long Beach resembles a semi-sovereign city-state. Technocratic and outside ordinary democratic political life, it has the power nearly equal to that of any state government to affect the way we live.[33]

It is as a hub in the circuitry of global commerce that this semi-sovereign port holds the most interest. Before the 1970s, when international trade played just a small part in the U.S. economy, few Americans beyond southern California thought much about the Port of Long Beach. Since the mid-eighties, however, the port itself has become a dynamic agent in its own right, with its own Washington lobbyist, in arguing for the opening of America to foreign commerce. Since 1980 it has offered berths to more than twenty shipping lines, mostly Asian (and these owned principally by Korean, Japanese, and Chinese firms), each leasing a terminal for several million dollars annually.[34] In 1990 the combined ports of Long Beach/ Los Angeles handled 100 million tons of cargo; five years later, Long Beach alone was carrying this volume, or 25 percent of America's international waterborne trade.[35]

Everything imaginable passed through the Port of Long Beach in 1995: 22 million tons of petroleum; 12 million tons of plastics, clothing, and furniture; and 1.2 million tons of food—nuts and fruits from Israel, Chile, and Italy, fish from Peru, shrimp from Thailand. Most of it was not destined for the Los Angeles basin but for discount stores in Kansas City, Missouri, and the deli counters in Wells, Maine.[36]

So much space was being opened for harbor expansion at this Long Beach complex that new space had nearly run out, forcing Long Beach/Los Angeles to spend millions for more dredging in San Pedro Bay.[37] So many megaships docked to unload their cargo that bottlenecks of all sorts began to hobble the port. The *Wall Street Journal* wondered in the fall of 1997 "how the transportation infrastructure was going to handle the country's growing appetite for goods." "Nobody was ready for so much freight."[38]

"THE UNTHINKABLE HAS HAPPENED"

But why had all this coordinated movement of goods and people, all this turbulent trade, come about in so short a time-span? How was it that in less than fifteen years so many trucks and ships and trains were moving so many goods on so many highways and through such extraordinary gateways as the Port of Long Beach? The answers are complex, to be sure. Some analysts see this commerce as an outcome of intensified global competition (attended by the collapse of trade barriers, and the government privatization of the economy in many countries) that accompanied the end of the Cold War. Others have looked at dropping interest rates, low labor costs, weak unions, or at what the *Wall Street Journal* called "the country's growing appetite." All these answers have merit, but I want to consider three conditions: the corporate mergers of the 1980s and nineties, which pressured business to distribute goods widely and quickly; government deregulation, which helped trigger both mergers and transport growth; and the promotion of intermodal transport.

From the 1980s onward, the United States has experienced the greatest merger movement in its history, with only a few letups, such as a crisis of short duration at the end of George Bush's presidency in 1991 when the stock market crashed. There have been merger phases before, times when corporate moguls erected giant firms to control markets, prices, and labor, and always to deliver goods with all due speed. The first great wave of mergers occurred at the turn of the century, when investment banker J. P. Morgan created U.S. Steel, the original $1 billion deal: oblivious to the goods themselves, Morgan's plan was to get for himself and other bankers reliable streams of income. The next phase erupted in the 1920s, with the concentrations in manufacturing, mining, gas, and electricity, then another in the 1950s and sixties with the popularity of huge horizontal firms or conglomerates often consisting of totally dissimilar businesses. But none of that compared in magnitude to the mergers of our own time, especially in recent years when, according to the *Wall Street Journal,* "the unthinkable has happened": since 1994, every year has set a record in the numbers and dollar value of the domestic mergers, from $347 billion worth in 1994 to $659 billion in 1996 and $991 billion in 1997.[39] The year 1998 reached the $1.6 trillion mark, equaling the combined worth of all the mergers completed between 1990 and early 1996.[40]

Mergers took place in a vast range of enterprises, from hospitals and pharmaceuticals to drugstores and book publishing. Telecommunications saw the coupling of four huge phone companies; two merged corporations alone controlled two-thirds of all phone lines in the U.S.[41] Mergers also shrank the number of long-haul railroads from forty-two in 1980 to four in 1998.[42] So, too, the airline business entered "the final phase of consolidation," according to one analyst at Salomon Brothers, with the six major airlines forming routing and marketing alliances with one another.[43] Shipping carriers, American and foreign, either merged or forged "strategic cross-border alliances," securing their grip on many lanes of commerce. "The inevitable and inexorable process of consolidation continues," said Ray Miles, president of London-based Canadian Pacific, of container shipping. "The whole concept of a national flag carrier is virtually dead. Across the board you are seeing the creation of truly global companies," observed John Reeve, a maritime expert.[44]

In the entertainment and media field, investment bankers managed the consolidation of the biggest movie theater chain in the world, linking together Regal Cinemas with United Artists Theater Group and promising to bring gigantic movie complexes—with identical movie fare but "loaded with amenities from better concessions to cozy love seats"—to anywhere in suburban America.[45] In the mid-nineties, industries from gold mining and gambling to hotels and department stores united together, each becoming the largest of its kind either in North America or in the world.[46]

In a time bursting with bravado about free markets, oligopoly also reared its face in banking, just as it did in real estate and newspapers. Perhaps the most startling bank merger of the era was the $69 billion union in 1998 of Citicorp with Travelers Corporation, though by 1995 banking was already well on its way to slimming down to a "handful of gigantic institutions," according to the *Wall Street Journal.* Thus continued the delocalization of the banking system, the moving of headquarters hither and yon across the country, and the liquidation, through the introduction of ATMs in every viable place around the world, of face-to-face banking (except in the case of lucrative mortgages and auto loans).[47]

Delocalization of ownership marked newspapers as well, with the Gannett newspaper chain devouring one family-owned and local newspaper after another to achieve an astonishingly uniform and predictable approach to reporting throughout suburban America; so, too, the *New York Times*—already owner of twenty-one regional newspapers, twenty magazines (including *McCall's, Tennis, Golf Digest,* and *Family Circle*), and several television and radio stations—acquired the independent *Boston*

Globe, for the sum of $1.1 billion.[48] Not surprisingly, the *Time's* editorial page, in the spirit of its own business method, told its readers, in three separate editorials over the course of two months, that they had little to fear from the "monster mergers" in banking. Of the Citicorp-Travelers merger, the *Times* observed: "The fact is that Citigroup threatens no one." Americans have "nothing to fear from huge banks," the paper reiterated a week later, "as long as there are other huge banks lurking in the same neighborhood," but how many big banks could be expected to fit in the same neighborhood?[49]

Real estate, long an atomistic industry made up of thousands of private, family-owned companies (like banks and newspapers) also consolidated into real estate investment trusts (REITs) or publicly traded corporations worth billions. Congress first created REITs in the 1950s to give average Americans the chance to invest in real estate the way they invested in stocks. Very shareholder-friendly, paying 95 percent of their net income in dividends, they were also *liquid,* allowing investors to withdraw their money at any time if investments failed or threatened to fail. This, of course, pressured REITs to succeed. For years, however, they attracted little capital. Then, after 1985, Congress lifted many restrictions and even permitted pension funds (a giant public reserve of money) to be invested in REITs. The result was a flush of publicly traded megacompanies (again, like banks and newspapers) with deep billion-dollar pockets, constantly on the prowl for opportunities.[50]

All these transactions belonged to the new era of global capitalism, an era that before the world fell victim to a vast financial crisis, promised to fulfill the hopes of the late-nineteenth-century American socialist Edward Bellamy, author of *Looking Backward* (1888). Bellamy fantasized the dawning of a true one-world economy, administered by state-owned firms, with all peoples joined into a single planetary consumer market by an intricate network of "pneumatic tubes" (through which all the goods would pass). The quaint tubes and state ownership aside, in the 1990s Bellamy was having his day, as the United States was "moving toward a period of the megacorporate state in which there will be a few global firms within particular economic sectors," according to Steven Nagourney, an investment strategist for Lehman Brothers.[51]

The wheelers and dealers executing these combinations were a motive force behind the new movement of goods on land, on sea, and in the air. Their mergers represented "the massive amounts of money on a world-wide basis" that "is looking for opportunities" and must find its outlets, to quote financial expert Adrian Dillon.[52] "If we only distributed pictures in the U.S.," explained William Mechanic, VP at Twentieth Century Fox, "we'd lose money. It takes the whole world now to make the economics of movie-making work."[53] The men behind these mergers sought global command of "the channels of distribution," to get their goods to people everywhere fast. "Companies that control the channels of distribution," said the *Wall Street Journal* in 1995, "are pushing a wave of consolidation." They are transforming "distributive work . . . into networks, coordinated by computers and communications technologies and used to build empires once considered too complicated or unwieldy to be managed effectively on a big scale or over huge distances." Today, the *Journal* said, "Connectivity is King."[54]

OPEN SKIES

Yet these companies could not have gone this far, indeed would not have existed at all, were it not for the second condition behind the movement of goods, the deregulatory policies of the federal government, which propelled the mergers and the revolution in transport. Since the late 1970s, Washington has followed a lenient antitrust policy and promoted deregulation, on the grounds that only "the marketplace should prevail," not government policy or management.[55]

Thus, government, since the late 1970s, has deregulated, or begun to deregulate, airlines, trucks, rail, and ships. Under presidents Gerald Ford and Jimmy Carter, the deregulation of the airlines commenced, igniting at first fierce competition but then drifting into extreme consolidation. In 1980 Congress passed the Motor Carrier Act, which lifted requirements for entry into the trucking business and caused the quadrupling of truck applicants in the first year; it paved the way for the rise of such large trucking firms as Schneider Inc. and J. B. Hunt, with their fleets of vehicles hauling cargo everywhere in America.[56] In 1994 Congress terminated the regulatory authority of states over truck movements within their borders, thus triggering interstate expansion by the trucking industry.[57]

In 1982 the Staggers Rail Act was passed, sponsored by Representative Harley Staggers, Sr. (Democrat, West Virginia) and shepherded through by ardent Jim Florio (Democrat, New Jersey), who considered this one of his finest achievements. The Staggers legislation limited federal authority to impose maximum rates on railroads, and it also freed railroads to sell off rapidly aging unprofitable lines, to explore a wide range of prices and services, and to combine with other forms of transport. It allowed shippers and carriers to enter into "confidential rate and service contracts."[58]

In 1998 Congress expanded the deregulation of the shipping industry, begun tentatively by the Shipping Bill of 1984. For years American shippers were under the thumb of a worldwide system of cartels, consisting of carrier lines grouped into what were called "conferences" that set transport prices. The 1998 law allowed U.S. shippers to make secret deals with carriers, thus eluding the power of the cartels. (It did nothing, however, to curtail the ongoing concentration of the industry globally or to repeal an old antitrust exemption, in force since 1916, which permitted carriers to group into cartels in the first place. It also favored the big U.S. shippers.)[59]

But Congress did more than deregulate individual transport industries. It also encouraged cross-modal consolidations. In 1983 it ended most of the regulatory controls enacted in 1935 to protect the fledgling trucking industry from rail competition; now railroads could freely merge and tap the potential of intermodal transport, that is, join with trucking firms and shippers to move goods swiftly, in a single transaction.[60] Ten years later, in 1995, Congress also removed the last prohibitions against common ownership of different modes of transportation. Back in the fifties, when trucking magnate Malcolm McLean had sought to acquire the Pan Atlantic Steamship Company (which he later renamed Sea-Land Services), he was forced by law to sell off most of his own trucking business, McLean Trucking. But by the late nineties, such obstacles had vanished, and not only was the company CSX the second-biggest railroad in America, it also owned the country's biggest barge business, several motor carriers, and the nation's biggest containership company (McLean's Sea-Land Services!).[61]

Throughout this entire time, the very word regulation tasted like bile in the mouths of such free market champions as Newt Gingrich and Richard Armey in Congress, as well as Clintonian New Democrats. So much was this the case that in 1995 Congress dismantled the Interstate Commerce Commission (ICC), which for decades had regulated competition among the railroads, and which the above-mentioned laws, in any case, had rendered irrelevant. In 1995 the ICC was replaced by the Surface Transportation Board, an independent agency, housed inside the Department of Transportation (DOT), highly receptive to mergers.

Congressional Republicans and Democrats, collectively, have done little to stop businessmen from doing what they have wished to do. Recent presidents have behaved similarly. Bill Clinton, for instance, has proved to be among the most pro-business, pro-merger presidents in history, certainly equal to Hoover and Coolidge, and probably surpassing Reagan. Echoing Theodore Roosevelt, but without Roosevelt's feisty faith in government supremacy over business, he explained to the *Wall Street Journal* in 1998 that mergers are "inevitable."[62] His Commerce Department, under all his secretaries (Brown, Kantor, and Daley), has acted as a virtual arm of American corporate business abroad by, among other things, setting up meetings between U.S. and foreign firms, and by providing firsthand detailed accounts of markets (maps, reports, guides) so that U.S. companies would know best where to invest.[63] Clinton's policies have moreover fueled the concentration of the transportation industry. In 1996 he allowed the merger of two big aircraft producers, Boeing and McDonnell Douglas, creating an "incredible powerhouse with massive technical, financial, manufacturing, and marketing resources."[64] Following in the footsteps of the Bush administration, Clinton's Department of Transportation also negotiated a series of "Open Skies Agreements"—"to create new pathways for commercial activity."[65]

These Open-Sky pacts deregulated travel between designated countries, giving each national airline access to the other's air space, limited only by the availability of landings and ramps.[66] As a way of persuading countries to join, the agreements granted special immunity from antitrust laws. They also permitted carriers to share costs, revenues, and customers, and to pool data about routes, fares, flier programs, and marketing. Since 1994, the government has negotiated agreements with nearly thirty countries, including Canada, Germany, Switzerland, Japan, Italy, and Peru. At the same time it has granted immunity to such big companies as United Airlines and Lufthansa AG; Delta Airlines and SwissAir; and American Airlines and Canadian Airlines International.[67] "This agreement will transform air transportation as we know it," said Gerald Greenwald, chair of United Airlines, of the Japanese-American accord. "It [allows] the airline industry to provide convenient access to virtually every major city in the world for the first time."[68]

Nothing better than Open Skies showed the direction Clinton and Congress wanted to take the country. The outcome, of course, caused "much stronger traffic growth" in passengers and commercial freight than ever in history and muddied further the boundaries between countries.[69] Along with the other deregulation policies, the new airline agreements helped to "partly denationalize national territory."[70] As Holman Jenkins, an editor of the *Wall Street Journal,* said of Open Skies, "one more citadel of nationalist chauvinism is falling, and the planet can't be the worse for it."[71]

THE INTERMODAL REVOLUTION

The last component in the creation of the turbulent river of goods was intermodalism, a far-reaching departure in transportation.[72] By the late eighties it was the fastest growing and most-talked-about feature of commerce; it joined trucks, railroads, and ships into a series of alliances "to maintain continuous flow throughout the entire transportation and transfer process," according to an authority on the subject, Gerhardt Muller.[73] Central to it was the creation of standardized containers to carry freight. Before the 1950s, longshoremen hauled goods off and onto carriers by hand and crane, which took a lot of time and many workers. In that decade, however, Malcolm McLean, an insightful, no-nonsense trucker from the South, who on his trips north was frustrated by "all that waste," came up with the idea of moving goods in standardized containers.

The Edison of the container revolution, McLean was born to poor parents in Maxton, North Carolina, in 1914. His father was a farmer and mail carrier, and McLean's first job was selling eggs. In 1934, after pumping gas, he bought his first truck and formed his own business, McLean Trucking, which soon matured into the largest in the South and took him as far north as Hoboken. It was in Hoboken, in fact, that he saw how much time was squandered transferring goods from ships to trucks to trains; he proposed instead that they be loaded in trailer-sized containers that could then be mounted interchangeably on truck chassis, the decks of ships, or railroad cars. Such containers, he believed, would greatly speed the flow of all kinds of commodities.[74]

McLean viewed transportation almost as an art form. Rather than thinking about specific modes of transport (trucks or ships, for instance), he fixed on streamlining the *process* itself. "The key to his thinking," said a colleague in 1979, "is transportation. He looks at things in terms of getting [cargo] from here to there at the lowest possible cost."[75]

In 1956 he entered the shipping business. He converted a World War II–era tanker into the first container-vessel, the *Ideal X,* which sailed out of Port Newark, New Jersey, to Houston loaded with fifty-eight containers. When it docked in Houston, few people observed that only a handful of men removed the cargo in just two days, whereas previously it would have required a week or more with three times as many men. A few years later McLean created Sea-Land, the first containership company, and soon a multimillion-dollar operation.[76]

Containerization did not succeed immediately. It was opposed by the many stevedores, the loaders and unloaders of cargo, who would be thrown out of work by it; ports and shipping companies also resisted at first, daunted by the capital costs required to accommodate the containers.[77] It had little impact through the 1960s, but it positively exploded in the 1980s with the invention of big lightweight containers able to carry freight in nearly any size and any volume. By the 1990s, almost 100 percent of the general cargo in industrialized countries moved in containers; animals, too, had been containerized. Circus elephants and tigers were packed into them. Thousands of head of cattle traveled in such boxes from America to Turkey and Egypt. Hawaiian ranchers even invented "cow-tainers," forty-foot, double-decked containers for cattle in which the animals stood up on their five-day journey to California for slaughter or sale.[78]

In the past fifteen years, moreover, rail and truck companies have created double-stack cars for these containers; tandem-trailers or Road Railers for use on the roads; and liftable steel trucks for use on rails. At the same time, many other businessmen besides McLean saw in intermodalism the promise of a tremendous future. Among them was Johnnie Bryan Hunt, trucking mogul from Arkansas and member of that famed trio of mass merchandisers (the other two: Don Tyson of Tyson chicken, the world's biggest poultry business, and Sam Walton of Wal-Mart Stores, Inc., the world's biggest retailer) who founded their businesses around the same time in one little corner of northwest Arkansas.

Born in 1927, Hunt, like McLean, came from poor Southern roots—in Hunt's case, sharecroppers and devout Christians. He drove a truck for twenty years and made his first fortune selling a new kind of chicken litter, an absorbent ground cover concocted from castoff rice hulls. In the early 1960s, with financing from Winthrop Rockefeller (future governor of Arkansas), he built his own rice-hull processing plant in the town of Stuttgart; in time, he churned out more chicken litter than anyone in America. He also invested in trucks and built a highly profitable business. He paid low wages and sent goods farther than anybody else. Soon trucking consumed his interest, and he took brilliant advantage of the government deregulation of trucking in 1980s. By that decade's end, he had fifty-three-foot trailers in his fleet. He opened fancy trucking terminals in St. Louis and Detroit, and he created a logistics department to match drivers with loads "for better use of equipment and on-time service."[79]

In 1989, Santa Fe Railroad invited him to link his company with theirs, since both served the same routes. He jumped at the chance to combine his trucks with the cheap fuel and cheap labor of the railroads; together Santa Fe and Hunt formed a system in which the cargo could move in standardized containers that fit on railcars. In time, he struck deals with six other railroads and invested millions of dollars in new containers. He devised his own system for hauling cars called AUTOSTACKER, and he contracted to carry Mercedes automobiles, among other luxury items, from the East Coast marine terminals to points far inside the country.[80] He also installed computers in his vehicles to predict the success or failure of shipments to defeat, or attempt to defeat, the weather in its capacity to hinder or halt the delivery of goods and, most of all, to track the whereabouts of truckers around the clock on an hourly basis and to protect against trucker errancy.[81]

By 1996 Hunt was running a billion-dollar company, with more than 11,000 yellow and white trailers and 7,500 truckers, driving, on average, nearly 50 million miles per month. He added a Hunt de Mexico and dreamt of an imperial legion of immense trucks—each one capable of demolishing signposts, strewing roads with rubber debris, forcing all non-truckers into slow lanes, off the roads, or into cold sweats, and sometimes causing extraordinary mayhem—on highways around the world, supplying "multimodal, containerizable transportation service to a global marketplace."[82]

The success of Hunt and McLean, as well as of other like-minded men, helped revive railroads, breathed new life into American trucking, and, in particular, made for the electrifying growth of the coastal marine terminals. By the 1990s, at Long Beach/Los Angeles ports, nearly 45 percent or more of all container cargo moved intermodally, and both ports boomed in part because they had introduced on-dock rail facilities, which moved goods directly to the sprawling downtown railyard in Los Angeles—thence elsewhere, deep into the country.[83] At Newark and Elizabeth, the busiest of East Coast ports and site of the first U.S. containerized cargo facility, intermodal rail, too, was in place and all port growth pointed in an intermodal direction.[84]

To visit these ports is to be at the vortices of intermodal mobility. Nowhere else can one see so much systematic movement or get such a sense of the mechanisms conceived and marshaled to deliver goods to Americans. An abstract, geometrical cleanness distinguishes these port terminals; since the 1960s they have been completely reshaped by intermodal mechanization, leaving them nearly bereft of longshoremen

(20,000 in the 1960s at the Port of New York and New Jersey; only 2,000 in 1998). What remains of an older human landscape, for example, at the Port of Newark and Elizabeth in New Jersey, resides mostly in the whimsy of the old street names (Algiers, Suez, Calcutta, and Mohawk) or in the Seaman's Church Institute, built in 1961 to serve the needs of the world's seafarers. Other living things can be found at these terminals, of course, concealed in warehouses or hidden in shipping crates, animals or birds, even the rarest tropical fish, many smuggled in, destined for intermodal delivery to municipal aquariums or pet stores.[85]

The federal government, too, put its trust in intermodalism, just as it had in mergers and on behalf of the same historical trend—the combining of industries in the interest of the rapid movement of goods throughout the country and the world. In 1991, both Congress and the White House, in a major piece of legislation called the Intermodal Surface Transportation and Efficiency Act (ISTEA), raised intermodalism to an exalted place in the heaven of American mobility. ISTEA (and later laws) authorized Congress to spend billions not only on the interstates but also on other key arteries, from two- and four-lane highways to what were called "high-priority corridor roads." It allocated money in every state to improve links between rail stations, seaports, and airports. It aimed for "intermodal connectivity" and for the "seamless movement of people and products," helping to "make the United States the most mobile nation in history."[86]

So far, this kind of legislation has fallen short of its goal, since ports, highways, intersections, terminals, and cities have been repeatedly overwhelmed by glut.[87] Nevertheless, "the United States," observed the *Journal of Commerce,* "has by far the best intermodal transportation network in the world."[88] ISTEA was reauthorized in 1995 as the National Highway

System Act and, again in 1998, in a $200 billion update that, among other things, legislated the building of a new interstate highway (I-69) stretching from Canada to Mexico and cutting through thousands of acres of farmland, forests, and countryside in the heartland of America.[89] In the late 1990s, moreover, the federal government continued to embellish on the achievement of the interstate highways. It worked to bring the palace roads (the ones drawing people out) and the provincial roads (the ones drawing people in) into closer relationship with one another. Interstates, corridor highways, paved and unpaved roads, the dirt roads of towns and villages, have been more in touch with one another, less parallel and more intersecting, than they have ever been in American history.

AT THE END OF THE ROAD

The intermodal advancements of the last fifteen years belonged to a transportation and distribution system that, along with the merged corporations and the government deregulation and support, constituted a juggernaut for more and more movement, for connections but not for connectedness. It was a power poised and ready to make its way across all boundaries, to find its way, compel its way, push, push, and push, fashioning America, as it had never been, into a grid of terminals and highways, of ports of entry and ports of departure.

The impact of these combined changes has, in many ways, been positive. As writer John McPhee has shown, for instance, road building has been an incredible boon for geologists, because it has blasted open great swaths of the earth's history, which otherwise would have remained hidden from view. The growth in ocean trade has also given new life to such port cities as Long Beach, Portland, Baltimore, and Norfolk; the future of such troubled cities as Los Angeles and Oakland now seems brighter as a result of the commerce (although the Asian crisis may stymie this progress). Some analysts have argued, moreover, that electronic highways have helped revitalize place, especially for many telecommuting professionals who now stay at home with "a chance to play an active role in civic affairs," as one said in 1995 in the *Wall Street Journal*.[90] (Technology, thus, doth make citizens of us all.)

The country's rush of goods, however, has also required new levels of advertising, more seductions, so that at the end of every road there will be consumers ready to part with their money. In 1970 the total investment in domestic advertising was $19.5 billion; in 1985 the figure rose to $94.7 billion. But by 1997—even as the number of advertising agencies had plummeted, merged into big global companies—the amount had surpassed $230 billion, easily more than the rest of the world's total. Television advertising alone increased from $3.6 billion in 1970 to nearly $50 billion in 1997.[91]

At the end of real roads, along nearly every interstate, there now appears a strip mall, another batch of warehouse retailers, or another sunburst of merchandising. In 1970 about 13,000 shopping malls existed in the United States, nearly all built after 1955.[92] By 1997 there were nearly 43,000 shopping malls—5,500 of them designated as large regional malls and often owned by the giant retail investment trusts (REITs)— crowding the margins of such cities as White Plains, New York, and Houston, Texas. "There's just too much retail chasing too few customers," said Leah Thayer, director of retail leasing for Hines, the Houston developer. Big-box retailers have "popped up on seemingly every vacant intersection," echoed the *Wall Street Journal*.[93]

At one highway intersection after another has come another feast of nonplaces supposedly designed by developers to be "real" places meant to make people feel secure and "at home." Some of these places, built like garrisons with their own police, have covered thousands of acres. Thus, just off Interstate 270 North near Columbus, Ohio, retailer Leslie Wexler, in partnership with New York developer Georgetown Group, has "transformed" a 1,200-acre entertainment-retail complex into an old-fashioned town center called Easton. He has arranged stores, theaters, restaurants and bars, hotels, video games, and even housing into something that looks like an old New England town, "themed" with nineteenth-century-style streetlights and architecture. In classic American-developer style, Wexler had pillaged the past to impose phony meaning on a contemporary consumer space.[94]

One has only to travel the country to see what more high-way retailing has achieved: along Interstate 35 in Minnesota's capital metropolis, Minneapolis–St. Paul, which boasts the Mall of America; along Interstate 90, which joins Rapid City, South Dakota, to Spearfish Canyon, once uncluttered open-sky country; or along Interstate 35, where it passes through Austin, once a cosmopolitan oasis untouched by malls. Like so many small towns, Hope, Arkansas, once had a thriving down-town. In 1995, when I visited, it was mostly boarded up. But on the edges of Hope, along the corridors reaching to I-30, where Hunt's yellow and white trucks whizzed by, I saw the usual strip malls, some dead, others living, filled with the usual suspects—Wal-Mart, Wendy's, Pizza Hut, etc.[95]

Many people have recognized the dangers posed by more roads or by widening the highways to promote more development, which invariably presages more retailing and then more highways, more trucks, and more congestion. Local residents—especially those in affluent towns and villages—have united to zone out more traffic, keeping what they have for as long as they can. Some have hired "place-oriented specialists" who know how to carry out "history-friendly" growth and to protect communities from the disorderly fallout that comes with commercial construction along interstates and near old-fashioned downtowns.

Most people, however, do not belong to upscale communities. They cannot afford to pay for place specialists who will think and argue on their behalf. Most people have neither time, money, nor even the knowledge to consider stopping the developers, the turbulence, or the traffic. They are forced to deal with the threats to place caused by an economy that aspires to perfect intermodalism, channeling goods and people across the continent.

But there is more to contend with than the landscape of roads and highways. People must also deal with a new landscape of the temporary that has come to overshadow their lives—new kinds of work and living, a new set of mores, more flexible and uncertain. This transformation, too, has weakened the fabric of place.

Two

The Landscape of the Temporary

Years ago, the poet W. S. Merwin wrote a futuristic parable about people who tire of remembering. To rid themselves of this burden, they get inventors to build machines that will do the remembering for them. Small and compact, easily worn on the body, the machines remember precisely. They sort out the conflicting signals, the mess of ordinary human memory, and simplify experience so that people are able to achieve their goals efficiently and quickly. In time, even "children will be fitted with these devices at birth" and "they will be given new ones as they grow older and can use them." That humans will be severed further from their usual selves will not bother anyone, for "the stages of such use will seem to reveal a new pattern in the growth of the individual and hence of the species." But then a horror will strike: the first man will lose his machine, becoming a "ghost," "incomprehensible" to everyone and to himself. A "terror" will pass through society, only to be forgotten as the people cope by denying the gravity of the crisis; they will grow even more dependent on their inventions. But, then, "one by one . . . with growing frequency," they too, will "begin to lose their machines."[1]

This grim little tale contains more than just a little truth for modern mobile managers and professionals. In 1996, William Herndon, for instance, vice president of technology and specialist in mortgages for BankAmerica Corporation, presided over a staff of 125 technicians scattered throughout the United States who managed part of the bank's computer system. A couple of years earlier, Herndon had given up his office to become a telecommuting executive. Armed with two kinds of computers, a wireless modem, a cellular phone, his own private 800 number, and a pair of "cowboy boots," he went on the road, free to convert every hotel room into an office space from which to monitor his "far-flung operations."[2] Alone in the wilderness, this paragon of portability wielded his IBM ThinkPad 760 ELD laptop computer to keep electronic guard over his staff and in contact with his business partners. Sometimes he needed to get around fast, so he carried a Hewlett-Packard palmtop, which fit neatly into his pocket. He was "more wired than anyone I know," said a friend. "With the right technology," the fifty-eight-year-old Herndon himself boasted, "I can do everything on the road that I used to do in the office." He delighted in carrying all his "techno-gear" in a green backpack.

But one day, he nearly lost his backpack in an airport. He thought someone had stolen it as it passed under a metal detector. He panicked. He confronted the attendants. It turned out he was wrong; the bag had gotten misplaced somehow. But he had had "an awful fright," he said. He had experienced his first Merwinesque moment.

Mobile businesspeople carrying remembering machines exist everywhere in America. They have helped create the landscape of the temporary, which has opened up over the last fifteen years in close relation to the expanding network of highways and roads. This landscape, of course, in one form or another, has long been on the American scene; for many it *is* the American scene, the best in America, in which place (or places) have merit only in "strictly pragmatic terms," as things to discard or forget once their uses have been explored and exploited.[3] It could just as well be called the landscape of the improvisational, the landscape of the flexible, or the landscape of the exchangeable and replaceable. In recent years, however, it has gotten bigger, emerging out of the economic universe, with its transnational firms, its rivers of goods, people, and data. It has presented as much a challenge to place as has the physical landscape of highways and gateways.

At least since 1985, the landscape of the temporary has been occupied by new classes of people: among them are the executives and managers who have left their home offices, and even their country, in search of opportunity and money. These people have willingly imposed on themselves an extremely flexible regime of work. Many have become *expatriates,* accustomed to temporary attachments; they see living and traveling abroad as an inevitable and desirable part of what they do. A huge pool of nonmanagerial temporary workers also belong to this landscape; in the recent past, such workers existed on the fringes, now they crowd the center of the labor markets. Along with these workers and managers, moreover, have come new kinds of temporary *housing* to serve them—"mansions" for executives, built to be quickly marketable; new chains of hotels and motels for mobile managers and professionals; and mobile homes for blue-collar men and women. For many Americans, rich or poor, the home has been reconceived to accommodate the new flexible patterns in work and management.

Many critics have deplored the existence of this landscape

of the temporary as a violation of what most Americans once imagined homelife and work to be; as much as any single feature of American society, it has discouraged settling down, made planning in the long-term hard—if not impossible—and transformed flux and uncertainty into normal, ever-present aspects of daily life.

Other observers—like late landscape writer John Brinckerhoff Jackson—have taken a different view. Indeed, Jackson, even though he understood profoundly how essential an abiding sense of place was to the well-being of any society, might also be called America's most significant modern-day philosopher of the temporary. He coined the phrase "the landscape of the temporary" and affirmed it as the most typical American landscape. It evolved, he thought, out of forms of mobility that have always distinguished (and enlivened) American culture; he maintained, moreover, that a new sense of place might even come out of the fluid margins and roadways of American life. If people create their own worlds (and I believe they do), then Jackson's teachings were as much a building block to the landscape of the temporary as anything else in America. He helped create an *intellectual* argument that, in its own right, helped other Americans defend and normalize the landscape of the temporary.

TRAVELING DADS AND THE EXPATRIATE STYLE

Business professionals of all types have pioneered the shift to flexibility, transforming temporary ties and relations into ordinary behavior. In the interests of global competition, they have accepted high degrees of "insecurity" and "ambiguity" (although they are paid good salaries for that acceptance).[4] "In this culture, we must find the sources of stability in ourselves," said Morris Schechtman, business consultant favored by many congressional Republicans, in his 1994 *Working Without a Net*. "Internal security nets are portable."[5] Rosabeth Kanter, consultant for Fortune 500 companies, has argued the same thing in her book *World Class* (1995). "Traditional values," she said, "are eroding," and we "must build new forms of security while embracing the emerging realities of flexibility, mobility, and change."[6]

By the mid-nineties, corporate managers were flying around the world more often, and more quickly, than ever before— here to sign a deal, there to play golf, here and there to convene a meeting, sign a deal, and play golf, all within a few days, sometimes on the *same day.*[7] There were so many flying executives and other business people that airports and hotels were overflowing.[8]

We might call many of these business people neo-expatriates, because they officially resided in their home country but were so often out of it as to be uncertain about where they were, or about what state or country they actually belonged to. (They were similar in this respect to the interstate truckers who moved the goods these men produced.) John Crompton, a snack-food executive with Pepsico in 1995, increased his air travel by 50 percent since the early nineties. E. V. Goings (good name), president of Tupperware in that same period, was not only versed in three languages, after months of language immersion, but had worked in Germany and Hong Kong. Barry Salzman, president of DoubleClick International, spent 75 percent of his time traveling in 1998, toting his requisite laptop to read his hundreds of e-mail messages daily and to help manage his global network of thirteen offices.[9]

Michael Lorelli exemplifies the peripatetic executive of the age. A "traveling dad," as he calls himself, he has gone from job to job, lived in place after place, and known years of jet lag, visiting over eighty countries. He helped run Playtex International, Clairol, Apple Computer, and Pepsico. As president of Pepsico's Pizza Hut International, he logged 300,000 miles. In the mid-nineties he presided over Tambrands Americas in White Plains, New York, maker of Tampax. While at Tambrands, he lived with his wife and two daughters in Darien, Connecticut, a community Vance Packard memorialized in his 1972 book *A Nation of Strangers* as a new kind of transplant town, known for its big residences where business managers lived temporarily, on their climb up the corporate ladder, and from which they commuted daily to New York. In those days, Packard wrote, the only people who showed much interest in the town's affairs were the "wives of the transient," who joined parent-teacher groups, served on the town government, and fund-raised (although their activities were always limited by prospects of future transplants to other places). By the nineties, even this reserve had dried up, as many traveling moms had joined husbands in pursuit of corporate careers.

In the fall of 1996, after Tambrands dissolved its Americas division to create a combined global operation, Lorelli, true to his destiny, pulled up "roots" and left Darien too, migrating to New Jersey to become president of a computer beeper-making business called Medicom.

By his own account, Lorelli paid a price for his chronic traveling, although not a price that seemed to slow him down. "You are away for as many as three weeks at a time," he admitted in 1996, shortly before moving to New Jersey, "then you come back and you're a zombie because you're exhausted."[10] So much time in the air, in fact, inspired him to write a children's book—*Traveling Again, Dad?* which was profusely illustrated by Drew Struzan, a California artist well known for his posters for Steven Spielberg's films *E.T.* and *Indiana Jones.* The

cover showed both author and illustrator waving from the windows of a corporate jet in the liftoff mode. Both men—it said
on the jacket cover—created the book because they "believe
that passing along our values is the true purpose of parent-
hood."[11]

The book is odd. Narrated by an animal—the family's ham-
ster, Awesome—it seems, on first impression, like an apology
from Lorelli to his wife and two young girls for leaving home
so often. But it is really a sentimental gloss on the landscape of
the temporary, amplified by Struzan's Pollyannaish drawings
and interspersed with snippets from family letters. It is unclear
throughout—indeed, it is never stated—what "values" are
being "passed on." "I'm going to miss you, Dad," says Awesome. "I wish you weren't going away." "Dad explained that
being away from the family now and then was part of his job.
Lots of moms and dads have to travel for work." The girls are
reassured: as Awesome points out, "the map on the refrigerator
helps us to keep track of Dad's travels."

Along with neo-expatriates like Lorelli, however, have come
the real thing: business expatriates who have lived abroad, man-
aging and creating investments, properties, and companies for
extended periods. Years ago, most people thought of American
expatriates as artists or various bohemians who fled the crass
money culture of their country to pursue some "higher" goal.
Most longed to become writers or artists; some died in Europe;
still others, like critic Malcolm Cowley in the 1920s, returned
home, burdened by guilt, to write memoirs begging for forgiveness for having left the country.[12] Cowley called his book
Exile's Return.

Since the mid-1980s, these literary types have been superseded by a different breed who have little interest in "higher
culture" and seek no forgiveness. Instead of fleeing money,
they have been bringing it to the world.[13] Among them were

young American investment bankers, real estate specialists, and techno-experts, who had invaded even Vietnam with their laptops and wallets, eager to make their first million. "We're creating a city here," Rachel Loeb from Kansas City, who sold skyscraper space to businesses eager to build in "new" Saigon, told a reporter, "and I'm selling it to the fund managers and CEOs of the world. I don't know many twenty-three-year-olds who can say that."[14]

In a burst of euphoria in 1995, the *Wall Street Journal* called people like Loeb the "footloose soldiers" of "history's mightiest cultural and commercial empire."[15] To some degree they resembled the peripatetic mining engineers, the Herbert Hoovers, of the turn of the century, but there were more of them, and they were much less animated by the need to return home to serve their country. Some were very "footloose" indeed, such as a clutch of American billionaires who notoriously moved abroad to escape the IRS.[16] Ted Arison, the "If you could see me now!" owner of Carnival Cruise Lines, the world's biggest such company, lived in Israel, a tax-free paradise for Americans. The Campbell Soup heir John Dorrance III acquired Irish citizenship. The Dart brothers, Ken and Robert, sons of Kenneth Dart, the billionaire founder of the biggest foam-cup company in the world, renounced their U.S. citizenship. One lived in London, the other in the Cayman Islands. Like Dorrance, they became Irish citizens.[17]

The Darts were a symptom of the bigger pattern, the movement of American firms abroad, which, in the form of subsidiaries or as direct foreign investment, had surpassed all other transnational business in the world.[18] But what did it mean that so many highly trained men and women—sometimes the most talented of Americans as well as the most money-hungry—no longer seemed to care for the places they came from and had lived in? How would they be made accountable, and to whom? How would they be taxed, and by whom? And, if they could not be taxed, how would they keep any sense of place at all?[19] Year by year, managers and executives who claimed flexibility as the mark of the most advanced human activity were absent from the country. "Place for me," one internationally mobile specialist said in 1994, is not something nailed down in time or geography, it "is a marker of change, chance, of opportunity."[20]

BRIGADES OF TEMPORARIES

Not only has management adopted absenteeism for itself, but it has imposed it on workers, skilled and unskilled, as well. Since 1980, new flexible labor reserves materialized, all configured to serve the interests of business, and all contributing to the further demise of the union movement. During World War II, union membership within the ranks of all nonagricultural workers had reached a record 35.5 percent, a figure that remained relatively stable into the 1960s. Following that decade, however, the movement stalled; by the seventies, it began a rapid decline. By 1995 only 16 percent of workers in the private sphere were in unions, and in 1998 the figure had dropped to 10 percent. The causes for this attrition were complex, but the most significant was the widespread reliance by business on cheap, flexible labor, a reliance that kept wages down, set worker against worker, and severely undermined worker solidarity.[21]

The new flexible labor pools included native-born Americans, skilled and unskilled, who worked under contract for short periods of time, traveled anywhere to take up temporary employment and often lived hand-to-mouth. Legions of foreign migrant workers also belonged to these reserves, as did immigrants, legal and illegal, many recruited into the country by hundreds of American firms—from the giant new meat-packing and chicken-producing factories of the South and Midwest to the fast-food chains and garment sweatshops on both coasts. Thirty years ago many of these businesses were unionized and paid good wages; in the past two decades, hundreds of thousands of nonunionized immigrants have toiled under conditions that most Americans would regard as intolerable.[22]

The last time management had this kind of control over labor was in the late nineteenth century, before the advent of unions and safeguards. It was at this time of great industrial growth that corporations, big and small, first produced "close to the market" ("just-in-time" may have been an American idea) and to create inexpensive labor pools that managers could draw on at will. "We hire men when we want them," said an employer around 1900. "We have no permanent work force."[23] Business also blocked all immigration controls, to keep what historian Alexander Keyssar calls "brigades" of inexpensive workers "sufficiently large to permit the demand for labor to fluctuate widely and often." "The presence of foreign-born workers enhanced the ability of employers to run their businesses . . . 'close to the market'" and "to regard all workers as potential members of the reserve," Keyssar writes.[24] These reserves, immigrant and nonimmigrant, reached levels of 20 percent of the workforce; they were found in every major trade or industry, each with its own surplus of unemployed, available workers. Few belonged to the middle class, however, since professional employment, from teaching to law, provided job security.[25]

Since 1980 we have returned to these earlier times but with big differences, not the least of which has been the rise of a giant temporary-help business that has systematized what in the late nineteenth century was a very messy activity.[26] Temporary-help agencies (as well as outsourcing firms, which they resemble) are *not* employment agencies but profit-seeking firms that recruit, screen, and rent workers whose employment lasts only so long as the employers want it to last. These workers, moreover, always come cheap and get few of the benefits given full-time workers (health insurance, vacation pay, sick leave, pensions, etc.); together with contracted-out labor, part-timers, on-call workers, and the self-employed, they represent upwards of 30 percent of all American workers (the percentage is far higher in metropolitan New York, Los Angeles, Miami, and similar places).[27]

Before 1980, when Americans thought of "temps" at all, they may have imagined contractors who "sold" secretaries or day laborers, foreign and native-born. Such temporaries still exist, of course, and in more abundance than ever, the result especially of congressional desire to meet the omnivorous labor demands of America's corporate farmers.[28] But three new things have happened. First, the business ballooned, with the numbers of temp firms soaring to unheard-of levels (from *800* in 1956, to *16,000* in 1993).[29] By the late nineties, moreover, the temporary-help industry had radically consolidated, reflecting the merger mania rippling throughout the economy, and producing "one-stop shopping" able to satisfy any temporary-staffing necessity, according to the *Wall Street Journal*.[30]

The second thing that happened was that the temp business sold skilled middle-class labor as well as cheap unskilled labor. It reached out, in other words, to cover such skilled professionals as lawyers, chemists, engineers, biologists, and accountants, to mention a few—the sort of workers Americans had rarely viewed as temporary.[31] Corporations of all kinds have depended on temporary skilled professionals as a way of controlling costs and competing worldwide with other firms; so much has this been the case that in 1997 the United States was the biggest market for such temporary employment in the world, accounting for about 40 percent of the temp market.[32]

This increase in the supply of professionals, moreover, included the recruitment of temporary skilled foreign workers, a practice ushered in after 1990 when Congress created a new visa category (H-1B). This law gave companies the right to employ skilled people cheaply from anywhere in the world on a temporary basis, so long as these institutions could prove that no Americans existed to perform these jobs.[33] Notably pro-business, the law allowed firms to lay off Americans and replace them with foreign workers who almost always got permanent visas after employment. It demanded no written proof that firms had first looked for Americans, and it created no sure way of protecting the foreign workers from low wages and other abuses, since by law the government had to wait for aggrieved workers to file complaints (and H-IB foreign workers almost never did, out of fear of losing their jobs).[34]

The new immigration law also spawned a near-vicious market in temporary foreign workers. By 1995 firms such as Syntel, Inc., in Troy, New York; Analytical Technologies, Inc., in Minneapolis; and Mastech, in Pittsburgh, had emerged to feed the appetite for such skilled labor. Founded ten years earlier by two Indian immigrants, Mastech proved the most predatory of companies in its quest for H-1B talent, selling its corporate customers H-1Bs in bulk. Its vulture recruiters "surfed the Internet, looking . . . for signs of distress [abroad], perhaps a currency collapse, or hostage event—something that [might] spur a software developer to forsake home for the suitcase-lugging life as a programmer for hire."[35]

A third thing happened to this industry: it generated *chains* that dealt with unskilled and skilled labor alike. For historical reasons that have not been studied well, Americans have shown remarkable aptitude for selling almost anything in volume through chains. In 1989, Glen Welstad, a forty-five-year-old businessman in Kent, Washington, founded Labor Ready, a temporary-labor chain selling manual work on a daily basis. Welstad, a graduate of the University of North Dakota, already had "chain store" experience: for years he was a franchisee of Hardee's Hamburger Restaurants and officer of Body Toning, Inc., and other chains. He was so good at his business, in fact, that he retired at forty. But Welstad was soon restless and returned fired up to start another kind of chain. He dreamed of creating the "McDonald's of temporary staffing for the manual labor market," with identical "stores" everywhere in America.[36]

Labor Ready hired unskilled workers, often immigrants who sold their labor on street corners (to the chagrin of many locals) to haul, lift, paint, and dig. Among the firm's leading clients were the movers of the country's new goods, the trucking companies, the warehouses, the big chains such as Home Depot and Bed Bath and Beyond. For wages paid by Labor Ready to the workers, the company got a fee from clients using the labor, covering wages plus profit; the workers, however, received none of the usual benefits paid to permanent employees. Labor Ready's trademarks were its "dispatch halls" or "stores," where workers gathered at 6 A.M. to be matched with their jobs (by managers who arrived at 5:30); its automated cash dispensers (because, as Welstad said, the workers preferred the "privacy" of cash); and its transport system (the company itself transported the workers to and from their sites). Labor Ready also boasted a software system, LabPro, that monitored, on an almost hourly basis, the success or failure of the various "stores." Such surveillance, like the one used by trucking firms to track truckers, pressured managers, who sold on commission, to sell labor fast and efficiently.[37]

The pressures paid off. In the early nineties, Labor Ready had only eight offices; by 1998, it was a publicly traded darling of Wall Street with more than 400 offices and revenues approaching half a billion dollars.[38]

The systematic chain-selling of temp labor, however, touched skilled workers as well. Tom Buelter, for instance, of Calabasas, California, founded a firm, On Assignment, Inc., in the early nineties to sell chemists and biologists. Buelter's strategy was to locate recent college graduates and customize them to employers short-term. By 1994 he owned forty-four branch offices and had placed thousands of "workers" into industrial labs around the country.[39]

HIGH-TECH AND THE ACADEMY

Global high-tech computer firms and universities exemplified best, perhaps, how far the temporary had penetrated into this skilled market. Consisting of a core group of managers plus a large community of "flexed" and "just-in-time" employees hired to carry out on-time projects, high-tech firms have long been wedded to temp agencies as "virtual human resources department[s]" for the "screening, testing, and training" of highly skilled labor.[40] They also raked the world for *young* skilled foreign labor, oblivious of where their employees came from, and exploiting to the hilt the government's 1990 immigration policy. Between 1992 and 1994 alone software companies like Intel, Netscape, 3M, and Microsoft scooped up nearly 110,000 H-1B workers.[41]

Voracious and pesty, high-tech companies lobbied again and again for an increase in the quota of such workers, on the grounds that the domestic supply could not meet the demand.[42] But since America's population was the third largest in the

world, nearing 260 million by the mid-nineties (in 1999 closer
to 275 million), and these firms cared little or nothing about
national borders, the truth lay elsewhere than in the lack of
domestic supply. "We want great flexibility," said a 3M executive, William McClellan, in 1995. "We want the ability to bring
our people in from Brussels or people in from Taiwan, to do
the work we need to do." "Because of globalization," argued
Motorola's CEO, Richard Eagle, "we have to move people
back and forth very quickly." Immigration lawyer Paul Parsons,
who worked for computer companies in Austin in the nineties,
summed it up: "Companies are frustrated. They want to hire
the best and the brightest. And they want to be able to move
their key people in quickly, often temporarily."[43] From the
managerial perspective, these best and brightest were the stars
of a fluid firmament, exemplary workers in the way illegal
immigrants (cheap, deferential, silent in the face of abuses, tolerant of high levels of mobility), models for American employees who might be "less willing to relocate" or more demanding
of respect.[44]

Global high-tech firms, along with other global companies
such as Proctor and Gamble and Ford Motor Company, have
worked hard to change the basic logic of the country's immigration policy, which historically offered a haven to the
oppressed of the world while, at the same time, protecting
American labor from unfair competition by foreigners. These
approaches were dated, global firms have argued, especially the
approach favoring the protection of American workers.[45]
Intel, Digital Equipment, Eastman Kodak, and others have
insisted that such protection merely "subsidized labor" in a
way similar to that of the protective tariffs that favored American goods over foreign. It belonged to the Old Time before
the "globalization of the marketplace." What was needed now

was not a policy to protect American workers, to say nothing of creating a refuge for the oppressed of the world, but rather one to subsidize American businesses, to "reflect the realities of the contemporary global marketplace," and to remove all the "stifling" obstacles to the "international movement of personnel."[46]

For years, high-tech firms, indifferent to the nation and its borders, have urged Congress to ignore the interests of domestic workers. They have, in other words, encouraged Congress to act as a willing agent in the destruction of national identity on behalf of creating richer transnational companies with little commitment to the country. In 1998 they succeeded in getting both the Clinton administration and the Congress—especially the market-oriented Republican majority, who disregarded the House's own report that "the shortage" of American workers had been grossly exaggerated and that companies like 3M, Motorola, and Xerox were even planning to fire thousands of workers—to raise the number of H-1B visas from 65,000 to 95,000 and to 115,000 annually for the years 1999 through 2002.[47]

Like other businesses headed by shrewd managers, universities, too, have turned to temporary and part-time instructors to teach students and run laboratories. Over the past fifteen years, at least, they have erected a two-tiered system that has closely followed the one that has arisen in business. The upper tier consists of a core of tenured faculty who get full health benefits and job security, plus such perquisites as paid sabbaticals and generous vacation time.[48] The lower tier of this system, in the early seventies around 20 percent of faculty but by 1998 43 percent, contains a swelling corps of people variously called "gypsies," "invisible faculty," or "the migrant workers of the academy."[49] Many are drawn from seemingly unchanging numbers of native-born graduate students, while others are postdoctoral candidates, native-born and foreign, whose numbers doubled from 17,000 in 1975 to 35,500 in 1995 and who worked like faculty but got low pay and no job security.[50] Close to 70 percent of all instructors at community colleges in 1997 were adjuncts or temporaries.[51]

The very existence of the upper tier depends on a beleaguered lower faculty. "Part-time faculty," said a department chair in a major urban university, "are the protection for the university. The tenured faculty can't be removed. The budget is fluctuating up and down. Therefore, the part-time faculty are the buffer. They take care of the budget surges and shortages." Another has said that "we buy cheap labor and we get what we pay for."[52]

Years ago, many Americans longed to join the academy, not only because of the intellectual adventure there but because it seemed to offer a world where spouses and children, as well as single people, misfits, and eccentrics, might get some sense of security and continuity, even after retirement. As Clark Kerr, former president of the University of California, observed in 1962, "the university, as an institution" aims to give four things to faculty: "stability," "security," "continuity," and a "sense of equity (they should not be suspicious that others are being treated better than they are)."[53]

By 1970 this culture, this world, had begun to disintegrate. What emerged in its place was a disorderly environment sometimes riven by feuds and fears, where tenure had ceased being a way to protect academic independence and had become instead a fortress in a storm and the property of an ever-shrinking few. Was a sense of place, to say nothing of loyalty to place, likely in this context, especially for the new brigade of temporaries?

URBAN AGGLOMERATIONS
AND TEMPORARY HOMES

For many businesses at the frontlines of the global economy, then, the last decade and a half have been banner years, marked by a steady flow of abundant casual labor, skilled and unskilled, in nearly every sector of the American economy. Such conditions of labor and management have made American businesses the most competitive and predatory anywhere. But many problems have accompanied this development.

One serious problem connected with this new economic universe has been the birth of huge urban agglomerations whose very character has been determined by the growth of contingent labor pools and whose identity as places is the very placelessness that afflicts them. Metropolitan New York and Los Angeles are among such places; the culture and economy of both are shaped by the decline of an older manufacturing base and by the ubiquitous presence of a casualized workforce, including temporaries, part-timers, subcontractors, and so forth. The informal work economy, which operates generally underground or beyond convention and law, and involves mostly recent immigrant labor (illegal and legal, children and adults), has brought together masses of people from every point in the world, people whose only bond is their contingency. Many of these people, in turn, exist to serve the interests of "urban glamour zones" occupied by an elite (financial-service providers of all kinds, bankers, planners, advertising people, and so forth) which itself has become accustomed to temporariness and which has little attachment to America except as a launching pad for careerist dreams.[54]

It has been these two groups—an avaricious, flexible elite and a large pool of poor, flexible immigrants—who have created the informal economy of New York City (as well as of the other cities). Without such an economy, which elected officials and policymakers throughout the state have done much to condone and even to decriminalize (including acquiescing to illegal immigration), that city could not function. New York City's own government spent $32.1 million in 1994, a record sum, on temporary workers, in an attempt to cut the public payroll.[55]

For free marketeers, such work conditions proved ideal because they exerted a strong "disciplinary effect on American workers" and kept wages down.[56] But they also stirred up corrosive insecurity, and it was around regions such as this that one could nearly feel it—the raw vitality, the struggle of many people, the anxiety on the subways or the streets. Following a pattern set years ago by other immigrants, the new migrants, the labor pools, also tended to form neighborhoods from which many hoped to escape, leaving behind spaces to be filled by more, similar, migrants, thus perpetuating the cycle.[57]

Another outcome of the growing landscape of the temporary has been the rise of newer kinds of housing for the affluent as well as the poor.

Temporary housing, of course, has always transcended class but never more so than in the past few decades. It has come in the form of "trophy homes" for wealthy entertainers and sports stars who buy goliath houses one year, only to trade them in the next for something bigger or more eye-catching.[58] Realtors have helped traveling dads, like CEO Michael Lorelli, find temporary housing, usually cookie-cutter colonial or French Renaissance mansions devoid of any personal touches introduced by occupants, homes which can be conveniently marketed any time the owners move on to their next job, state, or country.[59] After 1980 an array of luxury master-planned communities also opened up in suburbs, with golf courses and swimming pools, courting millions of affluent Americans "who move a lot" and want "instant community."[60] Designers and architects, too, have "rethought the home" and its furniture—"collapsible, lightweight, high-end design," "nothing heavy," to satisfy the flexible style of "the new professionals, just out of college, changing jobs every couple of years, people who are on the move."[61]

The lodging industry has also been busy serving the needs of mobile professionals and managers. Over the past ten years, American firms have built numerous chains of mid-level and economy hotels—from the merged Hospitality Franchises, Inc. (owner of Days Inn and Ramada Hotel), and Marriott International to the new "extended-stay hotels" such as Homestead Village, Wingate Hotels, and Extended Stay America. These chains have added thousands of new units to the world's supply, not only in the United States but also throughout Europe and in such countries as India, Brazil, Chile, South Africa, and China.[62] By the late nineties, businesspeople could travel almost anywhere and find reasonably priced hotels, comfortable places to hop into and out of, each one like the other, often with the same electronic tools (computers and voice mail), each reproducing the same air-conditioned, streamlined style dictated by their temporary nature.[63]

There are nests of these chains near every major airport and train terminal, around every conference center—temporary housing through which pass droves of flexible computer nerds, consultants on short-term assignments, global migrants, and high-level managers with their remembering machines.

These homes resemble the ones many professional Americans themselves live in when they are not traveling, utilitarian places to inhabit, leave, and recirculate. Far more than any other group of people anywhere, American businessmen (and most have been men) have been inclined to create a landscape of temporary housing because they themselves treat their own homes as temporary dwellings (despite their worship of home ownership). Years ago, many Americans did not think of their homes in this way, because such homes, especially farmhouses, embraced many things, from spiritual observance and cooking to childcare and apprenticeships. Such activities endowed the home with the power to "root people to the landscape," to quote J. B. Jackson again. Many people loved their homes, because they truly *lived* in them.[64] In modern times, the home—even as it has gotten obscenely bigger and families much smaller—has lost much of this character and, therefore, its capacity to connect people to place.[65] Such a situation explains why it has become so easy for so many people to leave their homes behind (since so little of any substance happens in them); and it also helps explain why so many Americans—not Europeans, not Asians—have been so temperamentally well suited to building the world's biggest hospitality empire.[66]

Temporary housing of all kinds, then, has been cropping up since the late 1970s, but because of its relative invisibility, most Americans think nothing of it. Other kinds of housing, however, for a different group of people, have not been so hidden from view. One can see them throughout the country but especially in the South (Florida, Alabama, Arkansas, Georgia) and the West and the Southwest (Wyoming, New Mexico, Arizona, and California). They dot highways and rural byways, forming agglomerations on a small scale, one might say. These mobile homes and trailer parks have often met the needs of poor and working-class Americans, many tied in some way to the demands of the casual labor market.

Mobile homes have long been a feature of this society, especially after 1960.[67] In the 1960s and seventies, however, skilled people—mechanics, electricians, carpenters, engineers, even a few dentists and doctors—were the largest group of owners, followed in number by: military personnel and their families, who moved from base to base; retired people looking for security in contained enclaves; and people who vacationed with small (and sometimes long) travel trailers.[68]

In the early 1960s, novelist John Steinbeck journeyed across the country in a mobile home with his poodle dog, Charley, a trip that formed the basis for his book *Travels With Charley.* Somewhere in Maine, he encountered a young family living in a big air-conditioned aluminum mobile home, fitted with an "immaculate kitchen, walled in plastic tile, stainless-steel sinks and ovens and stoves flush with the wall." He interviewed the young owner, a successful mechanic and welder and son of Italian immigrants. Steinbeck and his new friend talked of "roots" and of staying fixed in one place. But in a way that put him squarely in the mainstream of American culture, this man hated roots and fixity. He hated permanence and saw his mobile home as the best thing in the world.

"My father came from Italy," he told Steinbeck. "He grew up in Tuscany in a house where his family had lived maybe a thousand years. That's roots for you, no running water, no toilet, and they cooked with charcoal or vine clippings." "Fact is, he cut his roots and came to America." Steinbeck asked if he missed "permanence." "Who's got permanence?" he responded. "You got roots you sit and starve. You take the pioneers in the history books. They were movers. Take up land, sell it, move on." Steinbeck seemed persuaded. "Perhaps we have overrated roots as a psychic need," he said. Yet a few pages later, he complained about the weakening of "the poetry of place" or of local differences, which he blamed on the impact of "radio and television speech," as "standardized" as "white bread." "I who love words and the endless possibility of words am saddened by [this]. For with local accent will disappear local tempo. The idioms, the figures of speech that make language rich and full of the poetry of place and time must go. . . . Localness is not gone but it is going."[69]

Since Steinbeck's day, the main occupants of trailer parks have not been prospering welders or professionals but blue-collar Americans with a median income (in 1991) of $19,500.[70] The rise in the number of unskilled working-class owners after 1980, in fact, had transformed mobile homes into the fastest-growing sector of the housing market; by 1991, in nineteen states, at least one home in every ten was a mobile home, most bought by the working poor.[71] Elderly Americans, of course, still filled the trailer parks in Florida and elsewhere, often living in communities of considerable luxury and security; upscale recreational vehicles also remained popular for both the Wall Street and Hollywood rich.[72] But most of the trailer folk were poor; and the homes they owned were, of course, not very mobile at all but fixed in place. They did suit, however, the needs of the mobile people in them, people ready to change homes at a moment's notice.

J. B. Jackson, in his 1994 book *A Sense of Place, a Sense of Time,* said that trailers also resembled automobiles, impersonal and "easy to trade and sell." "When a better job becomes available somewhere else, the family can at least consider the wisdom of selling, and of finding similar accommodations wherever they go."[73] Jackson also noted what he thought were the many blessings of the trailer parks: the low costs, the ease of financing and maintenance, the convenience and comfort, and the fact that trailer living "brings with it no new responsibilities, no change or expansion in the traditional routine."[74]

But Jackson went further than this in an effort, partly, to counter those critics with grimmer, often more condescending thoughts about "trailer trash." He claimed that many of the new trailer parks (he focused particularly on parks in New

Mexico) actually represented new kinds of blue-collar "villages" that fostered openness and hospitality among people. They encouraged people to "go outside" rather than to stay inside and to rely on one another in the public square for pleasure and comfort. Such villages, Jackson argued, compared favorably with middle-class dwellings, which were divided into discrete spaces to ensure isolation, privacy, and limited interaction with neighbors. Mobile homes, on the other hand, were too confining to keep their owners holed up inside for very long. Vernacular rather than planned spaces, they were products of everyday uses, and they brought people together into something of an organic community, into a "super-family," or an "us," carved out of what Jackson called elsewhere "the landscape of the temporary."

J. B. JACKSON'S DOUBLE VISION

John Brinckerhoff Jackson was perhaps the first American thinker to devote an entire intellectual career to the exploration of "the landscape of the temporary." Almost single-handedly, in his books, through his magazine *Landscape,* and in his college courses at Harvard and Berkeley, he taught his students to "see" landscapes not as pretty pictures but as "a system of man-made surfaces on the surface of the earth."[75] He also knew better than anyone how highways and roads defined America. He made a ritual of ending his college course "The History of the American Cultural Landscape" (fondly known by his students as "Gas Stations") with an assessment of the superhighway.

The son of wealthy American bluebloods, he was born in Dinard, France, in 1909, and educated at Harvard. Almost from the time he learned to walk, he had a love affair with mobility.

"I am very pro-automobile, pro-car, and pro-truck," he said as an old man.[76] As a boy in the 1920s, he flew on airplanes in France; as a youth, he toured Europe almost annually—even on his first motorbike, a Christmas present in 1933. In his sixties, he often criss-crossed the country on a motorcycle. When asked in 1975 what kind of "new man" might appear in the future, he proposed "the man on the skateboard, in a kind of ecstasy of mobility, physical grace, and awareness."[77]

Jackson wrote about "mobility sports," from skiing to hotrodding, in almost religious terms, believing that they offered moments of such "intoxication"—in a "new landscape shorn" of the "gentler human traits" and "of all memory and sentiment"—that one might experience "a temporary reshaping of our being." "To the perceptive individual," he said, "there can be an almost mystical quality to the experience: his identity seems for the moment to be transmuted."[78] Like many other Americans, he sexualized mobility. He was an antinomian of the highway, seeking solitary insight in "a world of flowing movement, blurred light, rushing wind and water."[79]

Such a vision of motion relates to another possible source for Jackson's romance with this landscape. Unmarried and self-contained, he seems to have felt like a wanderer himself, which must have sensitized him to the temporary; and he identified with strangers. In an essay, "The Stranger's Path," written in 1957, he wrote eloquently of that part of the city which begins at the point "where strangers first disembark"—at the city bus terminals, truckstops, and rail depots—and ends with the "zone of transients" or that "special part of town" filled with "dives and small catch-penny businesses." Jackson showed little interest in the residential part of the city, occupied mostly by families. "Why have I always been glad to leave?" he asked. "Was it a painful realization that I was excluded from these rows and rows of (presumably) happy and comfortable homes that made me want to beat a retreat to the city proper?" In contrast, he wrote effusively about this Path, populated, he said, in "greater part" by "unattached men"—"men looking for a job or on their way to a job; men come to buy or sell one item in their line of business, men on a brief holiday." Where other observers might have shunned this urban zone as "more than a little shady," Jackson saw it as the "prime" entry point for "a ceaseless influx of new wants, new ideas, new manners, new strengths" into urban America, without which city life would die.[80]

But Jackson emphasized the landscape of the temporary for reasons that went well beyond the purely personal. From the early 1950s, when he started *Landscape,* into the 1990s, he believed that the United States was creating the modern version of this landscape, *was* a new landscape, on the threshhold of becoming what he went so far as to call "a new heaven on earth." Other landscapes had reigned before. In Europe the landscape had been made out of "stone," which expressed a "stable and well-ordered society respectful of the past." In America, in the early nineteenth century, there had been the "Jeffersonian agrarian landscape" (articulated as coherent independent farms), followed by the Thoreauvian landscape (with religious respect for Nature). But all these landscapes, Jackson argued, had been displaced by a new "fluid" landscape "devoted to change and mobility and the free confrontation of men." This landscape reflected an America "where land and buildings are increasingly thought of in speculative terms, where families move on the average of once every five years, where whatever is old is obsolete, and whatever is obsolete is discarded."[81]

Jackson created an intellectual tapestry that would for the most part fit the modern world of temporariness—with its myriad expatriates, its migrants, its temp agencies and hotels—

like a hand fits a glove. He believed that roads and highways functioned at the heart of American society. "What seems to bring us together in the new landscape," he said in 1994, two years before his death, "is not the sharing of space in the traditional sense but a kind of sodality based on shared uses of the street or road, and on shared routines."[82]

Jackson wrote repeatedly about adaptable structures invented by Americans, from the balloon frames of the nineteenth century to modern prefabricated housing. He first wrote about trailer parks around 1960, after visiting a mining encampment in New Mexico, where skilled artisans of all kinds lived in trailers, their "aluminum roofs gleaming in the sun."[83] He idealized these men as "wanderers in a landscape always inhabited by wanderers. They never settled down. The way they came out of nowhere, stayed awhile and then moved on without leaving more than a few half-hidden traces behind, makes them forever part of this lonely and beautiful country."[84]

Jackson never quit writing lyrically about such provisional groupings, even as the occupants changed to mostly poor working people. In 1979, in *The Necessity for Ruins,* he insisted that "the contemporary dwelling for all its impoverishment, for all its temporary mobile, rootless qualities" is "a transformer of spiritual energy" and "promises to capture and utilize more and more of this invisible, inexhaustible store of strength."[85] Five years later, in an essay titled "The Movable Dwelling," he remarked that the "real significance" of the trailers lay in "a kind of freedom we often undervalue: the freedom from burdensome emotional ties with the environment, freedom from communal responsibilities, freedom from the tyranny of the traditional home and its possessions; the freedom from belonging to a tight-knit social order; and above all, the freedom to move on to somewhere else."[86] And again, in 1994, in *A Sense of Place, a Sense of Time,* he came back to the same message (a little tempered by the facts, perhaps, but no less lyrical), seeing his blue-collar "villagers" as superb examples of America's displaced wanderers.

Jackson returned to these parks and camps because they confirmed something basic about his view of landscapes—that vernacular landscapes (those inhabited by ordinary people) were always transitory. He saw in mobile homes, in other words, the latest type of those vernacular communities he had found to exist throughout history, from the peasant villages of feudal Europe to the open adobe homes of New Mexico's Pueblo Indians. He set these dwellings against what he called "the political" and "aristocratic" structures created by "Established Power" (Jackson's term for the state), which strove to impress and control the people, anchor place, and enforce continuity. The vernacular landscapes, on the other hand, had an unenforced quality, flowering spontaneously, as need dictated, to serve ordinary people. In this context, then, not only were trailer parks American or Jacksonian, but they were inside the very nature of men and women.

There was a power to this analysis, but it tended to impart an almost genetic inevitability to various kinds of landscapes. It also obscured how Established Power imposed the landscape of the temporary on others. Jackson argued that the vernacular often equaled mobility; but just the reverse could be claimed: that ordinary people have longed for stability and permanence (as much as for their opposite), while Established Power, in its commitment to expanding markets, has preferred change. In the 1990s, the thrust of business, reinforced by the state, has been toward flexibility and dissolution of place, a fact that, for whatever reason, Jackson missed or ignored. He viewed capitalism as benign. He chose not to see the degree to which Established Power—the palace highways of the state—had impinged on the vernacular.

Yet for all his tendency to look for beauty and strength in the ephemeral, even in trailer courts and mobile homes, there was another side to Jackson: he did recognize the need for permanence and centeredness, for individuals as well as societies. "The permanent aspects of our environment are those which matter most," he argued in 1966. "A landscape allowed to expand to suit the temporary needs leaves a great deal to be desired. Each of us feels the need for something permanent in the world surrounding us, just as we feel the need for a permanent identity for ourselves."[87] He also saw the critical roles boundaries played in holding societies together. "It is well to remember that [boundary] means *that which binds together*," he argued in the same essay; "[it] is what makes it possible for a society to have its own individuality. And this is true of the individual holding also."[88] "Boundaries stabilize relationships," he said later. "They make residents out of the homeless, neighbors out of strangers, strangers out of enemies. They give a permanent human quality to what would otherwise be an amorphous stretch of land."[89]

Most significant of all, he understood the historical role of place in sustaining peoples. He urged Americans to fashion a public landscape with monuments and public gathering places (courthouses, post offices, etc.), "where we are particularly aware of our identity as citizens."[90] Of monuments, he said that they "serve as reminders of the past, symbols of another community to which we belong: the community of those who have died. If the public square is a reminder of the present, the monument is a reminder of promises made, or origins we are inclined to forget." A culture or country without "a sense of history," Jackson argued, is threatened by a splintering into subcultures, and by submergence in a world of legends and superstitions.[91]

Jackson also wrote eloquently of the lasting sense of

place that ordinary people made together, and nowhere more poignantly than in a 1984 essay dealing partly with his World War II experience when, as a second lieutenant in army intelligence, he joined the G-2 section of the 9th Infantry Division and took part in the invasion of Normandy. After the invasion, he spent a long, cold winter in the Huertgen Forest, sharing with "the men in companies and platoons" the same "military landscape."[92] As he recalled, he felt a profound bonding with the other men—all under the same threat of death, all as alive to the world around them as any men could have been; he also learned how landscape itself, broadly considered, might act as a critical medium for bringing "about a closer relationship between man and environment and between men."[93]

The "military landscape," he wrote, in an earlier essay invoking the same experience, "was the ugly caricature of a landscape." "Nevertheless, it . . . instructed us in what a good landscape, and a good society, should be." For here was a sense of place so thick, so dense and intense, that it could not fail to remind us of "spaces that never change and are always as memory depicted them."[94]

"This is how we should think of landscapes," he insisted, as ways to "satisfy . . . the need for sharing some of those sensory experiences in a familiar place: popular songs, popular dishes, a special kind of weather supposedly found nowhere else, a special kind of sport and game, played only here in this spot. These things remind us that we belong—or used to belong—to a specific place: a country, a town, a neighborhood. A landscape should establish bonds between people."[95]

Still, for all his understanding of the power of place, the lure of the temporary always returned to take precedence in his thinking, and always prevented him, finally (as I have said), from seeing how far the temporary had intruded into the lives of Americans. Again and again Jackson wrote with eloquence about the loss or destruction of old ways—the decline of self-sufficient and family-owned farms; the disappearance, in many parts of the country, of Sunday walks and of the "front yard." But he did not spend much time or thought on the "old ways"; his laments were often devices to prepare the reader for his central arguments: that (first) these things had died because they no longer performed useful functions, and (second) new landscapes were emerging that did perform useful functions. Underlying this approach, moreover, was Jackson's own addiction to the technologies of mobility, his refusal to consider the capitalist market system critically, and his distaste—which he shared with many other Americans—for being identified with the losing side.

This lure of the temporary prevented him, by and large, from appreciating fully the plight of those who lived in modern trailer parks. Jackson, of course, may have just refused to give up his original notion of these communities, a notion he formed in the sixties when he first spotted those gleaming homes in New Mexico and the skilled workers living in them. More important, he misconstrued the way in which such communities resembled the vernacular villages of the past.[96] Most modern trailer parks resemble such villages only in their poverty. They are extremely vulnerable, more so than Jackson was willing to admit. Often badly built, they can be wiped away by storms or tornadoes; greedy landlords can evict "undesirable" tenants easily by regularly raising their rents; and, most of all, trailer parks as a whole can be crushed by the shifting demands of commercial developers.

Like H-1B foreign skilled workers or adjunct university instructors, the unskilled workers in mobile homes seem perfectly suited to the demands of the flexible labor market: they often move on a moment's notice and with little protest. Yet, unlike many skilled H-1B workers or academic adjuncts, who ultimately—for the most part—have more freedom to dictate their own fates, these workers have little power to shape fate on their own terms (although many would deny that anyone should help them, least of all the federal government). In the winter of 1994, in Fairfax, Virginia, two hundred residents of a trailer park on land owned by Wal-Mart were displaced to make way for a new Wal-Mart store. A year later, in Everett, Washington, the managers of a planned strip mall forced the closing of the Olivia Mobile Home Park. By the decade's end, developers in Vail, Colorado, had leveled six trailer parks to make room for vacation homes. Hundreds of parks are in similar jeopardy, and only the owners' ingenuity, coupled with protection from the states, seems capable of slowing the removal of even more people.[97]

J. B. Jackson often missed much of this (although not always) because, on some critical level, he believed that everything that really mattered in life had a fugitive character, flaring up sometimes in a kind of brilliance only to vanish in the next moment. He himself was an urbane wanderer, a transient who managed to stamp the mark of the transient on a discourse that has shaped the way Americans think about landscape. His voice belonged to a significant chorus of voices made up of other temporaries, other singular singles of all kinds who have succeeded in redeeming the loner's wandering style as the most attractive style in modern America. But the need to instill a sense of permanence and stability, without which there can be no decent social order, is greater now than ever in our history; for the landscape of the temporary has more troubling features, more pitfalls, than Jackson ever imagined or chose to see—hundreds of thousands of detached managers with their remembering machines, millions of flexible workers, women as well as men on the stranger's path, drawn away from their homes, and the encroaching highways and roads, intermodal and otherwise, a global economy crashing into the traditional hearts of local cultures.

But this was not all: other changes were going on, too, just as subversive to place. They included the spread of a new service economy, at the core of which were tourism and gambling, each a challenge and an affront to place, each an attempt to rebuild place on a new foundation.

Three

"A Wonderful Sense of Place":
Tourism and Gambling to the Rescue

In the fall of 1995 I attended the White House Conference on Travel and Tourism, the first event of its kind ever held under the auspices of the federal government. It lasted two days, and the opening events had the feel of a revival, a political convention, and rock-and-roll concert all rolled into one.

On stage was a giant replica of the White House, bathed in blue and purple light, symbol of the institution that sponsored the two-day affair, and an image used as a logo on conference T-shirts and jackets. A Navy band played rousing patriotic tunes. Four gigantic video screens dispersed around the ballroom showed scenic views of America—beach shots, lake views with speedboats, neon-lighted nightspots, canyons, and deserts. John F. Kennedy's theme of "the New Frontier" was invoked again and again in speeches on video screens, a reminder to delegates that their goal—to win the tourist and travel war—was as crucial to America in the nineties as was Kennedy's aim in the sixties to beat the Russians in space. Seventeen hundred delegates from every state and five territories filled the ballroom, representing

the gamut of the travel and tourist industry, from travel agents
and hotel desk clerks to the CEOs of Hilton Hotels, Delta Airlines, and Alamo Rent a Car. Mayors, governors, and senators
attended, as did Vice President Al Gore and President Bill
Clinton.

Among the speeches was one by Jonathan Tisch, CEO of
Loew's Hotels, who told his audience that the United States "is
losing market share" in the international travel and tourist
business. "We're missing our greatest opportunity to sell the
best thing we have—ourselves." Americans have "a wonderful
sense of place," Tisch said, "so let's take advantage of that. Let's
sell that sense of place." "If we don't market our product, no
one else will."[1]

Nearly everybody packed into the gold ballroom of the
Sheraton Washington Hotel was in the business of selling
place. "We should market what we have," said Blanche Lincoln
of Arkansas, one of the many state tourist directors present,
"Our Indian mounds, the blues, the Civil War." Charles Gar-
field, host facilitator for the conference and a former NASA
official, asserted that "we have the greatest product on earth—
the U.S.A. But how do we market the U.S.A.?" Judson Green,
president of Walt Disney Attractions, warned, "We must market the brand U.S.A." or "our market share will be lost."

Many people in the room seemed to feel the gravity of these
claims, none more so than Bill Clinton, who knew, firsthand,
the economic power of the travel and tourist business. He grew
up in Hot Springs, Arkansas, during a period—1954 to 1965—
when that city was famed for its tourist attractions: its Versailles-
like bathhouses and hotels, such as the Arlington, among the
most elegant in the South; its numerous nightclubs, like the
Belvedere and the Vapors, on the east side of town, where
many people (including Virginia Kelly, Clinton's mother) came
to the play the roulette wheels and craps; and its long, big, pop-

ular Oaklawn Racetrack on the west side of town, which Virginia Kelly also frequented, just blocks away from Clinton's boyhood home.[2]

"This industry," the president said, "has been near and dear to my heart since I was a little boy," and "I have dedicated myself to helping" it "grow." Travel and tourism give us insight into "the common humanity of us all," he said. They allow us all to become "aristocrats," deepen our "understanding" of others, and help break down "the differences" that divide us. "They are also tailor-made for the global economy," "a powerhouse generating more than $400 billion in revenue and providing more than 10 percent of the world's income and employment."

Other speakers, among them Toby Roth, Republican congressman from Wisconsin (now retired) and the most zealous exponent of this industry in the House of Representatives, rang changes on these themes. Roth argued that "given that America's big companies are downsizing, all the new jobs are going to come from travel and tourism." This sector "is the wave of the future economically and politically." Greg Farmer, the undersecretary of the Tourist and Travel Administration (TTA) within the Commerce Department, and himself a product of the Florida tourist trade, pressed the New Frontier theme. "Thirty-five years ago," he said, "JFK gave us a vision. Today, we join hands to give all Americans jobs and equal opportunity. Travel and tourism is the rising star of the global economy." "This is a GROWTH INDUSTRY which touches every aspect of American business." He urged his listeners to imagine "all the bedsheets and bath towels for the 3.4 million hotel and motel rooms in this country."[3]

The late secretary of commerce, Ron Brown, agreed. Indeed, none more than Brown, whose attachment to this industry could hardly have been rivaled by that of anyone else in the Sheraton, felt the force of the rising-star argument and the meaning of all the bedsheets. The son of the manager of the Hotel Theresa in Harlem, he, like Clinton, had tourism in the bones. ("I grew up in a hotel," he told the crowd. He was "born into tourism," said his friend Congressman James Overstar.) He believed utterly, he claimed, in the promise of this great industry. It will "beat down barriers that separate nationalities." It will "open new doors" and "create jobs."[4]

A joint effort of Washington and the tourist and travel industry, this conference was held to promote a new national tourism strategy that would, as the event's media kit put it, "make the American travel experience second to none." The conference was organized, in fact, to inspire the industry to come up with its own national agenda (as Congress was about to cut off funding for the TTA) and to impress on the American public that it was no longer a fringe business but, in Clinton's words, "an indispensable part" of the new economy.

The conference testified to the status of the travel and tourist trades, which by the nineties offered more Americans more work than any other business outside of healthcare. But the conference stood for something else as well, something without which T and T would have been a much diminished enterprise. That something was gambling, or, more particularly, the casino economy, which had matured into a tourism staple. Historically, tourism and gambling were relatively separate activities (despite the example of cities like Hot Springs), but by the nineties they were almost interchangeable, mingling in new ways and places. Tourism and gambling as a team, as a blurred partnership in "entertainment and fun" (as the industry put it) had even infiltrated Indian reservations, which, despite their complex histories, many Americans often thought of as exemplars of place-rootedness.

But what did the future hold for such supposedly place-rooted communities when they marketed themselves to make money, treated place as mere fantasy and play, or no longer took it seriously as the historical backbone of cultural life? Tourism and gambling were central to the new service economy, and they were undermining place in an attempt to revitalize it.

"CRUISES TO NOWHERE" AND COSTNER'S DUNBAR

In the 1950s and sixties, few people cared whether or not Americans could compete in the international travel and tourist business. Let Bermuda, Monaco, or Greece sell themselves in marketing campaigns. The United States simply was what it was—a world power. In this climate, tourist dollars constituted only a small fraction of the nation's overall productive strength. By the nineties, however, not only was tourism employing more than 10 percent of the workforce (up from 6 percent in 1970) but American tourist and travel experts were agonizing about a "crisis in market share in the world's tourist and travel business."[5]

In many states (Utah, the Dakotas, California, Pennsylvania, Florida, Arizona, New Mexico, and others) and in many cities (New York, Los Angeles, Miami, Santa Barbara) tourism ranked first or second in importance as a source of wealth and employment. Counties, towns, and cities that had never relied on tourism before, had never thought of "selling place," now relied on it to make up for the drop in manufacturing; in this business, at least, Americans could not be undercut by corporations moving to Mexico or Indonesia. The natives still had their places, for what they still were worth, to sell.

In the 1990s nearly all of New York State, from New York City up through the Hudson River Valley and all along the old

Erie Canal, witnessed a decisive shift to tourism. Even New York's Putnam County, among the most rural and undeveloped counties in the state, created its first tourist bureau in 1995, to "bring in money" and "sell the area," as Republican county leader Robert Pozzi put it. "Putnam is the best-kept secret in the state until now," said the bureau's first director, Valerie Hickman, a recent immigrant from South Africa. "It's very exciting to see what's developing here."[6]

On the other side of the country, the people of Wallowa County, Oregon, out of desperation caused by the loss of mining and logging jobs, had even invited the Nez Perce Indians into the town to help build a brand-new tourism economy. In the nineteenth century, the federal government forcibly exiled most of the Wallowa Indians to an Idaho reservation, while those who remained behind were driven into Canada by angry whites; now, in one of the many curious twists of the age, the Nez Perce tribe was back in Wallowa, attracting "tourists by the busload," as a local resident reported.[7]

Indians themselves had turned to tourism as a way to survive on their reservations. Starting in the 1970s, tribes as diverse as the Hopi in Arizona, the Penobscot in Maine, and the Cherokee in North Carolina operated ski lifts, dammed rivers to build lakes for pleasure boating, and conducted powwows to capture the tourist trade.[8] From the late eighties on, many powwows—no longer unique ceremonies—were carnival events, spectacular drawing cards in which Indians from several tribes gathered to dance and sing, decked out in colorful feathers, and in beaded costumes worthy of Busby Berkeley. By the mid-nineties, Japanese, German, and English tourists were flooding into South Dakota, eager to live in a tepee for a week or more as part of a "cultural immersion" summer program offered by the Sioux tribes in the region.

Around the same time, the state of New Mexico established the first "full-fledged Indian tourism office" in the country.[9]

Year by year, casino gambling has also become big business. Before 1920, "there was only one place in the world where one could play roulette"—and that was Monte Carlo.[10] In time, other casinos were opened to serve the middle-class market on the Riviera and along the French coast near England.[11] But, in America before 1990, casinos existed only in a hot desert in Nevada, along the seedy beachfront of Atlantic City, and in Puerto Rico. Eight years later, twenty-eight states had casinos, some housed in more than seventy riverboats from Iowa to Illinois, self-contained gambling dens legally and culturally (if not literally) cut off from life on shore.[12] Casinos transformed old "drowsy shrimping port" cities such as Biloxi and Gulfport, Mississippi, into "tourism boomtowns," according to the *Wall Street Journal*.[13] On a smaller scale, floating crap game palaces called "cruises to nowhere" proliferated, docked along eastern cities from Florida to New York, ready to set sail for international waters in pursuit of the ideal nowhere setting for the toss of the dice.[14]

At the same time, Las Vegas, the world's premier gambling metropolis, underwent a burst of growth. A new species of casinos appeared after 1994, integrating theme-park rides, high-tech excitements, and a new family-friendly marketing approach. The Luxor Hotel, owned by Circus Circus Enterprises, was erected, a colossal Egyptian pyramid of black glass, across the way from the equally new MGM's Grand Casino/Hotel and blocks away from the Mirage's Treasure Island with its imitation tropical rain forest. The New York–New York Hotel/Casino made its debut in 1996, linked by a walkway to the MGM Grand, and noted for its phony Manhattan skyline with its giant Statue of Liberty and towering replica of the Empire State Building. In October 1998, at the heart of the Las Vegas Strip, mogul Steve Wynn planted his Bellagio Hotel/Casino; among its many unique features was a 8.5-acre lake and a Gallery of Fine Art, where visitors might view paintings and sculptures by Europe's and America's finest artists, from Monet and Van Gogh to Lichtenstein and de Kooning. By early 1999 Las Vegas contained more than 100,000 hotel rooms, a figure no other city in the world could come close to equaling.[15]

Then, of course, there were the Indian reservations, hardly what one might call nowhere. Indeed, these communities were supposedly unique places that Indians had struggled to transform from alienating prison camps imposed on them by the state into "islands of Indianness," controlled by Indians themselves, with historical identities, loyalty to ancestors, and a deep sense of place.[16] Since 1990, nearly 150 Indian tribes (out of 500) have built casino-type operations across the country from California to Connecticut.[17] Indians could take credit for bringing casinos to states, cities, and regions that never had them. The Pequots and Mohegans introduced casinos to Connecticut (grossing a $1.5 billion in 1997), the Oneidas to New York State, and the several Sioux tribes to Minnesota. The Confederated Tribes of the community of Grande Ronde operated Oregon's only casino, called Spirit Mountain; and the Kotenai tribe in Idaho managed the only hotel-casino complex in that state. The Puyallup Tribe in Washington State brought a $21 million casino riverboat, the Emerald Queen, to that city, its first Las Vegas–style gambling enterprise.[18]

Many tribal casinos were small-scale, often heart-wrenching attempts to escape poverty. The Oglala Sioux casino, the Prairie Wind, in Pine Ridge, South Dakota, sits in a corner of the nation's second largest reservation. The casino is a speck in a vast stretch of open plains where antelope run and a sea of rolling grass seems never-ending; it had done little by the late nineties to lift the poverty of Pine Ridge.[19] Elsewhere, however, many of the new Indian casinos, from the Viejas business near San Diego to the Oneidas' Turning Stone casino-hotel outside Rome, New York, were huge and rich, affecting not only the reservations but the regions in which they existed.

Gambling quickly became a highly lucrative feature of the tourist-entertainment universe. Developers everywhere sought to link tourism and gambling into a total package and to offer a diversified range of entertainment to children as well as adults. We must "integrate gaming with entertainment and retail," said Edward DeBartolo, Jr., chairman of Simon-DeBartolo Real Estate Investment Trust (the biggest of all the REITs), in 1995; this "is the wave of the future."[20]

Kevin Costner agreed with DeBartolo. The thirty-five-year-old Costner cleared a $60 million profit for his efforts in the 1990 *Dances With Wolves,* a film which emphasized the spiritual purity of Indians—in this case, the Lakota Sioux tribe in South Dakota—at the expense of the corrupt whites. In 1995, Costner, flush with the windfall from such films and looking for profitable places to invest it, embarked with his brother, Dan, on the erection of the Dunbar, a supposedly world-class vacation resort named for the character Costner played in *Dances With Wolves.*

The spot Costner chose to build on was a beautiful bluff just outside of Deadwood, South Dakota, from which one could see the Black Hills, with their green ponderosa pine, aspen, cottonwood, white birch, and willow. These were among the hills the Sioux viewed as sacred, the hills that were taken from them by the federal government in the 1877 treaties. No one better than Costner knew this history; his film had honored it and even inspired the local Lakota to make him and his brother, Dan, honorary members of the tribe.[21]

But little did the Indians know that the movie star planned

to convert their spiritual domain into what he called "the Switzerland of America." Costner got the property in a land swap with the U.S. Forest Service in 1995. A few years earlier he had purchased 585 acres in Spearfish Canyon, a slice of private property belonging to the Homestake Gold Mine Company (the biggest gold mining concern in North America) that happened to be nestled within the federally owned Black Hills. Costner bought the land, which Homestake no longer needed, only to encourage the Forest Service to take it in exchange for the land Costner *did* want—the 640 acres near Deadwood. In the tradition of "wise use," the Forest Service was eager to make the swap. The Service viewed the Spearfish Canyon site as having the same value as the Black Hills property (basing their determination on real estate standards, ironically enough). They wanted to incorporate it into the park system to save Spearfish from residential development, maintain its biodiversity in perpetuity, and preserve its natural beauty so that more and more people might be drawn into the region. After all, nearly 2.6 miles of U.S. Highway 14A, designated a National Scenic Byway under the Intermodal Surface Transportation Efficiency Act, was located within Spearfish Canyon.[22]

In the spring of 1996, Costner began in earnest to reshape his land into what his publicity literature called the "*largest* resort complex [to be] developed in North America in many decades."[23] The estate occupied nearly 840 acres and, when finished, would contain a 320-room hotel and conference center, four tennis courts, two pools, skiing and ice-skating facilities, health spa and sauna, an eighteen-hole golf course, nine retail outlets, a 3,000-seat outdoor amphitheater, a movie theater, an equestrian center, and a twenty-four-hour casino. By August 1997 his developers had completed a massive transplanting of trees to the site (since the previous leaseholder had stripped it of trees), the "largest [transplanting] effort ever attempted," according to Dunbar's brochure.[24] The golf course, too, had been seeded, and a rail bed for a train linking the resort to the airport in Rapid City was graded. But there were snags as well, unforeseen delays, fears that unless the betting limit imposed by South Dakota law (five dollars) was raised, the high rollers would not stream in. By winter 1999, the project had slowed to a crawl. A local news editor complained that "Costner has achieved nothing" but "to hold the town hostage." Still, many locals refused to lose faith. They had come to see Costner's kingdom as the lynchpin in the future "growth" of this part of South Dakota.[25]

JOBS, INDIAN SOVEREIGNTY, AND SOLOMON KERZNER'S MOHEGAN SUN

What lay behind Costner's fantasy of a new Switzerland in the Dakotas? Why, indeed, had so many people in just fifteen years turned to tourism and gambling as good ways of making a living? And why, for heaven's sake, were there casinos on Indian reservations? For some analysts, such as Paul Biederman, professor of tourism at New York University's Center for Hospitality, Tourism, and Travel Administration, answers to these questions could be found in one cause—the ever-expanding number of people, especially middle-class people in foreign countries with more money than ever in their pockets, and just as eager to unload it on vacations and cruises as Europeans and Americans had been over the past hundred or so years. These individuals, who lived in such places as Malaysia, India, and China, not only could afford cars, TVs, and computers but, as Biederman argued, they "longed to be tourists and visit the United States." Before 1998—after which the Asian economic meltdown threw a dismal pall over such longings—these people formed a kind of "built-in growth component," guaranteed to swell "for the next fifty to one hundred years."[26]

But hordes of tourists waiting to spill into America by sea and air were the least significant cause for the appearance of places like Costner's Dunbar. The tremendous growth of the airline industry with the number of commercial airplanes nearly tripling from 2,100 in the 1960s to nearly 6,000 in the late 1990s certainly played its part, permitting anyone with money to go almost anywhere and to see anything.[27] More important, however, were the internal economic causes, above all, the fundamental shift in the character of the American economy. As manufacturing, mining, ranching, logging, military spending, and family farming fell away as sources of work and income for Americans, governmental bodies around the country turned to tourism and gambling to make up the difference.[28] It was the logic of this reality that lay behind Bill Clinton's ardent defense of tourism at the 1995 Travel and Tourism Conference. It was this logic that made Rudolph Giuliani, mayor of New York City, a staunch supporter of tourism in New York and a serious advocate of bringing gambling to that city; and it was this logic that converted Christine Todd Whitman, blue-blooded governor of New Jersey, into an apostle for Atlantic City casino interests.

These economic conditions explained why Costner was bulldozing in the Black Hills: many local whites had welcomed the actor to the region because they had lost their jobs when the federal government closed Ellsworth Air Force Base in Rapid City. South Dakotan politicians, too, at all levels of government, saw in Costner's new Field of Dreams a boon for employment.[29]

And how was it that Americans could play roulette at such unlikely places as Indian reservations? The answer to this question boils down to one thing: the rehabilitation of Indian sovereignty that has taken place step by step over the past thirty years. During that time, Indian sovereignty has been rebuilt, first politically and culturally, and then, for some tribes, economically.

Before the 1960s the United States—except for a brief time between the world wars—had worked to destroy Indian sovereignty and to compel Indian assimilation into the American mainstream. After the late 1960s, however, the United States worked to promote Indian sovereignty and tribalism and *rejected* assimilation.[30] The government granted the Indian tribes new claims to sovereign status, indeed to such an extent that, as Richard White, an historian of the West, has written, it "ironically made tribes more important than they have ever been in Indian history."[31]

In 1968 Congress passed the Indian Civil Rights Act, which forbade the states from exercising civil or criminal jurisdiction on Indian reservations. Two years later, Richard Nixon, in an executive order, announced that "Indian acts and Indian decisions" would, from that time forward, determine all federal policy regarding the Indians.[32] This order was followed by a remarkable body of legislation and Supreme Court decisions that, altogether, "served as the vehicle for preserving tribalism in numerous Indian groups."[33] From the seventies to the present, moreover, both federal and state governments recognized the sovereignty of Indian groups. Indeed, it was ironic that at a time when many Americans were beginning to question (and even attack) the very idea of American sovereignty, they seemed sure that Indian nationhood should be reawakened and strengthened.[34]

This shift in government policy was in part animated by the collapse of Western imperialism and the rise of independent Third World countries; by the American civil rights movement; and by the spiritual needs of many middle-class white

Americans who were estranged from established religion and looked to some outside source for spiritual renewal and insight. Indian cultures, after years of being ignored or ridiculed by many people, were now elevated, even idolized by mainstream Americans as the source of cultural vitality (as they still are today).[35]

In the early 1970s, as part of this rehabilitation of cultural sovereignty, Richard Nixon also signed a law that restored to the Taos Pueblos in New Mexico 50,000 acres in the Carson National Forest, which contained the tribe's sacred Blue Lake, the "heart of their culture and site of their secret August pilgrimage."[36] Twenty years later, Congress was still midwifing the cultural rebirth of the tribes. In 1989 Congress passed a law to establish an Indian museum in the Washington Mall, a fitting symbol of the Indian renaissance on the national scene. The act also mandated that the Smithsonian Institution survey all its Indian artifacts, with the aim of returning them—"repatriating" them as Native American leaders called it—to those tribes that owned them originally.[37] A year later, Congress extended this law to nearly all other museums, stipulating that upon request they must return all "sacred objects and objects of cultural patrimony" to the relevant Indian descendants.[38]

It was in the context of this cultural-political rearmament of the Indian tribes that the federal and state governments also attempted to foster Indian *economic* sovereignty, so that the Indians—as presidents from Nixon to Clinton hoped—would get off the welfare rolls and "privatize" themselves.[39] Since the 1960s, the federal government provided the reservations with financial assistance, including the granting of water and fishing rights, designed to stimulate their economies along traditional lines.[40] But the biggest boon by far to many reservations turned out to be gambling, which Washington facilitated through the passage of the 1988 Indian Gaming Regulatory Act (IGRA), a radical act ushered through Congress by Representative Stewart Udall and acclaimed by Ronald Reagan, who, perhaps more than any other president, wanted to terminate Indian programs (but not the tribes) and launch privatization.[41]

The IGRA allowed any Indian tribe that could prove itself to be a tribe the right to operate tax-free on their own any form of gambling going on in its state. It also stated that any tribe that wished to conduct casino-type gambling had first to request negotiations for compacts with their respective states and, second, they had the right to sue those states in federal district court, if the states refused to negotiate (this right, however, the Supreme Court withdrew in 1996).

Given the current of revitalization set loose to promote Indian sovereignty, coupled with the existence of chronic Indian poverty and the experience many tribes already had in conducting low-stakes gambling since the 1970s (mainly bingo), the law seemed almost inevitable. But it had results that no one could have foreseen. Without consenting referenda or input of any kind from those *local* non-Indians who would have been affected the most by it, this federal law brought casino gambling to states that had never before had such activity. It unified American tribes (or at least their enriched elites) into one cohesive unit in a way that no other event or law had ever done, complete with Washington lobbyists, organizations, and magazines. It transformed some tiny tribes into little Kuwaits, governed by their own rules but able to shape the world around them.[42] To put it another way, this law—along with the whole effort to reempower Indian sovereignty—helped remake the American political landscape by adding yet another semisovereign entity to a growing community of such entities. Like the country's giant semi-sovereign port authorities (the ports of Long Beach, Los Angeles, Elizabeth, and so forth), and like its equally giant semi-sovereign research universities (discussed in the next chapter), these Indian casino empires belonged to a nearly autonomous and unaccountable institutional world, unique to this fluid, global age.

Perhaps equally as striking, the quest for Indian sovereignty brought to life a breed of non-Indian developers who cared nothing about Indians but saw in their supposedly nowhere homelands the perfect sites to house slot machines and crap tables. They included Lyle Berman of Minnesota whose Grand Casinos Corporation built, opened, and managed the profitable Mille Lacs and Hinckley casinos for the Chippewa Indians of Minnesota; also Solomon Kerzner, CEO of Sun International Hotels and a resourceful developer who, in 1998, owned more than thirty casinos in Europe, Africa, America, and the Bahamas.[43]

A native South African, Kerzner started his gambling empire in his own country during the heyday of apartheid, taking full advantage of the government's system of homelands. Kerzner focused on the homelands because their laws allowed gambling, while the rest of South Africa banned it. Moreover, the homelands were ideal places for casinos because they were not the products of actual black African history but the inventions of the white-controlled government bent on finding a way to segregate blacks from white society (except as reserves of cheap labor). In a way that eerily mirrored the resurgence of tribal sovereignty in America, the South African government urged the blacks to "return" to these "homelands" where they might reclaim their "tribal" pasts and cultures. It set up eight homelands (formed from hundreds of native reserves), each with its own constitution, its own legislature and cabinet, and its own system of education to transmit tribal culture. The desire, of course, was not to restore sovereignty (as in the American case) but to destroy it, and to ensure that the strategy worked, the government (especially during the 1980s) herded millions of blacks into the homelands, many of whom had long forgotten their tribal histories.[44] The outcome was not only worse poverty for blacks but the formation of corrupt tribal elites answerable to Pretoria and willing to enter into lucrative compacts with such gambling entrepreneurs as Solomon Kerzner.[45]

Kerzner drew up compacts with several tribes, granting him exclusive gambling rights, most notably in Bophuthatswana, just outside Johannesburg, where he built Sun City, the casino-hotel that billed such performers as Frank Sinatra and Liza Minnelli. In 1985 he was alleged to have bribed officials in the Transkei homeland, demanding similar exclusive rights to run a hotel-casino resort (the Wild Coast Sun) in Umtata, the Transkei capital, within reach of rich international tourists. In 1990 the attorney general of the Transkei, Christo Nel, charged Kerzner with criminal fraud, bribery, and corruption, and giving false witness before an investigative commission. Nevertheless, Kerzner was never convicted of any crime.[46]

Kerzner's South African casinos flourished until the early 1990s when anti-apartheid forces took over the government, dissolving the tribal homelands. In 1994, moreover, the South African government required that Sun International reduce the number of its casinos from seventeen to nine.[47] Kerzner shifted gears. He turned to America, where another system of homelands existed, many conjured up out of thin air by the Indian Gaming Regulatory Act. He set his sights, in particular, on the Mohegan tribe in Uncasville, Connecticut. Until the 1980s, this tribe had been defunct, having long ago (in 1861) *voluntarily* asked the state to break up the reservation by selling individual parcels of land to tribal members, thereby converting the Indians into American citizens and residents of Uncasville.[48] But the tribe—or the rump that still remained—resurfaced after Congress passed the 1988 law and, in 1994, with help from lawyers paid for by Kerzner, successfully got recognition from the Bureau of Indian Affairs as a legitimate tribe. Soon thereafter the Mohegans signed a deal with a developer, Trading Cove Associates (50 percent owned by Kerzner's Sun International), which developed and managed the casino and got 40 percent of all the profits. Kerzner's money hired the builders, the designers, the fantasists. The place was called Mohegan Sun. By the late nineties, it was the third-biggest casino in the country, with nearly 3,000 slot machines, hundreds of table games, a parking lot for nearly 7,500 cars, and a four-lane highway built for the tribe that allowed direct access from Interstate 395. The casino included twenty bars and restaurants and a big entertainment complex for children.[49]

The success of Mohegan Sun fed Kerzner's ambitions to become the preeminent casino player on the East Coast. In 1997 the New Jersey Gaming Commission approved his application for a license to operate the Resorts International Hotel in Atlantic City, which he had purchased earlier from entertainer Merv Griffin. No one on the New Jersey Commission seemed upset by his behavior in South Africa. One commissioner shook his hand after the proceedings and said, "Thanks again for investing in Atlantic City." Kerzner himself observed that "this allows us to expand even faster."[50]

TRAVEL AND TOURISM

Resourceful men like Kerzner and Costner, then, along with the reassertion of Indian sovereignty, and, above all, the reliance of Americans on services for employment and income, have given new status to the tourism/gambling industry. And they have so changed the dimension and nature of that industry as to make it into a threat to the sense of place.

Years ago, historian Daniel Boorstin in his book *The Image* discussed the difference between travel and tourism. Travel, he said, was an activity that almost compelled people to face the places they visited. People traveled on their own terms, followed their own passions and quirks, and accepted whatever distress came their way as the price paid for the pleasure gained. Modern tourism, on the other hand, insulated people from experiencing and knowing the world; through an elaborate set of protections (from arranged tours to air conditioning), it transformed travelers into passive consumers of painless adventure.[51]

This distinction has remained a sound one. At its best, tourism (especially when it approaches travel) can open people up to the unexpected and unknown. At its worst, however, it diminishes place, or the sense of place, by making it nearly risk-free to get where you want to go and—as part of the package— to feel entirely safe there (usually in chain hotels or motels of unrelieved sameness). Previously, when it was harder to get somewhere, the reward was usually more satisfying, the goal more desirable. In our time, however, "travel has become so easy that even the sedentary can reach just about any destination," to quote Lee Lescaze, writing in the *Wall Street Journal*.[52]

Worst of all, the "marketing of place" (as specialists in tourism call it), the selling of "brand U.S.A.," has trivialized countries and places. Disney president Judson Green said at the 1995 White House Conference on Travel and Tourism, that cities with "historic culture" will lose out unless they "sell this culture." "Dayton, Ohio," Green observed, "is blessed with the Lincoln-Douglas debates," but "the town is doing nothing to market those debates." But what will happen, Green asked, to the Lincoln-Douglas debates if the town decides to "sell" them aggressively? What will happen, indeed? Will Dayton cease to remember because it will not or cannot market its past? Or, if Dayton does choose to sell Lincoln-Douglas, what parts of the debates will it sell to mass markets? Will there be the usual trade-off between selling and understanding?

For all this, however, tourism, especially when respectfully and cautiously pursued, has often had a benign effect, even to the point of saving some endangered wilderness (e.g., Yellowstone Park) from the ashbin of history.[53] In some parts of the country, as well as elsewhere in the world, it has become a means for saving much unused farmland (as rural heritage) which would otherwise be sold off to developers.[54] However, when seen in relation to gambling, or when combined with gambling, the benign potential of tourism vanishes, as in the case of Las Vegas.

LAS VEGAS BLIGHT

For the past twenty years, most permanent well-off residents of Las Vegas have either taken refuge in self-contained residential subdivisions or fled to the sunny paradise of nearby Henderson. Most have made a trade-off, having come to Las Vegas to escape taxes elsewhere (the Nevada constitution bans income and corporate taxes) and with full knowledge that casino money ruled everything (the taxes from which also paid for whatever public services there were). Nevertheless, most residents have tried to act and live as if the city did not exist, although ironically they have never been able *visually* to escape the casinos (because the Las Vegas Strip can be seen from virtually any point on the compass).[55] The concrete reasons for this denial were no mysteries: Las Vegas is, for a city its size, among the most crime-ridden in America, its urban core suffering from terminal neglect, a condition fostered by the selfishness of Las Vegans who detest taxation.[56]

But Las Vegans, the rich as well as the poor who lived mostly in dilapidated North Las Vegas, have felt little attraction to the city proper for other reasons. Las Vegas is an American city *in extremis,* "the heart of the American dream," as Hunter Thompson described it, a metropolis where money stands out in all its naked glory.[57] It is a city that has pushed the placeless side of American life to its limits. For one thing, Las Vegas flouts nature. Without the Hoover Dam and Lake Mead—both only twenty miles away, both in their own rights interventions to defeat nature—it would vanish in a dry land that would soon overtake it.[58]

This sense of coming out of nowhere forms the backdrop for the other features of Las Vegas that make it inhospitable to people seeking stable communities: Las Vegas not only flouts nature, it flouts place and the past. Las Vegas flouts place because it serves only people on the move—transients, tourists. It is truly a cosmopolitan city, which people visit from all over the world, enticed in part by its nonjudgmental openness, which their own transiency facilitates and which the casinos, for obvious reasons, encourage.

Las Vegas also flouts the past (place). Here facades have more meaning than reality itself, the past existing as myth-fragments wrenched out of context—from imperial Rome and ancient Egypt to medieval Europe and New York City circa 1960. Here the casinos enlist the past to arouse the feeling of belonging to another world, of being swept up by some jet stream of fantasy. Gambling requires the freeing of impulse, and that freeing is sustained by a culture that says "Give in, don't hold back, let go."

In some ways, such a world is perfect for immigrants, because it says that no pasts matter and that anyone can be an American. From another viewpoint, it endangers immigrants (thousands of whom work in the Las Vegas casinos and hotels) or all those who want to build new bonds. How can people connect with a world that has no past, or that treats the past as fantasy and entertainment?

Las Vegas is a supremely democratic city, made so by money. The casinos exclude no one; the whole spectrum of human life walks Las Vegas Boulevard—the elderly, children, the crippled, all races, immigrants and tourists from every country, anyone who can pay the airfare to get into the city. That is why a replica of the Statue of Liberty, however absurd it may seem on first sight, belongs in this place. Las Vegas even contains a new Ellis Island Casino! Yet, at the same time, this democracy has nothing to do with political citizenship: it is a people's (a child's) playground, every bauble the contrivance of sharp managerial minds.

At the gold-lined Mirage, the city's most luxurious casino-hotel, Steve Wynn, the CEO, in 1997, put in an exclusive room called "the Salon Privé" for high rollers, precursor to his Gallery of Art in the Bellagio. Decorated with the finest European art (*real* Picassos, Monets, Manets, Matisses, Renoirs, Modiglianis) and with elegant dining spaces and golden toilet seats, it was accessible only to the richest gamblers.[59] Rooms like this one have been built in America for at least one hundred years, and all have captured the essence of capitalist culture—the hierarchy of wealth at the heart of the democracy of desire. Anyone might enter them so long as they paid. With enough money in America anyone could be king or queen (or senator); but for the losers, such rooms were locked shut, and Las Vegas reverted to the desert it really was.

A new generation of casino managers armed with MBAs from Harvard have tried, since the 1980s, to make Las Vegas family-friendly, an effort symbolized in Wynn's Mirage by an aquarium full of "endangered dolphins," as well as by a zoo full of "endangered cats."[60] In May of 1997 a little girl, left alone by her gambling father to play in the video arcade of one of the Las Vegas casinos, was raped and murdered at 3 A.M. in the casino's lavatory. Three months later, Steve Wynn opened his hotel to a conference of the nation's governors: the subject was—of all things—the care and development of children. Wynn's apostles were there, including Governor Christine Todd Whitman; but no mention was made of the child's death, overshadowed as her murder was by the attempt to link the casinos—Las Vegas—to a noble, moral cause.

Las Vegas reveals, in pristine form, the effects of a gambling-tourism economy, effects so toxic to traditional community life as to compel all who wish to settle down there willingly to do so in gated subdivisions. But wherever cities or towns have turned to tourism or gambling (or similar service-sector work) as their basic source of income, the same outcomes have occurred, if not to the same degree, certainly in kind. They have occurred, as well, on many Indian reservations, indeed in a way that illustrates how high the cost has been when place-rooted peoples turn to placeless activities to save their communities.

PRIMAL SENSE OF PLACE
AND THE WEB OF LIFE

Most Indian reservations have nothing in common historically with such cities as Las Vegas or Atlantic City: they were not the handiwork of developers but reputed homelands in which half of all Indians lived. Yet, many Indians have done all they could to entice Las Vegas into their communities, from hiring Las Vegas managers to designing their casinos and hotels in the most up-to-date Vegas style.

Some of the casino-reservations have begun to look and

feel like little Las Vegases. They draw the same kind of crowds, the same Balzacian mix of tourists and transients, giving rise to the same cosmopolitanism. They also resemble Las Vegas in their obvious theatricality and in their anything-goes atmospheres (if they did not, they would not be casinos).

Some tribes have even enlisted their own native culture to stir up the right kind of ambiance. The fanciest restaurant in the Mystic Lake Casino in Minnesota was decorated in 1995 with several Indian murals; one depicted an Indian chief sitting upright in a state of rapt meditation in an open, sunlit field.[61] "We are very proud," said Anthony Pico, chairman of the Viejas Band of Kumeyaay Indians, which after 1996 ran a casino (plus theme park and shopping mall) just outside San Diego, open twenty-four hours a day, every day, "that our casino is unique among most others to the degree that we drew upon our very own culture and heritage from the land and incorporated them into the structure's design." Even "the walls are the rich earth-tone colors and textures of the soil, trees, and flowers."[62] The Mohegans of Connecticut also dressed their casino in "the Mohegan Spirit," which, according to tribal historian Melissa Fawcett, "moves and breathes within the very rocks and trees of the Mohegan Homeland."

When the Mohegan business opened in 1996, Herbert Muschamp, architectural critic for the *New York Times,* and champion of Indian casinos, raved about its "primal power of place" with its "dense exhilarating forest of symbols." "The casino has actually revived the Mohegans' sense of tribal cohesion," he said. Muschamp even argued that the Mohegans belonged to a vanguard of moral liberators, which he viewed as a good thing. "The casino signifies the shattering of a moral taboo," he wrote. "Anyone old enough to be admitted to a casino grew up in a culture that placed gambling, along with cursing, drinking and prostitution, on the list of Bad Things. Indeed, in most parts of the country, gambling remains illegal. That is why the Indians have captured this market. Legally, Indians exist outside the borders of this country. They are exempt from the laws in which America's moral prejudices have been inscribed."[63]

Money and desire have also begun to pervade every aspect of reservation life, just as they do at Las Vegas and elsewhere. Money and desire, of course, bring on patrons. They also bestow immense economic power on many tribes, but with special meaning for Indians; for as tribal gambling wealth has grown, it has also distorted the economic side of Indian sovereignty (at least for some tribes).

This distortion, in turn, has had two major outcomes. First, it has jeopardized other forms of Indian sovereignty, which many Indians worked so hard to resurrect, and which helped reawaken an Indian sense of place and autonomy. One kind of place, in other words, has come at the cost of another kind, as money power has tended to pit tribal members against one another, undermining tribal governments, thereby threatening Indian *political* sovereignty. Even more important, it has led to the degradation of Indian cultural-spiritual traditions, at the heart of which has not been money and desire but the *condemnation* of money and desire, as well as respect for ancestors, devotion to "the sacred in nature," and a need to protect "the interlocking web of life," in the words of writer and teacher John Mohawk.[64] "Money was never that important before," Tim Giago, Sioux editor of the newspaper *Indian Country Today,* wrote in 1996, "because there was little of it, and when it was available, it was shared by all. [Now] tribes are abandoning their culture, traditions, and laws (written and unwritten). The money is just too strong a temptation. Would Crazy Horse, Chief Seattle, Chief Joseph or Geronimo be comfortable with the new direction? We know the answer to that."[65] "In our tribal society," observed Sioux Indian Thomas Pretends Eagle, "no one was hungry. Things were given freely, not hoarded. When you have enough, why more? Answer, why do I need more? There was nothing in Native society that could not be taken back into the earth."[66]

But Indian economic sovereignty has not only contravened other kinds of Indian sovereignty (or essential elements of place), it has also challenged the cultural sovereignty of those people who live outside the reservations, non-Indians who must suffer the wider fallout from an economy built on tourism and gambling. Many Indian casinos have begun to have economic predominance in their regions; numerous counties in Connecticut, upstate New York, Minnesota, and California have grown increasingly dependent on them for revenues and employment. These economies, in turn, have attracted a new group of real estate developers and investors determined to erect hotels, restaurants, and an "hospitality industry" in areas near the casinos. The casinos have also brought traffic, the widening of older highways, and new roads.

Years ago, Indians were afraid of roads, especially those laid by white men; the Indians saw in roads the doom of their cultures. When asked by a U.S. Census taker in 1897 why he feared the "white" institution of private property, a Tuscarora Indian replied that it was because there "will have to be outlets to it, and there will be roads all over it; it will be all roads."[67] Ironically, one hundred years later, Indians themselves were opening up the roads, not only into the reservations but into non-Indian neighborhoods as well. And where new roads did not exist, old ones were choked with gamblers, adding to the congestion caused by recent suburbanization.[68] Rural southeastern Connecticut, for instance, has one major north-south highway, Route 2, and for years it saw only light traffic. By 1996, however, 30,000 cars were delivering 50,000 customers to Foxwoods every day of the year.[69] In fall 1997 the tribe introduced a high-speed ferry, which carried gamblers directly from Manhattan to Foxwoods in Ledyard. The Pequots, moreover, aspired to the creation of an intermodal transport system, connecting airplanes, trains, and ferries into a "seamless whole," that would allow millions of people to visit their reservation "from all over the world."[70]

These roads, then, old and new, have aroused anxiety in many local non-Indians in North Stonington and Norwich, the towns nearest Foxwoods. Many local residents, unlike those in Las Vegas, have yet to make their peace with so much gambling-tourism; and they resent the federal government for having "imposed" the casino on them, through the IGRA, and *without* permitting a local referendum as to its merits.[71] In the past these people sympathized with efforts to reestablish Indian sovereignty (out of respect for Indian cultures), but by the 1990s they were beginning to feel otherwise.

Many Indian leaders themselves saw none of these dangers, or refused to give them any credence: they did not believe (or refused to believe) that their homelands had evolved into little Las Vegases or that they endangered anybody's culture. Some argued that the tribes had a right to change, the same as non-Indians, and that change and innovation were intrinsic to all cultures, at all times.[72] Other leaders were so desperate to end tribal poverty that they could not tolerate any attacks on gambling and tourism. Margo Anderson, chief of the Mille Lacs Band of the Ojibwa tribe that owns Grand Casino Minneapolis, defended her casino aggressively, arguing that it "saved the tribe" and "returned my people to dignity."[73] "I don't have any qualms about gaming," S. Verna Fowler, tribal leader of the Menominee tribe of Wisconsin, said, "because the need is so great. We just have so many needs to address."[74] Carol Cornelius, Oneida leader in Wisconsin, glowed in 1995: "When I walk into that casino, I'm overwhelmed. I think, 'My people did all this.' We've had five years to acquire all this business sense."[75]

Several Indians were less concerned with ending poverty than with getting rich, and had no trouble reconciling Las Vegas with Indian traditions, some viewing their casinos as "extension[s] of the strength and spirituality of [our] ancestors," others just making it up as they went along.[76] Nearly everything about both the Mohegan and Pequot tribes and their enterprises in southeastern Connecticut, for instance, was as fictional as anything the white-controlled government of South Africa ever imagined for the black homelands in the 1980s. The one bankrolled by Malaysian investors (Foxwoods), the other by a South African casino mogul (Mohegan Sun), they were the Madison Avenue fruit of the new global economy. The very ethnicity of the Pequot tribe, moreover, had to be re-remembered by a small army of anthropologists and non-Indian historians hired by the management for the many "Pequots" who, like their South African tribal counterparts, knew little about their ancestral ways (interestingly, one tradition that was found showed that the early Pequots detested gambling and drinking.)

Despite these affirming voices, however, there were others who condemned gambling as anathema to their culture. Doug George, a Mohawk leader and journalist, has repeatedly argued that "commercial gambling runs contrary to the ancestral Iroquois laws, and its spread has eclipsed [our] cultural survival and the effort to retain our language and our indigenous spiritual rituals."[77] Many tribes have voted down casinos in tribal referenda, including the Navajo in Arizona and New Mexico, the largest Indian community in the United States; the Alabama-Coushatta Indians of southern Texas, a very poor tribe with a high unemployment rate who nevertheless refused, by a large majority, to allow gambling on their reservation; and, for many years, the Senecas of upstate New York (although in May 1998 a majority did finally approve a gambling referendum).[78] Throughout South Dakota, moreover, when actor Kevin Costner swapped land with the Forest Service in his successful attempt to begin building Dunbar in the Black Hills, hundreds of Sioux denounced the deal. In letters to the Forest Service, not one Indian supported it. "The Greed of no man should over rule!" wrote James Testerman. Jesse Taken Alive, council chairman for the Standing Rock tribe, said that "everything is interconnected in nature, and the Sioux do not approve of any land ownership within the Black Hills." "*Paha Sapa* [Lakota for "the hills that are black hills"] is not for sale or trade," observed Burdell Blue Arm.[79]

Many Indians have clearly seen dangers for Indian culture in the presence of so much gambling-tourism on the reservations. But why should it have mattered to non-Indians? Why should other Americans have cared? For one thing, the renewed power of Indian sovereignty has returned in such force for so many tribes as to injure the stability of the non-Indian areas in which the casinos operate. In our time, modern tribes, governed for the most part by themselves, have been beyond the reach of non-Indian laws. In itself such sovereignty was not inherently such a bad thing; but after Congress passed IGRA, which permitted untaxable gambling to flourish on the reservations, historic sovereignty became deformed sovereignty, one too big for Indians or non-Indians to manage effectively.

Another reason why these new circumstances should have mattered to non-Indians relates to the integrity of place. For many Americans, Indian reservations long exemplified place-integrity; rooted cultures, they refused to break the link between selves and places. In the 1840s Thoreau expressed admiration for Indians because they were, he believed, nearer the "strength and marrow of Nature." Many years later, John Collier, the first director of the Bureau of Indian Affairs (in the 1930s), idealized the Indian way as an antidote to modernity. "They have what the world has lost," he wrote, "the ancient, lost reverence and passion for human personality, joined with the ancient, lost reverence and passion for the web of life." In our time, essayist Wendell Berry has said, respectfully, that for Indians "land was their homeland," and even though they "experience[d] movements of population, . . . in general their relation to place was based upon old usage and association, upon inherited memory, tradition, veneration."[80]

During his senatorial career from 1978 to 1996, New Jersey's Bill Bradley often visited the Sioux in South Dakota, where he witnessed their tribal dances and heard "the constant drumbeat and the high-wailing" that "took me back . . . to an earlier time, when dance was a part of a living tradition." In his 1996 autobiography *Time Present, Time Past* he argued that the Indian "spirit of place" had much to teach Americans, and he expressed awe for the ancient Indian "sense of harmony and balance." So great was his enthusiasm that it led him, in 1983, to introduce a bill in the Senate that, had it passed, would have returned to the Sioux 1.3 million acres of public land, including the site in the Black Hills where Kevin Costner later planned to put his new Switzerland.[81]

Many Indians themselves, of course, have agreed with these aims and ideas. They, too, have argued that Indians, far more than whites, have shown respect for the world around them, valuing it not as temporary landscape but as a permanent and "sacred geography." N. Scott Momaday, a Kiowa Indian and novelist, has said that in the way they "look at the world," "the Indian and the white man" diverge in almost "genetic" ways, which "I take" as "an obvious fact and a foregone conclusion." "The American Indian attitude toward the world," Momaday claimed, "involves a spiritual sense so ancient as to be primordial," expressing a "deep, ethical regard for the land." "Indians generally feel a sense of permanence in their land," insisted Armstrong Wiggins, a Miskito tribal member, "that non-Indians do not share. Non-Indians tend to be very nomadic, to view land as a commodity to buy and sell, and to have ancestral roots on other continents. . . . The idea of private, individual land is historically unknown in Indian communities." Onondaga chief Oren Lyons has observed that Indians "have these well-springs of knowledge about places that only aboriginal people would know because they've lived there. They have the long-term thinking required for proper context, context being life as it functions in the great cycles of life."[82] It was in the spirit of these convictions that many Indians, in our time, have fought to repatriate lost Indian artifacts and bones to their homelands, on the grounds that Indians severed from their places, are less than "spiritually whole," less than human.

Much of this thinking, on the part of both Indians and non-Indians, was pious and sentimental, and it exaggerated the differences between whites and Indians ("a foregone conclusion"?). But even if such thinking were all fantasy, it revealed in some measure the degree to which many Americans longed for a tradition of place—some sense of why places mattered at all or why they might be seen as worth defending—something their own culture did so little to supply or satisfy.[83] It was hard, nearly impossible, for most Americans to invoke a "tradition of tradition" (rather than a tradition of the new) without feeling un-American, "behind the times," or reactionary. In a book titled *Tradition,* the late sociologist Edward Shils observed that a language about ancestors and tradition has been largely lacking in this country. There has been no respected vocabulary of pastness in America, no recognized way to describe the costs when a people lack "an image of ancestry," fail to see "the unity of the past and present states," when they "lose the sense of being members of a collectivity which transcends themselves and which transcends their contemporaries."[84]

Yet despite the apparent lack of such a tradition, a need for it has always existed. That has explained why so many non-Indians have fantasized for so long about the Indian sense of place. Yet, ironically, many Indians themselves have given up on the past, to the point where they have become as bereft of a sense of place as whites. "Where are the Indians who still have an answer and are willing to share their wisdom with those who listen sincerely?" one Indian recently asked. "Probably most Indians will adopt materialism. But an alternative should be available for those who want it."[85]

Reliance on gambling and tourism has caused many problems in Indian country, above all by cutting into the fragile vestiges of a tradition of place. But wherever such service-sector employments as tourism and gambling have superseded other economic activity, the sense of place has been whittled away, compounding the impact of the other recent trends, which have also damaged the dignity of place.

Four

Educating for the Road:
American Universities in a Global Age

American universities have been as instrumental in forming the new world as have the intermodal highways and ports. The mission of universities may be intellectual, but they have exercised much economic influence as well—not by building read roads but by training people to build them and to think in terms of them, and to look at the world as a web of roads, real and mythical, for escape and opportunity.

What I have said applies especially to research universities, the interstate highways of America's educational system and the third in our unusual trio of semi-sovereign entities. Unlike the smaller educational institutions, which resemble the centripetal roads of local communities and neighborhoods, these universities are like the highways in their dispersive effects and in their contributions to mobility (not only geographic but economic and social). They rose to prominence, in fact, in the 1950s, when the interstates themselves were first being paved.

After 1980, research universities shifted from national to

global terrain. They embraced the transnational economy, striking alliances with companies around the world. Concerned about shrinking enrollments of native-born Americans, they turned to recruiting foreign students, foreign scholars, and wealthy immigrants. And they developed a new campus culture that welcomed all outsiders, withheld judgment in regard to a wide range of behaviors (in the manner of the casino culture), and showed little interest in fostering assimilation into American society, except into the American culture of "free market" consumer capitalism.

FROM NATIONAL TO "QUINTESSENTIAL GLOBAL UNIVERSITY"

Well into the twentieth century, America's universities and colleges rarely exerted the same influence on the national scene as did business or government. Even in 1940, only 14 percent of all high school graduates attended them, and what research was conducted was largely funded by foundations. After World War II, however, a seismic shift occurred in higher education, propelled at first by the G.I Bill, which brought millions of veterans to college and opened the way for the massive federal investment in education in the 1950s and sixties. In these later decades, moreover, when student and faculty numbers soared to record figures, universities—especially the research institutions—were beginning to look like cumbersome conglomerates. They had become so big, in fact, as to lack visible unity. Most were also relying for research monies on the federal government, which was replacing private foundations as the major funding source and which connected universities—more than ever—to the interests of the nation-state.[1]

By 1970 more than 50 percent of all high school graduates were going to college.[2] Many traveled far away for their education, even clear across the country, a pattern that democratized education while potentially limiting it as well; now parents had to pay not only tuition but also the cost of room, board, entertainment, and periodic visits with their children.[3]

In no other country did the fantasy of getting out and never returning, of mixing social with geographical mobility, become so prevalent as it did in the United States. The federal government, with its student loan programs, funded the mobility, and many elite campuses, whose reputations depended, in part, on having diverse student bodies, beckoned young people from every nook and cranny of the country.[4] Administrators, too, became more migratory; so did the faculty, whom one educator called in 1972 "the nomads of the twentieth century."[5] By the late sixties the concession to movement as a fact of life affected every faculty member, from fledgling doctoral students, whose success hinged on their willingness to teach in "nowhere places," to tenured professors, who compulsively "considered new job possibilities" to advance their careers. Such a concession may have modified the meaning of community for many faculty, detaching university livelihood from specific physical places and shaping it far more than it had ever been into something abstract (the academic community) to which anyone with credentials might belong and which could exist anywhere.[6]

In fact, so common did this pattern within higher education become that over time many people believed that the need for mobility was etched into the makeup of a whole class of people who hated real places but loved the disembodied freedom of the academy. "Having no concepts of links that cannot be broken," wrote Bill Bray, an American Indian, "Euro-Americans can pull themselves up by the bootstraps and plant themselves firmly in academic community, a community historically conceived to take care of them." "Aside from a few minor scrapes and disharmonies, they fit academia like a hand sliding into a glove."[7] The mentality of mobility saturated teaching thoroughly, as an expression of what the faculty had learned to accept as both inevitable and desirable. Who can say, moreover, how far this concession to movement reached into the character of what was taught, especially in the humanities and the social sciences where interpretation often outweighed knowledge or fact as central to teaching?

Nonetheless, despite the centrifugal trend of the system, with its bias against regional and local places (but closer ties to an abstract nation-state), universities still recruited mostly American-born students and faculty. Enough domestic middle-class wealth existed to carry the burden.

At the same time, many faculty refused to play the "mobility game," and instead settled down, often raised families, and got involved in the community life beyond the university. The majority of colleges and universities were also still local in character, educating students for work in surrounding regions. For all the mobility, the palette of higher education before 1975 remained place-oriented; it ranged from many community colleges and Bible schools to such historically black colleges as Spelman, Morehouse, and Fisk, and such regionals as Berea College in Kentucky (free to Appalachian residents) and the University of the Ozarks in Arkansas (free to mountain youth).[8]

Perhaps most interesting, many American campuses were exclusive physical spaces, segregated purposefully from the rest of society, antiurban in character and preoccupied with place-making to a degree unmatched or unknown by most university systems in the world (except the British). American universities and colleges, in fact, gave rise to "the occupation of campus planning," with its peculiar, almost old-fashioned fascination with special topographical features, from yards and groves to fountains and lawns, as historian of the university, Sheldon Rothblatt, has observed. "The American campus," Rothblatt writes, "was developed as and designed to be a place for growing up, an immense and sophisticated kindergarten, commingling personal retreats with public zones . . . , jealous of its perimeters and prerogatives."[9]

After the period 1975–80, however, this centripetal aspect of higher education began to give way before the more substantial centrifugal impulse, one not only national but now transnational in character. The great research universities, empowered by a constant stream of investment from the federal government, led this evolution.[10]

Some of these research institutions were old (Harvard, MIT, Columbia, Johns Hopkins, and so on). Still others had shed older identities, for example, New York University, which metamorphosed from a drab little commuter school at odds with its neighborhood (dirty, dangerous, radical Greenwich Village) into the Versace of American universities. By the 1990s NYU was one of the biggest landlords in lower Manhattan. Far from being a busy bee in the midst of hip, it now squatted like some giant spider at the heart of a nest of retail stores, restaurants and food outlets, chain bookstores, nightclubs, and theaters, a disarmed outsider culture over which the university presided and which it helped to create (Greenwich Village was no longer dirty, dangerous, or radical).[11]

By the late 1990s NYU was among nearly a hundred such mega-research institutions in the country, each with a private security force, an ever-rising tuition rate unpayable by most Americans, an endowment so enormous as to act as a buffer against nearly every economic storm, and a budget equal in value to a major Las Vegas casino (around $1 billion in 1997), though, alas, not as big as the budget of the Port Authority of

New York and New Jersey ($2 billion).[12] By the 1990s these institutions had become semiautonomous, even semi-sovereign bodies similar to the port terminals and the casino-reservations (similar, of course, in character; in influence, the universities, as a whole, far exceeded both these entities). "Campuses today are Athenian city-states," Vartan Gregorian, head of the Carnegie Foundation and former president of Brown University, said in 1996.[13]

By the nineties, moreover, many university presidents had adopted "internationalization" as the governing mandate of their incumbency.[14] Among them were George Rupp of Columbia and L. Jay Oliva of NYU. Rupp was an ordained Protestant minister with a doctorate in religion, the former head of Rice University before taking the Columbia position, and author of such books as *Beyond Existentialism and Zen: Religion in a Pluralistic World* (Oxford, 1979). In his 1995 *President's Report,* he wrote that "we intend to make Columbia an increasingly international community of teaching and learning. As distinct from institutions imbued with the provincialism of Western academic disciplines, [we] are moving more and more across boundaries." Columbia, in fact, "is well-positioned to be America's premier international university," a phrase he repeated again in his 1996 report.[15]

L. Jay Oliva, an historian of Russia, went one step beyond Rupp by dropping "international" for the more fashionable "global" as the way to describe his school's ambitions. "Through all my years at NYU," he said in a 1996 speech, "an international vision has been a fundamental part of our mission. . . . But now we have reached a level of institutional strength that permits us to take that vision to a new place . . . to open up the next century as the quintessential global university." "We plan to enter the next century," he told the *New*

York Times, twice in the same year, "as the world's first truly global university."[16]

This new global agenda took many forms, perhaps the foremost of which was immersion in the world's marketplace through the forging of partnerships with transnational companies.

PARTNERS WITH GLOBAL BUSINESS

Since the 1980s, research universities have cast beyond their historical base for bigger fish. They have dissolved the lines that once marked them off from the outside (lines already fuzzed before 1980) and implicated themselves deeply in the market—above all in the transnational market. As one NYU educator, pleased about this trend, put it, we have "outgrown" the old "bounded notion of the academy."[17]

This shift has resulted in the emergence of for-profit universities to convey practical knowledge, some doing business online as virtual universities.[18] But, above all, research universities have allied with transnational firms in the pursuit of economic development.[19]

Close contacts between industry and the academy were hardly new, of course, although in the past the federal government had mediated them in the form of defense contracts. The government still manages these relations in some measure today, but since 1980 they have become not only more frequent but more direct, fostered by universities in quest of revenues; by governors and legislatures determined to bring new industry to their states and willing to bargain away the kitchen sink to get it; and by firms (pharmaceutical, biotech, genetic) that had shut down their own research labs and were looking

to universities for ideas and knowledge. The federal government itself sanctioned this shift from mediated to direct relations. In 1986 Congress passed a law allowing universities and
business to collaborate in the pursuit of commercial patents;
and in 1990 it created the Advanced Technology Program,
which promoted links between universities and business designed to produce "high-risk, enabling technologies with significant commercial/economic potential."[20]

The very identity of the modern university, with its many
discrete faculties at odds with one another, each fighting for a
piece of the pie, played its part in clearing the way for an outside force besides the federal government to assert its claim.
"Initiative is shifting to the outside," Sheldon Rothblatt has
written, "where giant electronics firms and global pharmaceutical interests are clearer about their objectives."[21]

Most spectacularly, such contacts appeared as "research
parks" or "units of organized research" between universities
and firms in such fields as biotechnology, microelectronics, and
artificial intelligence. Operated by landlord-agencies, which
sold and leased properties to the various tenants, many of these
research parks resembled on a smaller scale the country's port
authorities in their structure and semi-sovereign character. In
1975 only ten such parks existed; a decade later, thirty; by
1997, nearly 140 were in business, many formed between universities and global industries and all managed in such a way as
to elude the burden of taxation (as "nonprofit" entities similar
again to port authorities).[22]

Among the grandest (and oldest) is Research Triangle Park,
a 6500-acre strip of buildings nestled in the piney woods of
North Carolina and ideally situated—like a huge mall—near
major airports and interstate highways. Begun in 1959 to serve
the research needs of a few big American companies (notably
IBM), it did not succeed until the 1980s, by which time firm

after firm had begun to participate (fifty by 1988) and the place had turned into a major landscape of its own, with several restaurants, a hotel, and many pay-as-you-go services. While the state built and kept up the park roads, most of the tenants supplied their own police, garbage collection, landscaping, and eating facilities. By 1990, nearly one hundred firms packed the park, including many from Asia, Europe, and Canada. All worked closely with the faculty of three nearby universities— Duke University in Durham; North Carolina State University in Raleigh; and the University of North Carolina in Chapel Hill.[23]

But the linkages between universities and transnational companies also flowered as *individual* partnerships, each seeking "new products and processes of economic value to society," in the words of Paul Gray, a former president of MIT.

University after university has signed on as partner with one or more of America's premier global firms, many at the cutting edge of "miracle-making" in computing and genetic engineering. Cows were cloned in 1997 by scientists at the University of Massachusetts, the outcome of a partnership with Advanced Cell Technology, a biotechnology start-up company in Worcester, Massachusetts. Around the same time, Pfizer, the global pharmaceuticals firm, formed a partnership with the University of Connecticut to create a laboratory for "joint research projects in which company scientists will work alongside professors and students." "If we want to be recognized as a world-class institution," the University of Connecticut's chancellor said of this marriage between private industry and the university, "we need world-class partners." In 1997 Virginia Commonwealth University secured a partnership with global Motorola, by promising to build a new $11-million engineering school—funded by the state legislature of Virginia—for the benefit of Motorola, which had begun construction of a new plant near the university (in 1998, however, Motorola stopped construction, leaving the university holding the bag).[24]

Among the most prolific of such couplings has been the one between Washington University in St. Louis, Missouri, and Monsanto, a bioengineering firm with global reach and famed for its "genetically improved" soybeans, its herbicides, and its "bovine growth hormones," each the progeny of Monsanto's "joint discovery program" with Washington University. This program, begun in 1982, matched scientists at Monsanto with those at Washington University to yield more than fifty patents of new drugs. In exchange for ownership of these patents, Monsanto doled out millions of dollars for nearly fifty research projects at the university's medical school. The school's researchers, of course, kept clean by doing only the "discovery" work, leaving the "specific drug design" to the Monsanto labs.[25] The program, in effect, transformed Washington University's medical school into a research arm of Monsanto.[26]

Ohio University, the University of Michigan, the University of Florida at Gainesville, Emory, Harvard, and, most impressive of all, Stanford and MIT have all courted alliances with business. In 1983 Stanford University, adept at such liaisons dating back to the 1950s when it pioneered the Stanford Research Park, opened the Center for Independent Systems, part of the School of Engineering and supported by "industrial partners" in the high-tech business, the soon-to-be superstars of Silicon Valley. At first it had only American corporations as members (Hewlett-Packard, IBM, Motorola, and so on), each paying an annual fee of $120,000 to participate in "any number of research areas." But in the nineties it invited European companies to join, then Asian firms, on the grounds that "in this new world order, everybody is transnational," as one Stanford professor put it.[27]

In 1998 Stanford took an even more audacious step: it cut a deal with Japanese-owned Yamaha to incorporate a new business called Sondius-XG, a company that made synthesized music for video games. No longer just an academic powerhouse, Stanford had become a "real" transnational business firm.[28]

Of all the institutions at the forefront of such relations none was "more merrily in bed with industry" than MIT.[29] In a 1997 essay on universities, Charles Vest, then president of MIT, complained indignantly that the federal government might cut back on funding to MIT. What has happened, he asked, to "our national will to excel?" We must "reaffirm a national commitment to excellence." But Vest was disingenuous; the government never seriously cut back on anything, despite some windy threats to do so; furthermore, in technology and science, MIT was notorious for its internationalism or for being a big "blurmeister," the university in need of federal dollars but oblivious to all boundaries or national differences.[30] Its stellar Media Lab, staffed by an army of futurists (experts in robotics and artificial intelligence), was acclaimed for its belief that all borders were breachable and that "given enough time and money, almost anything is possible."[31] "Ten to twenty years from now," Nicholas Negroponte, the Media Lab's director, said in 1997, "kids won't care much about countries."[32]

Michael Dertouzos, head of another MIT facility—the Laboratory for Computer Science—likewise observed in his 1997 book *What Will Be* that soon nations will no longer matter as "geographical" entities. "Language, culture, history, and religion are disengaging from geographic bounds, as many people emigrate or work abroad." "These forces are all losing their physical locality." Everybody, everything, has been set free, including Dertouzos; a holder of dual (U.S. and Greek)

citizenship, he wrote that soon "we will no longer be talking of the Greek nation as the physical country of Greece,
but as the Greek Network, linking the Hellenes around the
world."[33]

For years, MIT also boasted a degree program called "MIT
Leaders in Manufacturing Program," which allowed a whole
fleet of transnational companies, from Alcoa to Digital, to
"codify" what "principles should be taught and practiced in
the future."[34] Its Industrial Liaison Program assembled a glitter-
ing roster of partnerships with more than three hundred companies, most with global ambitions. Fourteen Japanese firms
provided nearly 20 percent of Media Lab's sponsorship in
1987. By the late 1980s, partly at taxpayer expense and without
taxpayer knowledge, globalization was already in high gear at
MIT.[35]

For many people inside and outside of the academy, such
partnerships had no downside. They offered an alternative to
dependence on hard-to-predict federal funding; they allowed
for the fast transfer of knowledge between universities and
businesses; and they created conditions ideal for the employment of recently graduated, technically trained men and
women. "Our leadership in technology today depends [on] the
bonding relationships that our universities have with industry,"
William Perry, former Secretary of Defense under Clinton and
professor of engineering at Stanford, said in 1998.[36]

For others, however, such partnerships only subverted what
was left of the boundedness of the university, and of its old liberal arts mission. "The university is being destroyed in bits and
pieces," one professor lamented.[37] Such partnerships also accelerated the entry of the schools into a placeless global system,
detaching them from the country (rather than from the nation-
state, which aided in this transformation) to which they owed
their existence.

RECRUITING FOREIGN-BORN TALENT:
THE "BRAIN GAIN" THESIS

Partnerships with global businesses, then, formed the bedrock for the new international identity of the research university. But there were other features of this makeover as well, including the recruitment of foreign-born students and scholars.

By the 1980s, American universities were competing fiercely for customers (students), particularly for students who could pay their way, but above all for wealthy foreign and immigrant students; as a result, many of the country's most elite schools saw a marked dwindling of the traditional majority group. In 1989, more than 60 percent of NYU's student body was native-born and white (while the figure for the school's native-born black students stood almost at zero); by 1993, for the first time in its history, there was no native-born American majority in the incoming freshman class.[38]

Mass immigration after 1975, of course, partly explained this transformation, and whatever one might think of immigration's overall impact on the country, it swelled the numbers of serious non-native-born students eager for an education and just as deserving of it as other young Americans.[39] But the general immigration levels alone did not fully explain the magnitude of the immigrant community on America's leading elite campuses, some of which—Berkeley, UCLA, Harvard, Columbia, Stanford, and so forth—had percentages of immigrant students well beyond 25 percent of the student body. These students were at these places not because they were enterprising immigrants but because a high proportion of them had affluent, college-educated parents who knew the money value of elite education and whose incomes far exceeded the American average.[40]

Besides well-off immigrants, universities also recruited

large numbers of foreign students, scholars, and researchers. This recruitment was "an arms race," as one admissions officer put it.[41] From the eighties on, school after school sent recruiters abroad—to Hong Kong, Seoul, Singapore—to rake in potential candidates, all able to pay whatever it cost to get to an American campus. Boston University even set up eight overseas recruitment posts to snag its prey, a policy imitated by other schools. By the eighties, schools were sizing up the world in much the same way that the tourist industry did—as a market with a seemingly bottomless pool of customers. The challenge was how to "sell" America's educational "products" in the world market and how to keep other nations—Australia, England, and Canada—from winning the lion's share of customers. "This is a product we are selling and that people are buying," said one educator. Others said that we have got to get "our market share" or we "have to sell what we have."[42]

In 1960 only about 40,000 foreign students, graduate and undergraduate, studied in American colleges and universities, a number, however, which began to rise in the 1970s as enrollments of native-born Americans as a percentage of the total began to drop.[43] By the late 1980s, when more than 450,000 such students attended American schools, the United States had emerged as "by far the leading provider of education to international students."[44] Even after the Asian economic crisis hit, foreign enrollments remained high, partly as a result of vigorous recruitment by American schools.[45] Many of these students paid their own way; as children of elite families, they could afford Yale or Cornell. At such places as Harvard, MIT, and the University of Miami, however, foreign students benefited equally with native-born Americans from "needs-blind admissions" policies, and they had the same access to financial help (this at a time when more and more native-born Americans could not afford to go to such schools).[46]

But graduate students, not undergraduates, formed the bulk of international enrollments. Most came from Asia (mainly China, Korea, the Philippines, and India), and, once again, they typically belonged to families at the very top economic and social tier of their societies, many accustomed to being waited on and eschewing all kinds of work "with the hands."[47] Most attended research universities and studied science and engineering. Throughout much of the 1990s, foreign students accounted for half of all Ph.D.s in mathematics, engineering, and science, well over half of all doctorates in civil engineering, nearly 40 percent in economics.[48] In 1996 universities awarded foreign nationals with temporary and permanent visas 38 percent of all doctorates in the life sciences or in such fields as biotechnology, gene therapy and engineering, biochemistry, molecular biology, environmental science, and agronomy.[49]

What was even more startling was the fact that a great percentage of these graduate students received financial aid, often at taxpayer expense in the form of federal "research grants," a "pattern" that "prevailed for years," according to David North, in a study for the Alfred Sloan Foundation.[50] Other countries did not subsidize foreign students (Britain, for instance, granted aid only to British citizens), nor did most allow foreign students the right to earn incomes (American college students in internships abroad were forced to pay out of their own pockets to work for foreign companies).[51] And only in America did so many graduate students stay in the country after graduation (since 1988, more than 60 percent every year), to find work as technicians in corporations, research park labs, or in universities.[52]

Indeed, besides recruiting foreign students, schools from Harvard to Berkeley hired thousands of foreign postgraduate scholars and faculty, a practice begun long before 1990. In the mid-seventies, in fact, the American Association of Universities, the lobby for research universities, urged Congress to permit more "professors and scientists" to immigrate on the grounds of "short domestic supply."[53] By the late eighties, the Association requested new visa categories and got them in the 1990 immigration law. One category, called the "Einstein exemption," gave "preference" to "foreigners of extraordinary ability"; the other, the H–1B category of migrant, let schools hire foreigners on a six-year basis, so long as they could prove no qualified Americans wanted the jobs (it was the same law, as we saw in chapter 3, that benefited business as well).

Between 1991 and 1995 the total number of Einsteins reached nearly 10,000 professors. In 1994 alone, more than 60,000 foreign temps—not just the Einsteins but all scholars, teachers, and researchers—came on board, with Harvard, Berkeley, MIT, UCLA, and Stanford getting the most. "The population of foreign scholars and postdocs is always growing here, believe me," said Lee Madden, assistant director of foreign scholar services at Stanford in 1994. "There's never a diminution in these numbers." Throughout the nineties, each year set a new record.[54]

Among the many flexible individuals on university payrolls, these foreign temps were called "the migrating workers of modern research, the hapless platoons of postdocs."[55] They belonged to many fields, but most were postdoctoral men and women (but mainly men, since countries like China and India restricted women's education) who specialized in such prestigious fields as particle physics and molecular biology. These people expected to parlay their temporary visa status into permanent residence in the United States. They worked long hours for tiny stipends, usually far less than industry paid for comparable work, without the protection of labor regulations or unions. Their employers were often full professors who did research at taxpayers' expense and from whom corporations often benefited, amounting to a hidden business subsidy.

Throughout the nineties, foreign workers on temporary visas held more than half of all postdoctoral positions in the United States (even as they were awarded, in some fields, nearly the same number of doctorates). Harvard, MIT, the University of California, Penn, and the like, depended on their labors.[56] The Johns Hopkins Medical School had one hundred such temps on hand a year, whereas Duke Medical School boasted two hundred a year, and the University of Maryland at College Park found room for one hundred foreign temp professionals yearly, along with more than 140 other international faculty members and researchers.[57]

So far had this practice proceeded that in 1995 more than one hundred native-born American scientists organized a group called the Network of Emerging Scientists (NES), with the intent of helping "highly trained, hard-working individuals" find "stable employment" and to publicize and confront what they perceived to be an inequity. Jenny Cohen, a physics Ph.D. who worked briefly at the Lawrence Livermore Laboratory in California, served as first director of NES. Cohen was born in Minnesota and educated in New Mexico. The mother of a little girl and a devoutly religious orthodox Jew, she was married to a Cornell-educated physicist and had longed for a stable career in science and to settle down. But she (and others like her) were forced to move from town to town to find work. "We've been moving for work ever since we left Cornell in 1987," she reported. She had also repeatedly lost out to temporary foreign professionals. "I care about people in this country," Cohen said in 1996. "I would like to see the people of this country given some type of preference."[58]

In the face of such objections, universities have continued

to justify their recruitment of foreign faculty, scholars, and graduate students (even as 75 percent of American workers themselves, many eager for an education, did not have college degrees).[59] One argument has been that international students and scholars enriched campus culture, added to its "diversity," and gave everyone insight into people "from all different backgrounds," as a Harvard official put it. "Foreign students" correct the "Eurocentric bias," echoed another educator from Georgetown University, "bringing a special angle Americans lack"—for instance, "the Brazilian, Chinese, Egyptian, Indian, or Indonesian way of thinking."[60] Others have emphasized economic arguments—the "cheap labor" supplied by the postdocs, graduate students, and faculty (although in some cases foreign faculty received very high salaries); or the "billions of dollars" spent by foreign-born students on tuitions, housing, entertainment, and food.[61] Still others have mounted no defense whatever but have explained the influx as a logical outcome of "free market prices" (people go automatically where they get paid the most) or of "the global restructuring process" beyond anyone's control (individuals cannot be blamed, in other words, for what "world forces" make them do).[62]

The economic rationales seemed the most correct, as well as the most obvious. But officials preferred another position in line with their global ideology, which said that it no longer mattered where skilled people came from or why. What mattered was *excellence,* getting the best students and the most cutting-edge faculty. In 1990 William Kirwan, president of the University of Maryland at College Park and spokesman for many university associations, testified on this issue before Congress, which was then debating the merits of immigration reform. "The subject of global interdependence," he said, in what was already a standard line, "is no more evident than in academia, where the development and exchange of knowledge is increasingly an international exercise. Ideas and learning know no national boundaries." Besides, he said, "the excellence of our programs" has rested on "the quality of faculty we are able to recruit from an international pool of teachers and scholars." Moreover, this dependence is greater today than ever, given the "shortage of world-class excellence in our university and college faculties. Academic institutions must have access to the very best . . . from this nation and from across the world. Merely being qualified would not be sufficient."[63]

This argument was flawed, not least because it was terribly wrong about the "shortage of world-class excellence" in America. Ever since the mid-1970s (if not earlier), American educators predicted that a scarcity of talent would cripple education and the economy and that unless American universities recruited foreigners, the nation would lose the competitive struggle or the "struggle for excellence." No such scarcity ever happened, however. What happened was glut, a surfeit of Einsteins in many fields—and especially in those fields (engineering, biotech, molecular biology, neuroscience, and so forth) that formed the foundation of the "new economy." At the same time, ever since the late 1980s, the available jobs in these professions have shrunk dramatically, with the results that an extraordinary pool of skilled labor—of young people unable to find permanent positions but, given the steep investment in their education, willing to take whatever they could—has been at the beck-and-call of universities and corporations.[64] Employers and "mature scientists" in need of lab technicians, of course, have celebrated this state of things, since they have enjoyed optimal access to skilled labor at bargain-basement prices; foreign nationals, too, have had cause for satisfaction, since they have received stipends exceeding anything possible in their homelands. For native-born Americans, however, the situation has been a disaster. It has produced for them what the National Research Council, a prestigious research body in Washington, has called a "crisis of expectations." Forced to compete with an ever-growing number of foreign nationals and compelled to find work that does not fulfill them, many have increasingly lost hope in the future.[65]

But Kirwan's position was flawed as well because it dismissed the gravity of what was once called the "brain drain." Years ago, statesmen worried that rich nations were robbing poor ones of desperately needed human capital. In the late 1960s, Paul Douglas, liberal senator from Illinois and an architect of workers' compensation laws during the New Deal as well as of later civil rights legislation, argued that "from the standpoint of the world and of the developing countries, it would be socially desirable that fewer scientists and technicians should migrate and that they should instead stay at home or return there after their training elsewhere." Douglas even suggested that the United States help set up "great international universities . . . in Asia, Africa, and Latin America to help train the most talented without deracinating them."[66]

Despite these concerns, hospitals and schools throughout the country turned heavily in the 1970s to immigrant professionals to fill jobs, spurred by a "brain drain" preference visa in the 1965 immigration law. By 1980 more than one-fourth of all immigrants who had arrived in the 1970s were technicians or professionals, including 7,000 Filipino doctors (1,000 more than the number of African-American physicians). Such use of immigrants reinforced institutional racism in the country, discouraging the training and hiring of native-born minorities. Nevertheless, anxieties about the international brain drain continued to dribble away, replaced in the 1990s by a fresh concept, the "brain gain." Even such an authority on the migration of talent as Jagdish Bhagwati, a leading international economist at

Columbia University, dropped the brain-drain concept for brain gain, although for a long time he had wrestled with the moral challenge of brain drain from different angles.[67]

The son of Brahmans (his brother was for years the chief justice of the Indian Supreme Court), Bhagwati was born in Bombay in 1934, and received higher degrees in England (at Cambridge University) and in the United States (at MIT). In the late sixties he returned home to India, only to complain about Indian policies that restricted the flow of scholars abroad. It was about this time, too, that he first defended the brain drain, on the grounds that India had little to offer ambitious people like him—no core, he said, of "eminent people to generate purely locally the kind of atmosphere and possibilities of continuing mutual discussions which alone can keep one on one's toes." India was so intellectually desolate, he argued in 1967, that "the talented Indian academic" who refused to leave would be "committing 'academic suicide.' "[68]

Bhagwati soon left India for a job at MIT, where he had second thoughts about the brain drain, thoughts he continued to have into the next few decades, as he struggled to put the phenomenon into some kind of moral light. He wondered, in 1976, "Which country does the mobile citizen 'belong to'?" "If there is international mobility of people," he asked, "how" can they be made accountable? Shouldn't "intellectuals at many levels" who had enjoyed so many advantages from their own countries and had prospered abroad be "taxed" or compelled to share with their brethren some of the benefits reaped from their migration?[69] Bhagwati believed that some kind of "global" tax plan, managed by the United Nations, might appeal to the "moral instincts" of the many eminent people who had left their homelands.

By the early nineties, however, Bhagwati had thrown in the towel, disavowing the brain-drain argument—and along with it any hand-wringing over taxation—for brain gain. In a co-authored article titled "Foreign Students Spur U.S. Brain Gain," versions of which appeared in *Challenge* and on the editorial page of the *Wall Street Journal,* he returned in spirit to a position he had advanced in the late 1960s. He argued that skilled migrants did not "drain" so much as "bring glory to their countries of origins"; and they "helped" their countries "through political lobbying in the U.S." America benefited, too, now more than ever. Singling out Indian students, he reminded his readers that these students were "among the best" who "have gone to the best institutions at home," graduates of India's government-funded "Institutes of Technology modeled on MIT." Korean and Taiwanese students, too, he noted, belonged to the "top" echelons of their societies. America was indeed lucky and should reward all these students—especially those in "science and engineering"—with "automatic green cards."[70]

Along with Kirwan and others, Bhagwati saw the brain drain as a blessing. But it was "the worst sort of imperialism," to quote Craig McCaw, founder of McCaw Cellular, because it separated the best-trained minds from their places, where many might have remained, as educators and builders. (Whether they were really the *best* minds, however, as Bhagwati said, was another matter; one might have found many more of them in the Bombay slums or elsewhere in rural India, where millions of Untouchables still live, doing the dirty work of the "higher ups.")[71] In 1968 V. M. Dandekar, an Indian scholar who never left India, said of Bhagwati that "he knows better and knows it too well that whatever the prestige of the individual Indian scientists abroad may be, it is the scientists working in their own countries, often anonymously, in poor conditions, improvising with native genius to overcome several handicaps in resources and equipment, who are bringing effective prestige to their countries in the world community."[72]

Bhagwati and others in the research universities glorified the divorce of brains from place, spirit from place. That divorce, moreover, helped to convert campuses into international enclaves, remote in many ways from the rest of America, especially for the majority of Americans unable to pay for elite education and at the expense of the many trained American professionals unable to find work in the academy. It added yet another level of mobility to an already established system of domestic circulation, carrying people away from their communities into the more anonymous space of the modern university and beyond into the placeless world of transnational enterprise.

CAMPUS AS OUTSIDER HEAVEN

The new university had one last aspect to it, which rounded out the internationalism shaped by the business alliances and by the recruitment of foreign-born talent. This aspect was a campus culture hospitable to the outside world in a way unlike anything Americans had known in the past.

Many universities have reconfigured campus intellectual life to meet the needs of non-native-born students. Earlier, when such students enrolled in America's best universities, they never encountered campuses that assisted them as universities do today. Since 1980, however, elite schools have provided international students with clubs, newspapers, magazines, and special societies. They have employed hundreds of immigration lawyers and foreign student advisers, whose sole business was to know the immigration laws and to help students and faculty understand and finesse them. One Indian-born scholar has observed that "most universities have so many international faculty" that "they've gotten used to [dealing] with how immigration works. . . . They have a person in the personnel office [whose] job is to handle all the relevant matters about foreign faculty."[73]

Friendly provisions, moreover, have accommodated nearly *all* "outsiders," domestic as well as foreign. In prior decades, schools sought to attract students with athletics, clubs, and "Greek" societies.[74] But, after 1980, they added to the menu of enticements; they tried to make campuses seem like utopian spaces in which most "outsider" voices (ethnic, racial, sexual) found expression and acceptance. Fed by an older stream of racial-gender politics and by the new immigration, "diversity practices" sprang up on many campuses to encourage students to "break the prejudice habit" and "embrace the Other."[75] An army of university administrators committed themselves to "de-provincializing" their student bodies (particularly the American-born students).[76] Obsessed with demography, they hired people for such new positions as "Multicultural director" or "diversity ombudsman"; they also redesigned their facilities to express the "multicultural" vision. The University of California, Santa Barbara, for instance, has both a large "Multicultural Theater"—explicitly to reflect the interests of Asians, Hispanics, African-Americans, gays, and lesbians—and a glass-enclosed multicultural space on the second floor of the student library, plainly visible and separate, where one can find the special gender and ethnic collections.[77]

Finally, universities founded a range of institutes and programs that directed the intellectual energies of the university away from national to global interests, from the inside to the outside.

In 1996, the College of Letters and Science at the University of California, Santa Barbara, created the Global and International Studies Program, a full degree program modeled after the recently created UCLA International Development Studies Program, and International Relations Program at UC, Davis. Designed to examine "transnational processes," postcolonial peoples, and "diasporic" men and women uprooted and in motion, the program was headed by Mark Juergensmeyer, professor of politics and religion and a practicing liberal Protestant minister. Though born in a small Illinois town, he viewed America as "dissolving territory" and hoped to prepare his students for "world citizenship."[78]

In the same year, the University of Chicago opened a new path in the humanities—"a new intellectual configuration," or a "new refashioning of the humanities," according to the *Chronicle of Higher Education,* a departure from its earlier conservatism. Scholars in history, literature, cinema, gender studies, and in several other fields abandoned the old paradigm to deal with transnationalism, the future of the nation-state, globalization, and a reassessment of the whole nature or character of "knowledge." In 1995 New York University created the International Center for Advanced Studies, headed by Professor Thomas Bender, whose central project was to study "the city in a pluralized world," evaluate "urban knowledges," and explore the character of "citizenship . . . in regional, national, and global contexts."[79]

Throughout their history, America's greatest universities aspired to do what Cardinal Newman, in his classic book *The Idea of a University,* said they should do—educate "the intellect to reason well in all matters, to reach out towards truth, and to grasp it."[80] American universities also often taught the world (or at least the elites of the world) what the world did not know about itself. A Japanese scholar who studied in the United States in the 1960s recently told an interviewer that he wanted to go to a particular American university because it "had the largest collection about South East Asia programs in the world. So if you [were there], you [didn't] have to go to South East Asia countries." An Indian-scholar observed of American libraries that "library collections on Asia are better in U.S. universities than those in Asia." Hungarian-born American historian John Lukacs, who immigrated to this country in 1946, was similarly impressed with what he found at American libraries. Living in Europe, Lukacs knew next to nothing about European history as a whole. "In Hungary, there had been no such thing as a course in European history at the Gymnasium or the university. It was in America, only in America, that entire verities in the history of Europe opened before my eyes."[81]

At the same time, insofar as American universities have emulated business practices and allied with corporations for revenues and status, they have exchanged what was left of an older form of open inquiry for a new internationalism tailored to the needs of the marketplace and indifferent to the life of the country. This trend showed up in ties to transnational business, in the ardent recruitment of skilled people from anywhere in the world, and in the creation of an outsider campus culture. It took form in the obsession with demography or race rather than place as a central university concern. And it appeared, above all, in the decline of the liberal arts mission, which had always been given a privileged berth in university life.

Increasingly, modern universities have come to resemble less the place-oriented institutions of the past than the populist casinos of the present. Like big casinos, they were also making a new cosmopolitanism, a vision without boundaries that domesticated the mobility of skilled elites around the world.

But this vision went well beyond the academy. It was bigger than the academy, although many academics helped fashion it.

It emanated, in fact, from all the things we have examined in this book, from the intermodal highways and the landscape of the temporary to the transnational companies and casino-dominated Indian reservations. It was the mentality, the ideology, of the new age we have entered.

Five

Cosmopolitanism and the Art of Mopping Up

On August 24, 1996, Walter Capps, candidate from California for a seat in Congress (which he would win that fall, only to die a year later), said in a speech before the Democratic Convention in Chicago that Americans "had no common history, no common ancestry, no common language, not even a common faith," nothing in common in any traditional sense. But they did share something, Capps observed, and that was "a common creed," a common set of universalist ideas, beginning with the idea that "all men are created equal." Furthermore, Capps announced, they were beginning to share a new sense of humanity, a new bond with all the strangers in their midst and around the world. We have reached the point, he claimed, where we must all "look into the face of any human being" and see ourselves.[1] A few years earlier, in 1993, Robert Jay Lifton, the noted sociologist, argued in *The Protean Self,* that Americans were developing a "place for many places." Without even knowing it, we have gone slowly but "inexorably" from "individual to family to social or ethnic group to nation," and now to "global belonging." "The human community has been radically broadened; our 'ancestor souls' populate the globe."[2]

These statements, among many such in our time, point to the rise of a new cosmopolitanism. Cosmopolitanism, of course, has a very long history. As a philosophy, it appeared as far back as ancient Greece, when the Stoic philosophers first proposed that men might give their primary allegiance to humanity as a whole rather than to their local origins. It emerged again from the eighteenth-century Enlightenment in the form of economic and political liberalism. Excited by the revolutionary new capitalism, thinkers such as Voltaire and David Hume believed that unobstructed trade anywhere—in which private individuals renounced their differences in the pursuit of wealth—would lead to heaven on earth. Cosmopolitan themes also took politically liberal form in documents like the Declaration of Independence and in the writings of Thomas Paine in the 1790s and William Lloyd Garrison in the 1830s, both of whom said "my country is the world." Karl Marx, too, inherited the Enlightenment legacy, believing that "workingmen have no country."[3]

Cosmopolitanism was more than a philosophy, however; it was also a general historical condition marked by creative interactions among diverse peoples that typified the richest civilizations since the beginnings of recorded history, as historian William H. McNeill long ago showed.[4] In its last enduring incarnation (between 1850 and the 1960s), such a cosmopolitan pattern was driven by Western (European and American) power and determined by Western interests, which, by 1920, had reached all across the globe, importing modernization (technology, science, capitalism) to the non-West and exposing the West to regular fruitful interactions with other cultures. At the same time, this cosmopolitan condition operated against the current of a more powerful nationalist and tribalist consciousness that overshadowed both European and non-European political life.

Cosmopolitanism carried other meanings as well, which more often than not associated it with specific places and individuals. For many people, it invoked a butterfly kind of behavior, a person who waltzed through life, dabbling here, dabbling there, never settling anywhere. For others, it suggested the city, especially the big city, and sophisticated urbanites who supposedly knew how to mix with anyone, enjoyed fine art and foods, spoke many languages, and accepted or tolerated many kinds of behavior. From this view, cosmopolitanism depended for its existence on the city, or at least on the idea of the city as a magnetic, free place. "I had the provincial's belief," remembered Indiana-born writer Darryl Pinckney, of his undergraduate days in New York, "that an interesting life could take place only in a great metropolis."[5]

By the 1990s, however, a new cosmopolitan mentality had taken up residence in the United States, broader than anything that preceded it. As a condition, it was beyond Western control and consisted of "many civilizations" in contention with one another; and it ran uniformly through established power in corporations, universities, and government.[6] As a philosophy, this cosmopolitanism little resembled the vision of the past, which often commented critically but not without sympathy on provincial foibles and that conjured up richly textured and fascinating places. This newer, more earnest vision advocated that all places, not just cities, become cosmopolitan. The vision had an almost conformist character and it broke entirely from conventional notions of place.

After 1980, this new mentality came in two basic varieties—one from the academy, the other from business. Liberal academics were the most prolific of the two groups, producing at least three kinds of cosmopolitanism: a multicultural outlook that divided people into groups and demanded that all marginalized peoples—or those viewed by multiculturalists as unfairly excluded by the majority culture—be fairly incorporated into systems of power; a fluid approach that invited interactions between groups and at the borders of cultures; and a postcolonial angle, developed mostly by emigré intellectuals, which singled out displaced and exiled individuals as America's key culture-makers. All struck at conventional and historical conceptions of place and loyalty. The business approach, intermingling with and shaping academic thinking, was simple but no less total in its cosmopolitanism; in it, one heard the jingle of casinos and the rush of the intermodal ports. Its basic contention was that the capitalist market, left to itself, would dissolve differences and bring on harmony.

VOICES AND BORDERS: NATIVE-BORN AND EMIGRÉ ACADEMICS

In the past fifteen years, many in academia have been talking cosmopolitan ideas and themes. Some of these people resemble the ancient Stoics who imagined that human beings might someday leave behind their local prejudices and embrace the "world as a whole." Among these are philosophers Judith Lichtenberg and Martha Nussbaum. A professor at the University of Maryland, Lichtenberg asserted in 1981, quite simply, that Americans exist in a "global world" and that "the limits of the planet are the limits of the world." "There is continual movement," she said, "from self to family to clan to tribe to nation, and ultimately to the whole human race."[7] Nussbaum, currently at the University of Chicago, has argued that we should just accept the fact that "we live in one world." "We are all born naked and poor," Nussbaum has said, ignoring the differences between the Rockefellers and the slum-dwellers, and we should learn to see all human beings as the same, with the same claim on our compassion. "We should recognize humanity wherever it exists, and give its fundamental ingredients, reason and moral capacity, our first allegiance and respect." "National boundaries" are not "morally salient," and "patriotism is very close to jingoism."[8]

Nussbaum struck a note agreeable to all cosmopolitans. At the same time, her downgrading of cultural particulars, which she repeatedly displayed in her writing, turned off many thinkers, in particular, the multiculturalists. Multiculturalists asserted that Americans have no common culture, to invoke the late Walter Capps once again. Not only was Capps a congressman from California; he was also, for many years, a professor of Religious Studies at the University of California, Santa Barbara, where he lectured on the "Voices of the Stranger." Capps did not think what most Americans probably believed—that they shared the same culture. For him, Americans shared only a loyalty to political principles. Otherwise, they belonged to their own cultures. Multiculturalists rarely defined what culture meant, but usually (for them) it was reducible to race, gender, sexual orientation, or ethnicity, all conditions, in other words, that bore little relation to real places (except, in the ethnic case, but then as somewhere left behind), indeed, that transcended place.[9]

The multicultural view has a long lineage in this country, dating back in its earliest version to at least the 1910s, and resurfacing in the late sixties, when many defended the outsider and argued passionately for a politics of inclusiveness.[10] By the nineties, however, multicultural cosmopolitanism was the prevailing view, expounded by many thinkers, among them Michael Walzer, political philosopher and contributor to *The New Republic*.

Employed for many years at the Institute for Advanced Study at Princeton University, with its serene and beautiful setting, Walzer has tried to form a coherent vision of inclusiveness and, in the process, he has become more and more multicultural.[11] He sees America not as a "union of states" but as an ensemble of "nations, races, and religions, all of them dispersed and intermixed, without ground of their own."[12]

He disputes those writers who think that too much cultural difference—too many self-asserting groups—harm the country. What pattern does that, he counters, is not multiculturalism but individualism, a long American tradition that Walzer admires but also fears because it cuts people off from their groups, making them isolated and lonely.[13] The groups, however—racial, ethnic, or religious—are the keys to true citizenship, the unifiers (not the spoilers) of American society, empowering people to take part in democratic politics. So indispensable are they to checking the worst effects of individualism, Walzer believes, that the state should be called in to protect and nurture group differences. Through whatever means necessary, "the state" should "produce hyphenated individuals . . . who will defend toleration within their different communities while still valuing and reproducing the differences."[14] At the same time, the state should embrace immigration. "We are a society of immigrants," Walzer contends, "and the experience of leaving a homeland for this new place is an almost universal American experience. It should be celebrated. But the celebration will be . . . hypocritical if we are busy building walls around the country. Whatever regulation is necessary . . . the flow of people, the material base of multiculturalism should not be cut off."[15]

If in the past, as American historian Gary Gerstle has said, "a powerful nationalism" "suffocated" the country's "hyphenated identities," by the 1990s no one was suffocating: the multicultural view held sway, reinforced by the weakening of Western influences and by the resurgence of ethnic-tribal identities around the world.[16] At its best multicultural cosmopolitanism argues for a tolerance for other people's beliefs and manners; at its worst, it puts people into groups with divergent identities, sometimes bordering on an older racialist thinking which talked of "German Science" or a "Jewish Science."[17] Many multiculturalists emphasize biology over history, race over place, demography over culture, as the driving forces in history, a position destined to offend many Americans. This particular form of cosmopolitanism, moreover, sees no hope for assimilation; indeed, it maintains that, ever since there were immigrants, the United States had "coerced" millions of people to "assimilate."[18]

But there is another side to academic cosmopolitanism, the fluid side, which insists that boundaries of all kinds—especially between groups—must be viewed with suspicion. "I revel in fluidity," said Cornel West of Harvard in 1994. "I always think that we are in process, making and remaking ourselves along the way." What we need, he believes, is a "transgender, transracial, transsexual orientation of social motion, social momentum, social movement."[19] ("We are becoming fluid and many-sided," Robert Jay Lifton writes in the very opening sentence of *The Protean Self.*)

Thus, the fluids, rather than dwelling on multiculturalism (which, to some degree, implies boundaries although not territorial boundaries), applaud the nimble self able to take many shapes.[20] This position, too, has roots in various strands of the American past—in the liberal, universalist outlook itself, which asserts that people are free to choose whatever identities they wished, impervious to where (or into what situation) they are born; in the bias of twentieth-century social science, which viewed progress as an outcome of the demise of old place relationships (those tied to land, villages, regions, or countries); in the secularization of the academy after 1920, which was carried out, above all, by liberal Protestant university presidents, who sought to establish a non-Christian international outlook on American campuses; and in the contributions of Jewish-Americans who entered the academy after World War II, many bearing an outlook hostile to exclusionary notions of place.[21] The fluid view could also be traced to the countercultural movements of the 1960s, which affirmed unimpeded self-invention.[22]

Modern fluid cosmopolitans, however, further radicalized this position; after 1980 they extended self-invention into all areas of life (gender, sexuality, race, anything once viewed as fixed or biological). They also turned their attention to the "border," the "borderland," the "boundary."

In 1990, editor of the *Journal of American History*, historian David Thelen, announced plans to publish articles on "border-land studies"—on how "individuals in the past construct[ed] multinational and transnational processes as they met everyday needs in the borderlands between cultures."[23] Around the same time there was a flood of books, articles, conferences, and dissertations dealing with borders. By the late nineties, the cult of the border had risen to new heights and borderland scholars treated borders as the source of all culture-making. "Culture is by nature heterogeneous," said José David Saldívar, professor of ethnic studies at Berkeley, "and necessarily works through the realm of borders."[24]

Some scholars even temporarily left their campuses to study life on the border, to document and photograph its fluidities. In 1996, Mary Ellen Wolf, professor of French at New Mexico State University, took leave from her academic job to photograph the many Mexican transvestites who made their living as prostitutes on the border between California and Mexico.

Wolf admitted (in a journal interview) that "it's become all too common now to think of the border as a metaphor for fluidity, and in this way forget that it's a real place." Yet she could not resist revealing in her pictures "the stories of crossings that take place in multiple registers and on a daily basis." Besides, she confessed, "I find myself wanting to cross, to go away from myself and the institution that I'm identified with. Of course, it would be wonderful to learn if any of the theory debated and absorbed in the university has a connection to life as it is lived, to life in the streets, and, in this case, to life in the borderlands."[25]

Besides singling out life on the borders for special scrutiny and praise, some academics also believed that the *transgression* of borders was the best way to achieve the best humanity.

Richard Sennett, sociology professor at New York University, stands out as a fascinating and complex exponent of proteanism, often taking positions that are at odds with one another. In his most recent book, *Corrosion of Character* (1998), which deals with the impact on work of modern capitalism, he seems opposed to proteanism and to the crossing of boundaries.[26] Flexible corporate practices, he says, have transformed workers into "fragments" and made them accept "instability," "uncertainty," and "incompleteness" as normal. The new capitalist order has forced workers into chronic acts of "becoming." Above all, it has robbed workers of their power to form "sustainable narratives" and, thereby, undermine trust. Character, Sennett argues persuasively, cannot develop when people have little control over their own life histories. "Flexibility," he insists, "cannot give any guidance for the conduct of ordinary life": only "durable and sustained paths of action" can do that.[27]

Yet, in nearly all his other work, Sennett admires the very qualities which, in this book, he criticizes.[28] In *Conscience of the*

Eye (1990), for instance, a book about Christianity and cities, he argues that life flourishes when people reject "fixed" categories of identity and engage "the incompleteness" of the "outside" world. Maturity begins when people "tear down the walls that keep them inside," when they let the outside inside, and when they abandon those Christian ideas that have nurtured "interior" reflection and a stable sense of self. Christianity supports qualities, Sennett says—permanence, completeness, sequential order, the "inner life"—that have kept people from responding to the diversity of the urban outside. Moreover, these qualities don't even exist, especially in the big cities. What does exist, Sennett says, are "strangers," "impermanence and chance," "discontinuity and disorientation," "fragmentation," and "chaos" which people must accept if they wish to live well and humanely. "Displacement rather than linearity," he says, "is a humane prescription."[29]

For Sennett, in this book and others, a mature humanity comes not when people seek wholeness or linear narratives, but when they encounter the unstable *borders* of society. "In the ecological structure of ponds or on the wild land," he says, invoking a biological analogy to illustrate his point, "the most intense activities take place at contested borders. . . . Less conflicted spaces behind the borders are less active. The social center is at the physical edge."[30] Sennett's purpose is to show that creative life happens not in the cores of societies but at their "permeable" perimeters.[31]

But there is more; for Sennett also believes that wisdom begins when people risk reaching across boundaries in the act of becoming. "In crossing a boundary," "people can see others as if for the first time." "Recognition scenes that might occur at borders are the only chance people have to confront fixed sociological pictures routinized in time." "At a boundary one transgresses one's identity, as one had known it in the past."

"Self-understanding occurs when suddenly a person becomes aware of crossing boundaries."[32]

On their face, the multicultural and fluid sides of academic cosmopolitanism seem at odds; but they are, in fact, quite at home with each other. For one thing, both, in differing degrees, consider such concepts as "difference," "otherness," and inclusion as central to their vision. Robert Lifton, a fluid cosmopolitan, affirms what he calls "multilocalism" and says "inclusiveness is vital." David Hollinger, an historian at Berkeley, argues in his 1995 book *Postethnic America* for "postethnicity" or for a mentality that generates "cosmopolitan instincts" without forfeiting the ethnic "rootedness" of the past.[33] At the same time, advocates of both views share an anxiety about territorial place, which pulls people in, defines their lives, and establishes clear laws and standards of exclusion and inclusion.

From the multicultural angle this view is expressed in Walzer's notion that America is not a state in any territorial conventional sense. "The fundamental contrast between Europe and America" is one "between territorially grounded ('tribal') and groundless ('multicultural') difference," he says. In America, Walzer's "ethnic particulars" are suspended in air, perpetually adrift like milkweed seeds, never touching ground, a position Walzer (and other multiculturalists) think also determines the character and limit of patriotism in America. In terms of land, language, and common memories, American patriotism does not exist at all, Walzer thinks. What patriotism does exist—what really does unify Americans—is directed not at places but at political principles or abstract ideas of justice, which all must defend if they wish to go on living as "ethnic particulars."[34]

Fluid cosmopolitans think similarly about place. Thus, Sennett argued in 1995 that traditional ways of organizing places had only cemented differences and excluded others. What we need now, he claims, is a fluid sense of place forged within the "fleeting and fragmented" elements of urban life where strangers meet. "Place-making based on exclusion, sameness, or nostalgia is socially poisonous and psychologically useless," he insists. "Place-making based on more diverse, denser, impersonal human contacts must find a way for those contacts to endure."[35] Impersonality "must" offer the ground for "a more sociable, truly cosmopolitan existence."[36]

After 1980, finally, another group of academics, all emigré intellectuals, contributed their own postcolonial variation to the academic cosmopolitan theme. Fleeing countries that seemed torn in pieces, most of these scholars had "no positive feeling for the state at all," as one postcolonial academic has said.[37] They arrived in this country disposed to see America itself as a land in pieces. And they also added their own angles, above all those of exile and diaspora.

In recent years, a vast literature has emerged to describe the ordeal of all people in motion. Much of this literature, however, differs from that of the past, which often depicted exile, and even simple migration, as terrifying and blighted. The philosopher George Santayana wrote in 1912 that "the most radical form of travel, and the most tragic, is migration."[38] Years later, in 1978, Orlando Patterson, Harvard University sociologist, echoed this view; in an article on migration in Caribbean societies, he observed the "deleterious" impact that incessant "mobility" and "uprootings" had had on regional Caribbean cultures, forming a "modal personality devoid of trust" and preventing the rise of "relative stable structures" basic for enduring social health.[39] Recent fiction, too, recounts the tragedy of exile. In 1996, W. G. Sebald published the hauntingly beautiful *The Emigrants,* a novel based on experiences of three members of his family who were exiled from Germany as a result of the Nazi assault on the Jews. Sebald showed what happens when a culture dares to expel its most loyal citizens, whose "beautiful names" were "so intimately bound up with the country they lived in and with its language." Such evictions end in death or despair for the exiled and for the exiler (and for all those touched by the exiling mentality), in a world "hopelessly run down" and "ruined . . . by the insatiable urge for destruction."[40]

By the 1990s, however, exile was for the most part no longer understood as tragic by many educated commentators—despite the misery in places like Bosnia or the Congo—but as worthy of "celebration."[41] Many people also invoked diaspora to describe what they thought to be their experiences in America. Years ago, the concept of the diaspora was confined mostly to the traumatic experience of Jewish exile; but just as in the case of "outsider" and "border," the term "diaspora" has been freed of its dire trappings and redefined to reflect the identities of many mobile groups, even tourists.[42]

The new group of migrant intellectuals in particular have laid claim to the dynamics of exile and diaspora.[43] Among the most influential of these scholars have been highly educated Asian Indians who grew up "in the elite sectors of the postcolonial world," as one of them has written.[44] They carried with them to America memories of humiliation, inflicted first by the British and then by their own Indian states which had worked to dismantle the system of privilege from which many in this group had benefitted.[45] Critics of nationalism, sensitive more to its pretensions (or, as Prasenjit Duara, historian at the University of Chicago, has said, to its "ubiquities, changeability, and fungibility") rather than to its merits, they looked at such concepts of nation-state and citizenship largely as Western propaganda foisted on the world. Among the many international scholars recruited by universities and colleges, they were after 1985 "pacesetters" in the American inquiry into all aspects of "place," from nationalism and borders to migration and patriotism.[46]

Three scholars in particular, all like Duara at the University of Chicago, have much shaped the character of this postcolonial position—Dipesh Chakrabarty, Arjun Appadurai, and Homi Bhabha. Chakrabarty teaches postcolonial theory and "subaltern" history (India's version of bottom-up history) and sees the nation-state, citizenship, and even "linear" history itself, as fabrications of Western imperialism. Intellectually, he wants to "provincialize Europe," and although he gets a good salary at one of the world's most prestigious universities, he condemns both universities and history as collusive players in the Western game of "repression and violence." He longs to "write over the given and privileged narratives of citizenship other narratives of human connections."[47]

Born in Bombay, India, and educated in Britain, Appadurai, an anthropologist, migrated to the United States in the 1970s.[48] Twenty years later, he headed a "globalization project" at Chicago, funded by the MacArthur and Ford foundations.[49]

Appadurai has written widely on transnational subjects, but in no piece has he been more provocative than "Patriotism and Its Futures," written in 1992 and republished in his 1996 *Modernity at Large*.[50] Appadurai argues that millions of people live today in a "deterritorialized" condition, the result of the near-collapse of the "nation form." "Key identities," he insists, "now only partially revolve around . . . place." "In the postnational world we see emerging, diaspora runs with, and not against, the grain of identity."

Appadurai sees this condition as a healthy one, partly because nationalism was always "the last refuge of ethnic totalitarianism." But it is especially healthy because it should challenge societies to devise a "new language [and politics] to capture the collective interests of deterritorialized groups."[51]

This challenge, Appadurai believes, can best be met by the

United States, the least national of nations, indeed no nation or country at all. America is the world's "greatest apparent falsification," "a fascinating garage sale for the rest of the world." Appadurai scoffs at the idea that an "Americanness" unifies the country, and he deems the "melting pot" a vain fantasy. No one really "belongs" in this place, he claims. America, he contends, is merely "one node in a postnational network of diasporas," a "diasporic switching point to which people come to seek their fortunes but are no longer content to leave their homelands behind."

The existence of diasporas, moreover, is why America offers the best site for the future; here the Third World outcasts, long despised, might create a "new Americanism" unlike any in history, "a delocalized transnation." Here a new patriotism might emerge, not tied to the "sovereign nation," nor to any traditional American "locality" but to other sovereign locations. If only Americans would accept what they have become—a diasporic people with no ties to historical places—then a new order might emerge. All it would take would be for Americans to lift the movers above the settled, diasporics over the natives, strangers over themselves.

Like Appadurai, Homi Bhabha was born to an upper-caste Indian family in Bombay and educated in Britain. Bhabha's appointment at the University of Chicago was greeted by administrators as "a coup for the university."[52] The move pleased Bhabha, too, for it brought him into contact—as he said—with "a whole range of stellar individuals" and into a place where he might study "vernacular cosmopolitanism" and "the structures of modernity in a transnational context."[53]

Bhabha's work—especially his major book, *The Location of Culture*—shows the usual postcolonial revulsion for the Western nation-state and for citizenship.[54] Like Appadurai and Chakrabarty, he seeks a "radical revision of the human community," not from the angle of "soil and place," but from the point of view of "the marginalized, the displaced, the diasporic," and the "border." He also sees the new culture emerging from "the freaks of culture displacements." For him, as for the others, "national cultures" must give way to "sovereignties" that transcend place—gender, race, ethnicity, sexuality, the migratory condition itself. "It is from those who have suffered the sentence of history—subjugation, domination, diaspora, displacement—that we learn our most enduring lessons for living and thinking," he says.[55]

Bhabha's contribution to the cosmopolitan debate has been to harden the placelessness already present in American academic cosmopolitanism. Uninhibited by affection for any traditions of place, he and his postcolonial colleagues have given more life to the central view that America is not really a place at all but mostly an idea, a state of mind, a condition open to continual amendment, a road rather than a destination.

"OUR VALUES ARE GLOBAL"

As formidable a creation as academic cosmopolitanism is in all its forms, there is another form that surpasses it in reach and power: market cosmopolitanism. Market cosmopolitanism emerged after 1980 in much of the business world. It replaced Marxism (with which it once competed) in the sweep of its internationalist ambitions. This cosmopolitanism, however, is one of money not of workers. It is the thinking of those who, at the very least, are averse to any kind of fixed national boundary, anything that might limit the flow of ideas, money, goods, or people.

Market cosmopolitans share many of the above academic liberal themes. But what distinguishes the market version from the others, however, is, obviously, its aim—money and profit—

which inevitably determines how long and to what degree any business might remain committed to any liberal idea.

Many businesses, as well as business journals and consultants, have adopted the new market cosmopolitanism in both its multicultural and fluid forms. Think tanks, too, trumpeting the glories of the cosmopolitan market, have sprouted in the nation's capital.[56] Among the most ideologically unique has been the Cato Institute, a medium-sized organization in Washington, D.C., founded by Ed Crane in 1979 and housed in a blue-glass building on Massachusetts Avenue, ironically just across the street from a bronze statue of labor unionist Samuel Gompers. Market libertarians all, the men at Cato have urged that all obstacles—religion, nationalism, patriotism—be modified or dumped before the god of Productivity. No group has so acclaimed the privatization of everything, the deregulation of everything, the stripping away of most governmental safeguards, the free movement of everything from money to migrants. Their influence has reached into the minds of such leading Republicans as Texans Richard Armey and Tom DeLay.[57]

Businesses, too, have hoisted the cosmopolitan banner, promoting "diversity" among their workers, and pursuing "multicultural marketing" for their customers. Like their academic contemporaries, they view the United States as a "culture without a center" and pursue niche-thinking in terms of race, gender, and ethnicity.[58] Many firms also display the fluid-protean-open-borders approach, none more so than the bankers and financial managers who reaped the most from the deregulation of the world's money markets, as well as from the spread of electronic and intermodal technologies, which facilitated rapid trading in huge volumes.[59]

"When I look at a map of the world," says John Doerr, top venture capitalist in Silicon Valley who arranged the financing for such firms as Netscape and Sun Microsystems, "I don't visualize it in terms of . . . countries. Instead I see Internet packages or E-mail messages flowing between various points."[60] "It is a matter of complete indifference to the chief financial officer of any major company whether one sells capital notes in New York, Hong Kong, or London. Decisions are made on the basis of rate and availability, not geography," writes Walter Wriston, in his 1992 book *The Twilight of Sovereignty.* Former head of Citicorp, a bank with hundreds of branches around the world, Wriston also argues that new technologies have made "obsolete" "the old political boundaries of nation-states."[61]

"Boundaryless behavior is the soul of today's GE," said Jack Welsh, CEO of General Electric, in his 1994 annual report. "Simply put, people seem compelled to build layers and walls between themselves and others, and that human tendency tends . . . to cramp people" and "smother dreams."[62] "The real work today," observes Whirlpool's CEO, David Whitwam (sounding rather like Homi Bhabha or Richard Sennett), "takes place at the boundaries."[63] Throughout the nineties, gambling moguls have created "international marketing programs" to bring high rollers from around the world to their casinos. "This is going to be an international clientele," said Ralph Sturges, chief of the Mohegans, of his Mohegan Sun Casino. We want "visitors from all over the world," said Steve Wynn of the Mirage Casino-Hotel in Las Vegas.[64]

As for the major port terminal directors, they have long thought of themselves as efficient businessmen on the frontlines of the "new international world order," erecting "commercial bridges between nations," and—through marketing offices around the world—aggressively recruiting new clients to fill berths and terminals.[65] Their approach has been inclusive, technocratic, managerial, and cosmopolitan. As far back as the 1940s, the Port Authority of New York and New Jersey demanded that "the barriers of provincialism" be thrown down and that a nonpartisan vision come to the fore. Today, that port leads as an evangel for the globalization of the greater metropolitan region.[66]

High-tech companies have readily accommodated the diverse workforce they helped create, and have forged an ideology to fit the vast markets they command. Among the heaviest users of foreign skilled labor, they have all adopted "boundaryless" multicultural policies.[67] "Today," said Ray Smith, CEO of Bell Atlantic, in 1995, "businesses [seek to claim] citizenship in the global community by replacing the declining significance of *place* with the ascending significance of *people*."[68] By 1996 IBM had established thirty-two "global diversity councils," according to Ted Childs, vice president for IBM's "global workforce diversity," to make sure that "we value contributions by people who are not 'American.'" "We are global in scope, our values are global," said Nicole Barde, Intel's diversity manager.[69]

Along with these companies are many business newspapers and magazines, notably *The Economist* and the *Wall Street Journal,* both with editorial offices around the world, and both in tune with the cosmopolitan view. To be sure, the *Wall Street Journal* is schizoid about cosmopolitanism. It endorses both the multicultural and the transborder approaches, the former found mostly in its B section, where the paper's regular column "Business and Race," written by Leon E. Wynter, often discusses the latest data on group niche-marketing. On its editorial page, however, the *Journal,* led by editor Robert Bartley, reviles multiculturalism. Bartley recommends instead a pure vision of "free markets, free trade, and open immigration." In 1993 he wrote scathingly about "cosmopolitan elites," by which he meant the "do your own thing" people who thrust on the American people the "selfish" values of the "1960s."

Three years later he bemoaned the "decline in standards" and warned that "the very rationality of capitalism"—if left unchecked by "economic necessity or religion"—"will eat away its 'bourgeois' moral underpinning." Around the same time, however, and in a way that ate away at his own moral underpinning, he said that "the big trends of the age transcend national boundaries and national sovereignty." "In the end, newly empowered individuals throughout the world will make their own decisions minute by minute, expressing emotional demands and creating financial markets." "In the 21st century, we will be ruled not so much by the writ of politicians but by the logic of markets."[70]

American Demographics, a slick magazine published for over twenty years by Dow Jones, publisher also of the *Wall Street Journal,* seems to inflect nearly every article in a cosmopolitan direction.[71] Its editors, who claimed to have brought demography "out of the shadows," have advocated "multicultural marketing." They have published handbooks on how to squeeze the most out of the group niches, offering material on practically every lucrative identity market from singles who refuse to have children to lesbians and gays who, according to a recent piece, constitute "a separate tribe" with "distinctive mores and fashions." At the same time, the magazine has showcased the fluid culture of America's new class of young "self-navigators," professionals who boast a "new value structure" and "who seem to 'drop in' on and migrate between different ways of living."[72] In a fall 1997 piece, "Matters of Culture," it argued "conclusively" that "cosmopolitan Americans outnumber those with less open cultural views."[73]

Finally, there are the individual consultants, who through their writings have done a great deal to popularize market cosmopolitanism. Among them are Joel Kotkin, a ubiquitous business consultant and senior fellow at the Pepperdine University School of Business and Management in Malibu, California; and Rosabeth Kanter, professor at the Harvard Business School and popular consultant to America's biggest companies.

Kotkin, a frequent contributor to the editorial page of the *Wall Street Journal,* asserted in 1995 that the future belongs to the "rich and affluent voters" who work in the mobile "new economy," hate "small town culture," and believe that "economics, not morality, is the key challenge facing society."[74] Kotkin believes that "borders" are the centers of the new order of things, and he is attracted to what he calls "global tribes" or the world's most ambitious emigrés set loose from their homelands to float about in quest of alliances with transnational firms. "These global tribes," he wrote in his 1993 book *Tribes: How Race, Religion, and Identity Determine Success in the New Global Economy,* "are today's quintessential cosmopolitans, in sharp contrast to narrow provincials. As the conventional barriers of nation-states and regions become less meaningful under the weight of global economic forces, it is likely such dispersed peoples—and their worldwide business and cultural networks—will increasingly shape the economic destiny of mankind."[75]

These groups, he observes, are "diasporic," in touch with their "homelands" only in their fantasies, and they make ideal entrepreneurs because they possess "the traditional diaspora values of enterprise and self-help."[76]

Like Appadurai and Bhabha, Kotkin sees America as merely one node in a network of global diasporas, not as a country in any conventional sense. He even thinks that the British settlers on this continent were not settlers at all but the "most important and enduring diaspora" in American history, never connecting with America and never ceasing to dream about Westminster Abbey or the white cliffs of Dover.[77]

A few years after writing *Tribes,* Kotkin dealt directly with the changing character of place in America, recognizing that some kind of adjustment had to be made if people were to accept the cosmopolitan order. "For ten years, the idea of place has taken a beating," he said in a 1997 op-ed piece for the *Los Angeles Times,* yet "many Americans still crave some sense of identity unique to the places where they live"; and today, only big cities, rather than homogeneous suburbs, have the wherewithal to supply this sense of identity. But Kotkin has almost no historical imagination, and his approach resembles the strategies of the tourist industry. The Old World is dead, according to him, so we must create a "new sense of place" out of "the new economy," not out of the past. Here Los Angeles especially shines for its many "place options," including "Koreatown, Little Tokyo, the San Gabriel Valley and Westminster's Little Saigon," "the Latino shopping districts," Venice Beach and Burbank, and such "shopping areas" as "the Fashion District, Los Feliz Village, and Sherman Village in the Valley."[78]

Rosabeth Kanter, besides advising firms and teaching at Harvard, has written many books of guidance for businesspeople. In her 1995 *World Class: Thriving Locally in the Global Economy,* perhaps the most tendentious statement of business cosmopolitanism of the decade, she attempts to prove that global companies do not destroy local communities so much as build them up.[79] She also distinguishes "cosmopolitan" businessmen from what she calls "the locals" (people with unneeded skills) and "the isolates" (the unskilled), both of whom have experienced the pain of dislocation and layoffs.

Kanter's cosmopolitans have all the characteristics mentioned above, especially "flexibility, mobility, and change." They "value choices over loyalties," seek to "tear down the invisible walls between countries," and long to "break through the barriers" that limit choice. They "respect differences" and understand "the elusive" and "elastic boundaries of identity."

The locals, on the other hand, "value loyalties over choices," "define" themselves "primarily by particular places," and pursue "opportunities confined to their own communities." Opposed to letting the outside inside, they "try to preserve and even erect new barriers, most often through political means."

Kanter shows little sympathy for the locals, and even less for the isolates, those without any skills at all. These people, she says, are "provincial." They "fear invasion" and "dread the power of cosmopolitans, they fear their mobility." The locals "take pride in being Americans," which only masks "envy" of "outsiders or foreigners," who "are seen as doing better than insiders." The locals and isolates also seem to want to deny themselves what "most people" desire—"quality goods," the "best goods" from "the global shopping mall."

Kanter claims that communities throughout America, if they want success, must yield to the power of the cosmopolitans. Firms, too, of course, should contribute to their communities and be good "citizens"; but the larger burden falls on the locals. "Stay-put workers" who have "dug in roots" "must" accommodate "the migrant managers who are comfortable moving operations—and themselves—anywhere." The locals must, in other words, make way for those who do not value context except as a means for achieving more and more wealth.

Kanter believes that everywhere, not just somewhere, must be cosmopolitan. "Cities need their own foreign policy." They "must open their connections to the world" and "destroy" the "walls in the mind." "Those who lack the mental flexibility to think across boundaries," Kanter concludes, "will find it harder and harder to hold their own, let alone prosper."

UNPRECEDENTED ALLIANCE AGAINST PLACE

Corporate executives, academics, and postcolonialists have together brought cosmopolitanism into the mainstream. They seem unified in their views—above all, in their phobia for place. They see place and everything associated with it (memory, the past, tradition) as confining and as negatively discriminatory. In every case, they prefer weak fluid boundaries that exclude no one and encourage transgression to the maintenance of old neighborhoods or the protection of established communities, both local and national.

The multicultural side of cosmopolitanism appears to support place, but what it supports is not place but communities based on "essences" that pretend to "unite" people into identities only vaguely or uncomfortably tied to place.

In light of the new cosmopolitanism, America emerges more than ever as a transparency without a history and as a land of free-floating individuals without strong loyalties who view life as a theater of never-ending options. So, too, the apostles of this approach tend to look on Americans who have "too much interest" in their own localities as intractable and limited, if not dangerous. These cosmopolitans, in other words, form an ideological threat to the interests and well-being of most Americans.

This convergence of views is remarkable, but what is even more remarkable is how both liberal and left-wing thinkers concede to market dominance and, in the process, bring into question some of their dearest positions. Liberal cosmopolitan academics have espoused views worth defending: inclusion of those peoples unjustly shut out from positions of power; compassion for strangers ruthlessly torn from their homelands; historical study of those groups (working-class, minority women and men) who have been ignored by historians and other analysts in the past; and respect for the cultures and philosophies foreign to our own. A great deal, too, is worth saying in defense of moving across boundaries (both in and over time) to experience the unfamiliar, the new. All these qualities keep us alive as well as humble; they need to have (and *do* have) a place in nearly every conceivable sphere of life, from politics and business to music and sex. Cosmopolitanism generally, especially when cultivated within specific places, or when harmonized with traditions of place, can only enrich the character of the whole culture in which it exists.

But many liberals and leftists have often seen nothing but this side of the equation and sacrifice too much to market ideology, because that ideology, as many of them know, has become the vehicle for the realization of their dreams. Their emphasis on difference and identity, insistent as it is, has helped undermine the assimilationist achievements of the period between 1920 and 1975. Liberal academics have also worked to abolish the very category of the outsider, to say nothing of the condition itself. Some outsiders, however, should remain outsiders, not only the obvious ones (criminals) but all those who have felt like outsiders and who might wish to remain outsiders if only because such a perspective might make them critics, observers, or artists. (The problem is, of course, outsiderness cannot be created or managed into existence.)

By the late nineties the constant drumbeat for flexibility and self-invention had gone too far, not only because it blotted out the merits of place but because it failed to address how few Americans could really invent themselves and to what degree their "mobility" and "flexibility" had nothing to do with their own free will but had been imposed on them by others. Nationalism, without a doubt, had menaced the world, especially in the hands of centralizing elites or, as historian John Lukacs has said, in the fascist case, as it was "rooted in the racial and tribal bonds of the people."[80] But love of country or patriotism "rooted in a particular place" (rather than in any race or biological grouping) was quite another matter; it was a necessity for social health. Patriotism at its best, inspired by a history of shared sacrifice in a shared country, was not racist or exclusionary; it was democratic, civic-minded, and inclusive, devoid of the hatred that so often arises out of communities based on race or ethnicity.

Most Americans, it could be argued, want or need some kind of bond to the country (or region in the country) they know and have grown up in, some larger sense of place among all places to admire, love, and defend.

Today, many people look on cosmopolitan consumerism as a good thing, the best we have or can expect to have, because it keeps people to themselves in their pursuit of wealth and forces them to live peaceably with others and to withhold judgment. But market cosmopolitanism, unchecked by any countervailing power, is the most exclusionary of all cosmopolitanisms. Whole worlds that do not have market value are exiled as more "places" are contained within the reach of the invisible hand. Thus, in the name of freedom and choice, market cosmopolitanism tends to exclude those things that give the most meaning to life for most people—the fullest possible sensual experience of the world; vocation; spiritual life; pursuing a goal or truth regardless of costs; friendship, family, children; and, of course, place itself.[81] The profit motive may facilitate innovation, but unfettered markets merely extend the shrinking of choice—more goods and money but fewer real choices—to a wider canvas.

The market world of choice boils down to this: on the

micro level, it *does* mean, as Kanter says, that consumer choice rules; but on the macro level, it means that those with the capital and the agenda create the context, the boundaries, the entire culture within which ordinary people make their choices. Most Americans, in other words, have little control over the larger arena in which they choose their goods and services. In the mid-sixties, sociologist Milton Gordon wrote that educated Americans talked constantly about universal man when in fact the world was extremely diverse. Today, conversely, we babble on about diversity when, in fact, we are all becoming more and more alike, especially in global cities where the capitalist market exerts its fullest impact.[82]

It is in this context, then, that the liberal, left-wing forms of cosmopolitanism seem to be playing their most significant historical role, for by denigrating place and fostering everything connected to mobility and choice, they actually fortify the context for more market expansion, cheer on the strategies of opportunistic migrants, and mop up after unscrupulous developers and politicians have bulldozed neighborhoods, regions, and whole countries.

Current cosmopolitanism seeks a world in which long-lived attachments (to family, home, town, city, country) mean little or nothing and must be swept away or tailored to suit the tourist industry. Is this the kind of cosmopolitanism to which we are all now heir, not one animated by one civilization but driven by many civilizations, the fluid mentality of everywhere and nowhere?

But there can be no culture built under unstable protean conditions, mainly at the borders, or by strangers. Any culture that hopes to endure, to say nothing of thrive, must be formed and sustained at the centers not at the edges. America cannot be reimagined out of the materials spawned by geographical frontiers and urban edges, because it is at those very edges and frontiers where the world's pimps and con artists congregate the most and where the market forces are most Darwinian, most virulent, and most subversive to the making of any kind of decent, collective life.

Conclusion:
Veblen Revisited

The building of highways and gateways, the rush of trucks and trains, the spread of temporariness in work and life, the reliance on such service industries as gambling and tourism, the place-hostile activities of universities and government, and the rise of a new cosmopolitanism have all come at the cost of ties to towns, cities, and regions, and to the country itself.

Many valuable things we take for granted and which give to life much that makes it worthwhile, however, cannot flourish without a sense of place. Artistic creativity, for instance, requires it. While artistic performance of the highest quality can happen anywhere, the best of art has been created by people living in a particular place. The examples of this are so legion—from Yasunari Kawabata to Johannes Brahms—that they hardly bear reciting. Can world art or world music be art or music in any way that matters?[1] Novelist William Trevor, in his *Excursions in the Real World,* writes that "fiction insists on universality, then equally insists that a degree of parochialism can often best achieve this." One hundred years ago, Alice James, recluse sister of William and Henry James, put the same matter another way, if more roughly, in her diary: "The paralytic on his couch can have, if he wants them, wider experiences than Stanley's slaughtering savages." These are commonsensical notions, but in today's climate they might pass as profundities as well as warnings.[2]

A strong sense of place, along with the boundaries that shape it and give it meaning, not only fosters creativity but also helps to provide people—especially children—with an assurance that they will be protected and not abandoned. In our time, many people are riveted by the worst kinds of sexual predation, by child abuse especially. But in a society or culture bent on dismantling boundaries as a regular fact of life and inclined to exalt a borderless mentality, no one should be surprised that other boundaries—especially those shielding children—should provide so little power to defend. Yet it is indisputable that children need a sense of place (along with an acceptance of boundaries that define and establish the safeness of place) in order to become self-reliant. This sense of place should be ideally created by parents (not by state authorities or by police), who care for and love their children and who give to place the feeling of "indestructibility" which every child needs. "Where firm boundaries are needed to give meaning to content and control to spontaneity, and do not hold," observed child analyst D.W. Winnicott, "there will be an increase in the number and power of antisocial individuals, tipping the balance against the mature in society."[3]

Without a sense of boundaried place, finally, there can be no citizenship, no basis for common bonds to others, no willingness to give to the commonweal or to be taxed, even lightly, in behalf of the welfare of others. To be sure, the boundaries of place may, in the nature of things, "exclude the outsider or stranger," as J. B. Jackson once observed in *The Necessity for Ruins.* But as Jackson also observed, boundaries "stand for law and permanence," "create neighbors," and "transform an amorphous environment into a human landscape."[4] A living sense of a boundaried place, some kind of patriotism beyond love of abstract principles, is the main condition for citizenship.

This living sense always has a provincial character. It takes shape first as connections to families and friends, then to neighborhoods, towns, and regions, and finally, to the nation and the world. It is through the formation of this *sense of place,* beginning with the home and parents, that people develop their *loyalty to place,* but it is only after the earliest concrete ties are formed that the bigger connections can be forged; the process cannot begin the other way around.

Cosmopolitan thinkers who believe that the real threat to the planet comes from the failure on part of ordinary people to break loose from their provincial roots and to embrace "the stranger" and the "world at large" have got it backwards. The real threat arises from the spread of powerful global forces indifferent to provincial needs, forces that have ripped to shreds local commitments and have forced millions of souls into unwanted dispossession and exile. The real threat does not come from strong provincial commitments: it comes from their absence. People strong in their sense of place possess the conviction to decide how they will live; at the same time, they are often more able and willing to *include* others because they have little or nothing to fear from outsiders or foreigners. It is only fragile boundaries—or the feeling that people have no control over their own world—that produces the worst forms of exclusionism, that eats away at citizenship, and that leads, finally, to reliance on centralized state power to manage, dictate, order, or forbid.

"Centralization of state power in the national government,"

said Josiah Royce in 1908, "without a constantly enriched and diversified provincial consciousness, can only increase the estrangement of our national spirit from its own life. On the other hand history shows that if you want a great people to be strong, you must depend upon provincial loyalties to mediate between the people and the nation."[5] In America of the 1990s the bureaucratic state has become more invasive than it has ever been (despite vaunted congressional attempts to cut it back in the interest of freeing up the "free market"). On the other hand, the cultural center of the country, with all its various places and historical associations, has grown ever more atomized and vulnerable.

Everything I have discussed in this book, from the market gateways and highways and the big research universities to the cosmopolitanism of business and the academy, has contributed to the destruction of a sense of place and to the transformation of America into a country of exiles. If the process continues with the same degree of intensity, we can only expect greater reliance on state power—more prisons, more police, more attempts to manage or manipulate minds—to compensate for the failure of Americans to remember and protect their places.

Thorstein Veblen had provincial loyalty inside his own name. He was named for his mother's father, Thorstein Bunde, who, in turn, was named for his farm, Bunde, in Norway.[6] To own a farm was a great achievement in Norway, for a farm possessed a worth that went well beyond its commercial value. It imparted high status which the place-name signified; by custom, farmers attached it to their ordinary Christian names and patronymics. But not only did Veblen carry the place-name of his grandfather, he also bore the memory of his grandfather's dispossession. After relying on lawyers for some costly litigation, Thorstein Bunde was unable to pay them back and they took his farm. To lose one's farm was the greatest humiliation any man could have suffered at the time, and Thorstein Bunde, defeated by the loss, died at the age of thirty-five.

Veblen's father, Thomas Anderson, grew up as a tenant on the farm of Veblen, after his own father, too, had his property taken from him. Impoverished, he immigrated to the United States in 1847, determined to establish his own farmstead. With help from a friend, he gained access to forty acres of land in Wisconsin but was forced off his claim by "Yankee speculators," whom he would despise for the rest of his life. A superb craftsman as well as an innovative farmer, he acquired another farm (though inadequate to meet his needs) and built a house in Cato, Wisconsin, where his son Thorstein was born (and which stood for more than one hundred years).[7] In 1865 he moved for the final time, to Minnesota, where he got the land he dreamed of, more than two hundred acres of it. He farmed, planted orchards, kept bees, and built the barns and dwellings. (His wife, Kari Bunde Veblen, on the other hand, drove the reaper, made the butter, cheese, and soap, wove cloth, sewed garments, and carded wool.) Until 1864, he was known as Thomas Anderson, but in the year he purchased his new Minnesota land, he reasserted the farm name of Veblen. He went to court to have his name changed to Veblen, and he made the deed out in the Veblen name. In Norway, he was a tenant *on* Veblen, bearing the burden of his own father's dispossession. In America, he *owned* Veblen, reclaiming the reputation and respect his father—and his father-in-law—had lost.

Thorstein Bunde Veblen's name, then, contained memories of displacement and loss, of determination to find and then stay put, and of a dignity and pride in ownership that surpassed all commercial ambition. It reminded him always of his obligation to connect with some place and to stay there. It was also like tinder, ready, under the right conditions, to ignite a fury in him—against himself as well as against others. In 1920, when he visited his cabin in California, he faced not only what he thought to be an act of dispossession by a greedy landlord but also his own failure to take responsibility for his property, his own place; the result was a violent act of destruction far out of proportion to the gravity of the cause.

Very few Americans have names that resonate with such history, names which might remind them of their own need to connect to the places in which they live. Many of us have been overtaken by conditions that obscure why places (and the past in them) should matter. Some of us prefer not to remember the past at all. It would be a good thing if we did.

Notes

INTRODUCTION: VEBLEN IN SILICON VALLEY

1. R. L. Duffus, *The Innocents at Cedro: A Memoir of Thorstein Veblen and Some Others* (New York: Macmillan, 1944).
2. Author's visit, May, 31, 1997. On the Silicon Valley rich, see *Business Week,* August 25, 1997, pp. 66–69, 126, 130 (the entire issue is devoted to high-tech industries); "Hot Young Companies, New Millionaires Fuel Silicon Valley Boom," *Wall Street Journal* (hereafter *WSJ*), October 8, 1996, p. 1; "Two Friends Hunting for Gold in Silicon Valley," *BusinessWeek,* August 10, 1998, p. B1. According to *BusinessWeek,* there were 186,511 millionaires in Silicon Valley in 1996 (p. 126).
3. Duffus, *The Innocents at Cedro,* p. 159. For this discussion, I have drawn on Duffus, pp. 93, 130–32, 154; Joseph Dorfman, *Thorstein Veblen and His America* (New York: Viking, 1935), pp. 271–74, 455–57, 496–98; Peter C. Allen, "The Cottage by the Creek," *Sandstone and Tile* 9:3 (spring 1985), pp. 1–10.
4. Duffus, *The Innocents at Cedro,* p. 131; Dorfman, *Thorstein Veblen and His America,* pp. 455–56.
5. Thorstein Veblen, *Absentee Ownership and Business Enterprise in Recent Times: The Case of America* (New York: B. W. Huebsch Inc., 1923), pp. 33–36, 51–59, 135.

6. See Gary Snyder, *A Place in Space* (Washington, D.C.: Counter-point, 1995), pp. 222–23. For another discussion of place, see Dolores Hayden, *The Power of Place: Urban Landscapes as Public History* (Cambridge: The MIT Press, 1995). But Hayden's arguments are burdened by an ideological commitment to multi-cultural group theory; thus, all groups—ethnic and racial groups, workers, women—should have what Hayden calls their "territorial histories."

7. John Brinckerhoff Jackson, *A Sense of Place, a Sense of Time* (New Haven: Yale University Press, 1994), pp. 151, 160. Edward S. Casey, a philosopher at the State University of New York at Stony Brook, also has many informative things to say about place and, generally, takes a position similar to Jackson's. See his *Getting Back into Place: Toward a Renewed Understanding of the Place-World* (Bloomington: Indiana University Press, 1993); and *The Fate of Place. A Philosophical History* (Berkeley: University of California Press, 1997).

8. Quoted in George W. Pierson, *The Moving American* (New York: Alfred A. Knopf, 1972), p. 117. A hundred years later Thornton Wilder wrote, without regret, that "from the point of view of the European an American is a nomad in relation to place." An American is "differently surrounded; he has no fixed abode but carries his home with him; his relations are not to place but to everywhere, to everyone . . ." (*Ibid.,* p. 117). The Tocqueville quote appears in Witold Rybczynski, *City Life* (New York: Scrib-ners, 1995), p. 109. For a synthetic treatment of the literature on the mobility trends of the mid-nineteenth century, see Peter A. Morrison and Judith P. Wheeler, "The Image of 'Elsewhere' in the American Tradition of Migration," in William H. McNeill and Ruth S. Adams, eds., *Human Migration* (Bloomington: Indiana University Press, 1978), pp. 75–84.

9. For the impact of the "ebullient" demand for cotton (the word is Gavin Wright's) on western migration, see Gavin Wright, *The Political Economy of the Cotton South* (New York: W. W. Norton, 1978), pp. 15–24; and for population figures, see D. W. Meinig, *The Shaping of America* (New Haven: Yale University Press, 1993), vol. 2, p. 307.

10. Josiah Royce, *California* (New York: Alfred A. Knopf, 1948; orig.

pub. 1886), pp. 185–94. For three excellent books on these migrations, see Malcolm Rohrbough, *Days of Gold: The California Gold Rush and the American Nation* (Berkeley: University of California Press, 1997); John D. Unruh, *The Plains Across* (London: Pimlico, 1992), pp. 58–65; and John Mack Faragher, *Sugar Creek: Life on the Illinois Prairie* (New Haven: Yale University Press, 1986), pp. 45–52.

11. Rohrbough, in *Days of Gold,* has emphasized the frequency with which communities were undermined by this migration (pp. 58, 62, 83). On land speculation, see historian Paul Gates, who long ago showed how it dominated American society and economy in the nineteenth century. In the years 1835–38, 38 million acres of public lands were sold, 29 million of which were acquired through speculation, much of it purchased by bankers and banks; the peak years, however, were 1854–58, when speculators confiscated and resold Indian lands. See Paul Gates, "The Role of the Land Speculator in Western Development" (orig. pub. 1942), in Allan C. Bogue and Margaret Beattie Bogue, eds., *The Jeffersonian Dream: Studies in the History of American Land Policy and Development* (Albuquerque: University of New Mexico Press, 1997), pp. 6–22.

12. See, on this, Rybczynski, *City Life,* pp. 15–34, 109, 110–30; and on patterns of European mobility, see Charles Tilly, "Migration in Modern European History," in McNeill and Adams, *Human Migration,* pp. 48–68; and Hagen Schulze, *Germany: A New History* (Cambridge: Harvard University Press, 1998), pp. 120–36.

13. David H. Bennett, *The Party of Fear* (New York: Vintage, 1995), p. 62; Edward K. Spann, *The New Metropolis: New York City, 1840–1857* (New York: Columbia University Press, 1981), pp. 23–44; Roger Daniels, *Coming to America* (New York: Harper Perennial, 1990), pp. 121–265. For a good account of the terrible passage to America on packet ships, see David Hollett, *Passage to the New World* (Great Britain: P. M. Heaton Publishing, 1995), pp. 121–90.

14. Walter Nugent, *Crossings: The Great Transatlantic Migrations* (Bloomington: Indiana University Press, 1992), pp. 6–9.

15. Timothy J. Hutton and Jeffrey G. Williamson, *The Age of Mass Migration: Causes and Economic Impact* (New York: Oxford University Press, 1998), pp. 165–74.

16. Arthur Mann, *The One and the Many: Reflections on the American Identity* (Chicago: University of Chicago Press, 1979), p. 77.

17. John Higham, *Send These to Me* (New York: Atheneum, 1975), p. 48.

18. On protectionism, see Alfred E. Eckes, Jr., *Opening America's Market* (Chapel Hill: University of North Carolina Press, 1995), esp. chapter 4, pp. 59–99; on passports, see David Burner, *Herbert Hoover: A Public Life* (New York: Alfred A. Knopf, 1979), p. 73; on the absence of controls on financial transactions, see Barry Eichengreen, *Globalizing Capital: A History of the International Monetary System* (Princeton: Princeton University Press, 1996), p. 3; and Doug Henwood, *Wall Street* (New York: Verso, 1997), pp. 106–14. On the full international character of the age, see Karl Polanyi, *The Great Transformation* (Boston: Beacon Press, 1968), pp. 1–200.

19. Between 1880 and 1920 American mass manufacturing businesses used every means, including blocking all immigration restriction, to create what labor historian Alexander Keyssar called "brigades" of low-wage workers. See Keyssar, *The First Century of Unemployment in Massachusetts* (New York: Cambridge University Press, 1986), p. 62.

20. See on this transformation, David Montgomery, *Workers' Control in America* (New York: Cambridge University Press, 1981), pp. 91–114, and *The Fall of the House of Labor* (New York: Cambridge University Press, 1987).

21. For a recent history that partly chronicles the use of government troops from 1875 to 1910, see Anthony Lukas, *Big Trouble* (New York: Simon and Schuster, 1997), pp. 103–18, 225–39, 261–65.

22. On the American mining engineer's worldwide reputation at the turn of the century, see Clark C. Spence, *Mining Engineers and the American West* (Moscow, Id.: University of Idaho Press, 1993), pp. 1–17, 278–317.

23. Spence, *Mining Engineers and the American West,* pp. 143, 278, 286, 301; and William Leach, *Land of Desire: Merchants, Power, and the Rise of New American Culture* (New York: Vintage, 1994), pp. 352–53.

24. I have laid out this history in *Land of Desire.*

25. Josiah Royce, *California* (New York: Alfred A. Knopf, 1948; orig. pub. 1886), pp. ix, 182.

26. *Ibid.*, pp. 174–85.
27. Josiah Royce, *Race Questions, Provincialism, and Other American Problems* (Freeport, New York: Books for Libraries Press, 1967; orig. pub. 1908, essay written 1902), pp. 68–69.
28. *Ibid.*, p. 68.
29. On these tendencies, see Josiah Royce, *The Philosophy of Loyalty* (Nashville: Vanderbilt University Press, 1995; orig. pub. 1908), pp. 103–10; and Royce, *Race Questions,* pp. 61–71.
30. Royce, *The Philosophy of Loyalty,* p. 54.
31. *Ibid.*, p. 104.
32. *Ibid.*, p. 110.
33. Royce, *California,* pp. 180–81.
34. See Faraghar, *Sugar Creek,* pp. 51–52, 144–45; and Unruh, *The Plains Across,* pp. 322–23.
35. Reprinted in Robert Finch and John Elder, eds., *The Norton Book of Nature Writing* (New York: W.W. Norton, 1990), p. 196.
36. George Orwell used the term "without bootlicking" to describe American life in the mid-nineteenth century. "There was poverty and there were even class distinctions, but except for the Negroes there was no permanently submerged class," he wrote. "Everyone had inside him, like a kind of core, the knowledge that he could earn a decent living, and earn it without bootlicking." Sonia Orwell, *Such, Such Were the Joys* (New York: Harcourt, Brace, and Company, 1945), p. 162.
37. Alexis de Tocqueville, *Democracy in America* (New York: Doubleday Anchor, 1969), p. 237.
38. For the best single discussion of American patriotism, see Merle Curti, *The Roots of American Loyalty* (New York: Columbia University Press, 1946). Little of any value has been written on patriotism, but see essays on nationalism by George Orwell, especially "Notes on Nationalism," in George Orwell, *Such, Such Were the Joys* (New York: Harcourt, Brace, and Company, 1945), pp. 73–97; books by John Lukacs, esp. *Confessions of an Original Sinner* (New York: Tichnor and Fields, 1990), pp. 3–4, 141, 191–96; and Lukacs, *The Hitler of History* (New York: Alfred A. Knopf, 1997), pp. 113–27; and John Bodnar, ed., *Bonds of Affection: Americans Define Their Patriotism* (Princeton: Princeton University Press, 1996). For an unpersuasive, strained attempt to deal with loyalty

from a liberal perspective, see George Fletcher's *Loyalty* (New York: Oxford University Press, 1993).

39. Quoted by Donald Pisani in "Forests and Conservation, 1865–1890," in Charles Miller, ed., *American Forests* (Lawrence: University of Kansas, 1997), p. 23. For history of this movement, see this volume and Roderick Nash, *Wilderness and the American Mind* (New Haven: Yale University Press, 1982), pp. 108–81; and Samuel Hays, *Conservation and the Gospel of Efficiency* (Cambridge: Harvard University Press, 1959), pp. 36–190.

40. On this treatment, see Edward Spicer, "American Indians, Federal Policy Toward," in Stephen Thernstrom, ed., *Harvard Encyclopedia of American Ethnic Groups* (Cambridge: Harvard University Press, 1980), pp. 114–22.

41. Higham, *Send These to Me,* pp. 58–59.

42. For different perspectives on this matter, see Richard Alba, *The Transformation of Identity in White America* (New Haven: Yale University Press, 1990), and Mary Waters, *Ethnic Options: Choosing Identities in America* (Berkeley: University of California, 1990). Alba thinks that white Americans, after years of ethnic conflict among themselves, have now begun to think of themselves as "European-Americans . . . in opposition to the challenges of non-European groups (316)." Waters maintains that Americans still connect to their "ethnic" pasts but only weakly, freely choosing, whenever they wish, to be Irish this month or Italian the next, or whatever, depending on their ethnic mix. Both books are simplistic and mechanistic. Both also do not accept the idea that Americans may be, well, Americans.

43. Quoted from his essay "The Forgotten American," written in 1969 and republished in Peter Schrag, *Out of Place in America* (New York: Random House, 1970), pp. 14–34. Schrag's view of Americans contrasted sharply with the notion held by one of Schrag's contemporaries, sociologist Milton Gordon, who argued that most Americans by the 1960s got their "sense of peoplehood" (to quote Gordon), not from being Americans but from being "Negroes, Jews, and Catholics" as well as "white, Anglo-Saxon Protestants" (Gordon, *Assimilation in American Life* [New York: Oxford University Press, 1964, p. 77]). Gordon's view became over the years the dominant view. See, for instance,

Michael Novak's *The Rise of the Unmeltable Ethnics* (New York: Macmillan, 1972), which declared emphatically that ethnic "inheritance colors the eyes through which we discern what is reasonable, fair, cause for joy, or for alarm." "Each of us is different from any other," Novak said, "and yet our similarities with some others tend to cluster around shared ethnicities (p. 320)." See also Alba, *The Transformation of Identity in White America* and Waters, *Ethnic Options,* note 42.

44. John Steinbeck, *Travels with Charley* (New York: Bantam Books, 1963), p. 208.

45. Quoted in Mann, *The One and the Many,* p. 172. Mann also wrote that "in the early 70s census," conducted by the U.S. Bureau of the Census, "close to 80 million Americans did not identify themselves by origin or descent." In 1975, John Higham, respected immigration expert, said that "contrary to some claims, we are not all ethnics. Everyone has sense of ancestral belonging, but many Americans, much of the time, feel little ethnic identification." See Higham, *Send These to Me,* p. ix.

46. In 1960, English novelist Lawrence Durrell observed in a travel piece in the *New York Times* (hereafter *NYT*) that Americans abroad seemed always able to identify other Americans by the states or counties or regions their compatriots came from, simply by listening to accents. To Europeans, Durrell said, most Americans all seemed the same. "The great big nations like say the Chinese or the Americans," Durrell went on, "present a superficially homogenous appearance; but I've noticed that while we Europeans can hardly tell one American from another, my own American friends will tease each other to death at the lunch-table about the intolerable misfortune of being born in Ohio or Tennessee—a recognition of the validity of place which we ourselves accord to the Welshman, Irishman and Scotsman at home. It is a pity to travel and not get this essential sense of landscape values." From "Landscape and Characters," collected in Durrell, *Spirit of Place, Letters, and Essays on Travel* (New York: E. P. Dutton, 1969), pp. 156–63.

47. Timothy J. Hutton and Jeffrey G. Williamson, *The Age of Mass Migration: Causes and Economic Impact* (New York: Oxford University Press, 1998), pp. 232–33, 245. After World War I and the

imposition of immigration quotas, "the globalization–inequality connection was broken" (p. 245).

48. See Vernon M. Briggs, Jr., *Immigration Policy and the American Labor Force* (Baltimore: The Johns Hopkins University Press, 1984). Labor historian David Montgomery also writes that "closing the door to Europeans accelerated the stabilization of ethnic communities in industrial towns and cities. It reduced the rate of return to Europe to less than half its prewar level, increased the proportion of women among those let in to roughly half the total, and encouraged foreign-born residents to apply for citizenship as some protection against deportation." See Montgomery, *Fall of the House of Labor,* p. 462.

49. Robert Reich, *The Work of Nations* (New York: Vintage, 1992), pp. 43–57; and Alan Ehrenhalt, *The Lost City* (New York: Basic Books, 1995), pp. 90–110.

50. See, on this historical tenacity, Frederick Hoxie, "From Prison to Homeland: The Cheyenne River Indian Reservation Before World War I," *South Dakota History* 10 (Winter 1979), 1–24.

51. John Bodnar, *The Transplanted: A History of Immigrants in Urban America* (Bloomington: Indiana University Press, 1987), p. 212.

52. Schrag, *Out of Place in America,* pp. 12–13. Alan Ehrenhalt's book on Chicago in the 1950s, *The Lost City,* captures the place-oriented character of the times.

53. George W. Pierson, *The Moving American* (New York: Alfred A. Knopf, 1972), p. 29. See also, Kenneth T. Jackson, *Crabgrass Frontier: The Suburbanization of the United States* (New York: Oxford University Press, 1986), for another view of this historical pattern. "The American population," says Jackson of the nineteenth-century tendency, "was very transitory. The United States was not only a nation of immigrants, but a nation of migrants." Yet, "despite such mobility, permanent residence was considered desirable, and, then as now, home ownership was regarded as a counterweight to the rootlessness of an urbanizing population" (pp. 50–51).

54. Peter Berger, *The Homeless Mind* (New York: Random House, 1973), pp. 75–77.

55. On decline in mobility rates in the 1970s, see Larry Long, *Migra-*

tion and Residential Mobility in the United States (New York: Russell Sage Foundation, 1988), p. 52.

56. "No-Fault Divorce Law Is Assailed in Michigan and Debate Heats Up," *WSJ,* November 5, 1996, 1; for a fine account of the way expanded social security and federal housing loans facilitated mobility, see Deborah Dash Moore, *To the Golden Cities: Pursuing the American Dream in Miami and L.A.* (Cambridge: Harvard University Press, 1996), pp. 27–63; and, for a journalistic, data-filled portrait of the *extreme* mobility patterns of educated Americans in the 1990s, see "America's Most Educated Places," *American Demographics,* October 1995, 44–51.

57. "Geographical Mobility: March 1993 to March 1994," *Current Population Statistics,* P20–485 (Washington, D.C.: Department of Commerce, Bureau of the Census, 1995), viii.

58. Louis Winnick, *New People in Old Neighborhoods: The Role of Immigrants in Rejuvenating New York's Communities* (New York: Russell Sage Foundation, 1990), pp. xv–xvi. For current immigration figures, see *Statistical Abstract of the United States 1997* (Washington, D.C.: Department of Commerce, Bureau of the Census), 10–13; Bureau of the Census, "Current Population Survey" (Washington, D.C.: March 1998), 111; National Research Council, *The New Americans* (Washington, D.C.: National Academy Press, 1997), 3–4, 34–36. By 1996, immigrants and their children constituted 56 percent of the population of New York City; by that time as well, immigration to California had exceeded all rates reached in the past (see *Los Angeles Times,* April 9, 1997, A1, A14; and *NYT,* December 1, 1997, B3.

59. On this subject, see Vernon Briggs, Jr., *Mass Immigration and the National Interest* (New York: M. E. Sharp, 1992); Vernon Briggs, *Immigration Policy and the American Labor Force;* and Stanley Lebergott, *Manpower In Economic Growth* (New York: McGraw Hill, 1964).

60. For the modern accumulation of immigrant "social and civil rights," see Saskia Sassen, *Globalization and Its Discontents* (New York: New Press, 1998), pp. 23–25. On welfare, see economist Thomas Sowell, who pointed out in 1996 that "fewer than 5 percent of the immigrants from Britain and Germany went on wel-

fare after arriving in late twentieth-century America, but more than one-fourth of the immigrants from Vietnam and nearly half of those from Cambodia did" (Sowell, *Migrations and Culture* [New York: Basic Books, 1996], p. 388). In New York, over 40 percent of the Dominican population was on welfare in the late 1990s.

61. Sanford Ungar, *Fresh Blood: The New Immigrants* (New York: Simon and Schuster, 1995), p. 368. This view has been widely argued, but see Winnick, *New People in Old Neighborhoods;* Peter Sahlins (provost of New York's State University system in Albany), *Assimilation, American Style* (New York: Basic Books, 1997); Joel Millman (staff reporter for the *Wall Street Journal*), *The Other Americans: How Immigrants Renew Our Country, Our Economy, and Our Values* (New York: Viking, 1997); and Ruberto Suro (reporter for the *Washington Post*), *Strangers Among Us: How Latino Immigration is Transforming America* (New York: Alfred A. Knopf, 1998).

62. For percentages of Hispanics and Asians, see Jeffrey S. Passel and Barry Edmonston, *Immigration and Race: Recent Trends in Immigration in the U.S.* (Washington, D.C.: Urban Institute, 1992), table 8; and National Research Council, *The New Americans* (Washington, D.C.: National Academy Press, 1997), pp. 37, 113–23. Immigrants did not disperse as they did, for the most part, in earlier waves, although many small towns experienced heavy inflows; for a small sampling of documents, see "East Meets West in the Heart of Texas," *BusinessWeek,* November 13, 1995, 18E–2; David L. Wheeler, "Sociologists Watch as the Heartland Adjusts to a Wave of Immigrants," *The Chronicle of Higher Education,* June 27, 1997, B2; and *The Index to Immigration Hot Spots* (Washington, D.C.: Center for Immigration Studies, 1996).

63. The best study to document this effect is William H. Frey's "Interstate Migration and Immigration for Whites and Minorities, 1985–90: The Emergence of Multi-ethnic States" (Populations Studies Center, University of Michigan, October 1993); for his update, confirming the same trend, see William Frey, "The Diversity Myth," *American Demographics,* June 1998, 39–43.

64. Lawrence Mishel, Jared Bernstein, and John Schmitt, *The State of Working America 1998–99* (Ithaca: Cornell University Press,

1999), prepared by the Economic Policy Institute, Washington, D.C., pp. 120, 182. On the negative impact of mass migration on the wages of unskilled workers and on equality generally, both in our time and around 1910, see Hutton and Williamson, *The Age of Mass Migration,* pp. 231–36, 248–52.

65. See the following discussions of dual citizenship: "Immigrants' Pressing Drive for Dual Nationality," *Migration World* 25, no. 1/2 (1997), 12; Peter H. Shuck, "Dual Citizens, Good Americans," *WSJ,* March 18, 1998, A22; "Dual Citizenship is Double-Edged Sword," *ibid.,* March 25, 1998; "Torn Between Nations, Mexican-Americans Can Have Both," *NYT,* April 14, 1998, A12; and "Pledging Allegiance to Two Flags," *Washington Post,* June 6, 1998, 14.

66. Quoted in Lukas, *Big Trouble,* p. 479.

67. "The New Immigrant Experience," *NYT,* July 22, 1998, A18, editorial. For another *Times* celebration of New York City, see "Many Nations, One Big Party," *ibid.,* August 14, 1998, E1.

68. On the poorer immigrants as the principal victims (along with poor, unskilled native-born Americans), see James P. Smith and Barry Edmonston, eds., *The New Americans: Economic, Demographic, and Fiscal Effects of Immigration* (Washington, D.C.: National Academy Press, 1997).

69. According to Benjamin Barber, political scientist at Rutgers University, the only Americans who have a right to call America "a place" are the Indians; "the rest of us came from somewhere else." See "National Conversation," C-Span, September 2, 1995.

70. The United States, historian Hans Kohn, expert on nationalism, wrote in 1957, "is the embodiment of an idea" or a "structure of ideas about freedom, equality, and self-government." "To be an American is not . . . a matter of blood," observed novelist Robert Penn Warren, but "a matter of an idea—and history is the image of that idea." Penn Warren is quoted in Michael Lind, *The Next American Nation* (New York: Free Press, 1995), p. 221; Hans Kohn is quoted in Russell A. Kazal, "Revisiting Assimilation: The Rise, Fall, and Reappraisal of a Concept in American Ethnic History," *American Historical Review* 100:2 (April 1995), 460. The classic statement of this argument is Louis Hartz, *The Liberal Tradition.*

71. Bauer, speech before "Toward Tradition," a conference convened

by Jewish-Americans for Tradition, Washington, D.C., September 22, 1997; Newt Gingrich, *To Renew America* (New York, Harper Collins, 1995), p. 30; Dole speech, C-Span, May 26, 1996. Bauer was paraphrasing a quotation from Winston Churchill. For similar arguments, see Seymour Martin Lipset, *American Exceptionalism* (New York: W. W. Norton, 1996), p. 31; Maurizio Viroli (professor of political science at Princeton University), *For Love of Country: An Essay on Patriotism and Nationalism* (London: Clarendon Press, 1995), pp. 8–13, 164–85; Arthur Schlesinger, *Disuniting of America* (New York: W. W. Norton, 1992); and Roger M. Smith, *Civic Ideals: Conflicting Visions of Citizenship in U.S. History* (New Haven: Yale University Press, 1997).

72. Quoted by Jacob M. Schlesinger, "U.S. Economy Shows Foreign Nations Ways to Grow Much Faster," *WSJ,* June 19, 1997, 1. This interview took place in the context of a meeting in Denver where Clinton explained to visiting European leaders why the American economy, given its "labor flexibility" and "entrepreneurial risk-oriented spirit," was so superior to the economies of other nations.

73. Quoted in David Hollinger, *Postethnic America* (New York: Basic Books, 1995), p. 141.

74. Lewis H. Lapham, "Who and What Is American?" *Harper's,* January 1992, 46.

75. Janet Wolff, *Resident Alien* (New Haven: Yale University Press, 1995), p. 148.

76. Bharati Mukherjee, "Beyond Multiculturalism: Surviving the Nineties," in Ishmael Reed, ed., *MultiAmerica* (New York: Viking, 1997), p. 454.

77. Isaiah Berlin, *Against the Current* (New York: Viking, 1980), p. 352.

78. Royce, *The Philosophy of Loyalty,* pp. 115–16. The full quote is:
> Now, in our country we do not want any muted hatred of sections. But we do want a hearty growth of provincial ideals. And we want this growth just for the sake of the growth of a more general and effective patriotism. We want the ideals of the various provinces of our country to be enriched and made definite, and then to be strongly represented in the government of the nation. For, I insist, it is not the sect, it is not the

labor-union, it is not the political partisan organization, but it is the widely developed provincial loyalty which is the best mediator between the narrower interests of the individual and the larger patriotism of our nation.

79. Wallace Stegner, *Where the Bluebird Sings to the Lemonade Springs* (New York: Penguin Books, 1993), p. 72; Wendell Berry, *Sex, Economy, Freedom, and Community* (New York: Pantheon Books, 1993), p. 22.

80. Fei Xiaotong, a Chinese anthropologist who studied in the United States during World War II, praised Americans but lamented their indifference to the past, to place and memory. He was lonely all the while he lived in America during the forties. "American children," he wrote in 1944,

> hear no stories about ghosts. They spend a dime in the drugstore to buy a Superman comic book. . . . Superman represents actual capabilities or future potential, while ghosts symbolize belief in and reverence for the accumulated past. . . . How could ghosts gain a foothold in American cities? People move about like the tide, unable to form permanent ties with places, still less with other people. . . . In a world without ghosts, life is free and easy. American eyes can gaze straight ahead. But still I think they lack something and I do not envy their lives.

On Xiaotong, see R. David Arkush and Leo O. Lee, eds., *Land Without Ghosts: Chinese Impressions of America from the Mid-Nineteenth Century to the Present* (Berkeley: University of California Press, 1993), pp. 171–81.

1. INTERMODAL HIGHWAYS AND GATEWAYS, VISIBLE AND INVISIBLE

1. Eno Transportation Foundation, *Transportation in America. A Statistical Analysis of Transportation in the United States,* supplement to the 15th ed. (Landsdowne, Va.: Eno Transportation Foundation, 1998), p. 7. For truck lengths over a ten-year period, see Gerhardt Muller, *Intermodal Freight Transportation* (Landsdowne, Va.: Eno Transportation Foundation Inc., 1995, 3rd ed.), p. 70; and U.S. Federal Highway Administration, *Federal Size Regulations for Com-*

mercial Motor Vehicles (Washington, D.C.: 1997), pp. 4–5. On maximum lengths in Arkansas in 1994 for tractor semi-trailers, see
U.S. Department of Transportation, *1997 Comprehensive Truck
Size and Weight Study,* vol. 2, Issues and Background, Draft (Washington, D.C.: June 1997), tables II-3 and II-17.

2. Karl Polanyi, *The Great Transformation* (Boston: Beacon Press,
1968), p. 18. For more recent discussions of this period, see
William H. McNeill, *The Rise of the West* (Chicago: University of
Chicago Press, 1963, 1990), pp. 726–92; Samuel Huntington,
Clash of Civilizations (New York: Touchstone Press, 1997), p. 51;
Paul Krugman, *Pop Internationalism* (Cambridge: MIT Press,
1995), and Barry Eichengreen, *Globalizing Capital: A History of the
International Monetary System* (Princeton: Princeton University
Press, 1996), p. 4. Polanyi never argued, however, that a totally
free market reigned in the nineteenth century or, for that matter,
has ever reigned. For a similar position, see Eric Hobsbawm, *The
Age of Extremes: A History of the World, 1914–1991* (New York:
Pantheon Books, 1994), pp. 573–74.

3. Quoted in William Leach, *Land of Desire* (New York: Vintage,
1994), p. 356.

4. Roads have long been viewed as radical interventions, usually
connecting cities (although today they connect suburb to suburb
more than they do city to city or suburb to city). See Robert
Redfield, *The Primitive World and Its Transformations* (Ithaca: Cornell University Press, 1953), p. 56:

> It is the city that makes world-wide and conspicuous the self-
> conscious struggle to maintain a traditional ethos, as it is the
> city, in the first place, that traditional morality is attacked and
> broken down. The conflict on the religious or ethical level
> between city and country, urbanite and peasant, sophisticated
> mind and simple villager or tribesman, is an ancient and
> familiar theme. . . . In the Maya village of Chan Kom, to
> which my mind ever reverts in these connections, my good
> friend, a certain thoughtful villager, saw with dismay the
> coming of the highway that would bring the evils of the city
> to the peasant community his own leadership had built.
> Recoiling from the consequences he had not foreseen of an
> urbanization for which he had put forth great effort, he

began to view the city as a source of moral evil. "With the road will come drunkenness, idleness, vice," he said.

5. I would like to thank Mary Furner for pointing this out to me. We greatly need a new history of transportation, but see, for a recent informative and general history, James E. Vance, Jr., *Capturing the Horizon: The Historical Geography of Transportation Since the Sixteenth Century* (Baltimore: The Johns Hopkins University Press, 1990). See also, for America in particular, George Rogers Taylor, *The Transportation Revolution, 1815–1836* (New York, Rinehart, 1951); John Lauritz Larson, " 'Bind the Republic Together': The National Union and the Struggle for a System of Internal Improvement," *Journal of American History* 74 (Sept. 1987), 363–87; Alfred D. Chandler, Jr., *The Visible Hand: The Managerial Revolution in American Business* (Cambridge: Harvard University Press, 1977), esp. pp. 79–203; and Muller, *Intermodal Freight Transportation,* pp. 7–14.

6. John Brinckerhoff Jackson, *Discovering the Vernacular Landscape* (New Haven: Yale University Press, 1984), pp. 24–25. I have borrowed the distinction between "centrifugal" and "centripetal" roads from Jackson. Others, too, have adopted these distinctions; see especially Phil Patton, *Open Roads: A Celebration of the American Highway* (New York: Simon and Schuster, 1986).

7. Historian James Flink has argued that "the goal was to reorder society to accommodate increased automobile use and ownership, and therefore increased automobile production." See James J. Flink, *The Automobile Age* (Cambridge: MIT Press, 1993), pp. 368–73; for similar analyses, see David James St. Clair, "Entrepreneurship and the American Automobile Industry" (unpublished diss., University of Utah, 1979), pp. 167–68; and Henry Moon, *The Interstate Highway System* (Washington, D.C.: Association of American Geographers, 1994), pp. 1–21. For a different perspective, see Phil Patton, *Open Roads;* Tom Lewis, *Divided Highways* (New York: Viking, 1997); and, more recently, Fred Barnes, "In Praise of Highways," *Weekly Standard,* April 27, 1998, 15–18. All three writers argue against the notion—held by Flink and others—that "the Road Gang" (or the "auto oligopoly," plus gas and oil industries) played the major role in fostering the growth of the highways.

8. Robert D. Yaro and Tony Hiss, *A Region at Risk: The Third*

Regional Plan for the New York–New Jersey–Connecticut Metropolitan Area (New York: Island Press, 1996), p. 29.

9. James H. Johnson (CEO of the Standish Group International, Inc., a specialist in electronic commerce), "Realities of the Virtual Enterprise," an unpaginated advertisement, *Business Week,* December 4, 1995.

10. *Wall Street Journal* (henceforth *WSJ*), April 30, 1998, B4; Gus Welty, *Railway Age,* September 1996.

11. U.S. Department of Transportation and the Bureau of Transportation Statistics, *National Transportation Statistics 1997* (Washington, D.C.: 1997), pp. 6, 24, 33, 209. Interestingly, too, the number of private airports has *increased* from 10,461 in 1985 to 12,809 in 1995, while the number of public airports has *declined* from 5,858 in 1985 to 5,415 ten years later.

12. "People in Alaska eat, sleep, are born, sometimes die on airplanes," Ted Stevens, Senator from Alaska, said on floor of the Senate in 1996 (C-Span, Oct. 2, 1996). According to *The Atlas of the New West,* "airports capable of private jet landings" had a greater presence in the West after 1980 than did ranches or mining shafts" (William E. Riebsame, General Editor, *Atlas of the New West.* A Project of the Center for the American West, University of Colorado at Boulder (New York: W. W. Norton, 1997, pp. 71–72). On "too many airports," see *Journal of Commerce,* June 29, 1998, 8A.

13. *National Transportation Statistics 1997,* p. 7; and U.S. Department of Transportation and the Bureau of Transportation Statistics, *Transportation Statistics Annual Report 1997* (Washington, D.C.: 1997), pp. 228–29.

14. *National Transportation Statistics 1997,* p. 225; Rosalyn A. Wilson, *Transportation in America 1997* (Landsowne, Va: Eno Transportation Foundation Inc., 1997), p. 9.

15. On San Diego, see "U.S. Border Towns Suffer From post-Nafta Syndrome," *WSJ,* August 28, 1998, pp. B1, B4; on Woodstock, Vermont, see "War Is Declared as Giant Trucks Invade Tiny Towns," *WSJ,* September 16, 1998, pp. B1, B4.

16. Interview with Don Lotz and Dimitri Rallis, port analysts, Port Authority of New York and New Jersey, World Trade Center (N.Y.C.), April 20, 1998.

17. The lengths of trucks, as well as their access to many highways and roads, was limited by the 1991 ISTEA legislation; see "Big Rigs Could Barrell Down Roads," *WSJ*, June 16, 1997, B1. As this article indicates, states and cities frequently sought exemptions from the federal law.

18. Anna Wilde Mathews, "Mr. and Mrs. Grimm Get a Load of Shrimp Cross Country, Fast," *WSJ*, February 3, 1998, A1, A8.

19. Phone interview with Thomas Klimek, transportation analyst, Bureau of Transportation Statistics, Washington, D.C., May 18, 1998; see also U.S. Department of Transportation, *1997 Comprehensive Truck Size and Weight Study,* vol. II, "Issues and Background," draft (Washington, D.C.: 1997).

20. On the number of truckers, see American Trucking Association, *American Trucking Trends* (Alexandria, Va.: ATA Statistics Department, 1997), pp. 2–5; on the government's pledge, see *WSJ*, November 3, 1998, p. 1; and for an account of a "lost" trucker who drove down the wrong road and destroyed a footbridge on Saw Mill River Parkway in New York State, see *Journal News,* November 3, 1998, p. 2B.

21. *Transportation Statistics Annual Report 1997,* p. 212.

22. *Port of Long Beach Annual Report 1996* (Long Beach, California), pp. 4–5.

23. "Shifting Trade Routes Affect American Ports," *WSJ*, September 16, 1996, A1; and "As U.S. Seaports Get Busier, Weak Point Is a Surprise: Railroads," *WSJ*, September 19, 1996, A1, A14.

24. On America's decline as shipping power since WWII, see Muller, *Intermodal Freight Transportation,* pp. 32–33; on increase in international trade, see *Transportation Statistics Annual Report 1997,* p. 212.

25. Tim Ferguson, "Imports Ahoy!," *Forbes* 158:6 (September 9, 1996), 100–2; John Davies, "Skipping the Waves," *International Business* 9:5 (May 1996), 26–28; and Tony Carding, "Looking Back Over Thirty Years in Ocean Transportation," *Intermodal Shipping,* July 1995, 18–21.

26. For this observation, see Tom Baldwin, "A Gigantic Ship Squeezes In," *Journal of Commerce,* July 24, 1998, 1A, 8A.

27. On July 29, 1998, the Coast Guard and Maritime Transportation Subcommittee of the House of Representatives held a hearing on "The Needs of the U.S. Waterways Transportation System."

Nearly all those who testified invoked the *Regina Maersk* to illustrate the "competitive" challenge to American ports posed by
megaships; see especially the testimony of Lillian Borrone, director of commerce at the Port Authority of New York and New
Jersey; and John Arntzen, president, ACTA Maritime Development Corporation (transcript of testimony, in author's possession,
courtesy Ed Lee, staff of the Subcommittee on Coast Guard and
Maritime Transportation). On the *Regina Maersk,* see *ibid.,* June 6,
1998, 1A, and July 27, 1998, 2B; and *Containerization International,* March 1996, 73.

28. "The National Economic Significance of the Alameda Corridor,"
    Long Beach Harbor, February 1994.

29. For descriptions of this port (and others as well), see Charles F.
    Queenan, *Long Beach and Los Angeles: A Tale of Two Ports* (North-
    ridge, Calif.: Windsor Publications, 1986); Committee on Pro-
    ductivity of Marine Terminals, *Improving Productivity in U.S. Marine
    Terminals* (Washington, D.C.: National Academy Press, 1986).

30. On this shadowy world, see Donald Axelrod, *Shadow Government:
    The Hidden World of Public Authorities* (New York: John Wiley and
    Sons, 1992).

31. This pattern applies to all such port authorities; see Axelrod,
    Shadow Government, pp. 15–17.

32. Interview with Bruce Lambert, trade analyst, Harbor Square
    Administration Building, Long Beach Port, April 11, 1997. See
    also "The National Economic Significance of the Alameda Cor-
    ridor" (Alameda Corridor Transportation Authority, February
    1994; prepared by the Authority of the Port of Long Beach).

33. On the number of port authorities, see Axelrod, *Shadow Govern-
    ment,* pp. 238–40. For an account of the origins of the Port
    Authority of New York and New Jersey, the parent of Long
    Beach et al., see Jameson Doig, "Regional Conflict in the New
    York Metropolis: The Legend of Robert Moses and the Power of
    the Port Authority," *Urban Studies* 27:2 (April 1990) 201–32. Doig
    shows how port managers overcame the "provincialism" of local
    political control in New York City to impose their own "apoliti-
    cal" dominance on a region. See also Doig's forthcoming history
    of the Port Authority of New York and New Jersey, *Empire on the
    Hudson* (New York: Columbia University Press, 1999), especially

chap. 12, "Breaking an Airline Monopoly" (draft courtesy of Professor Doig).

34. George Murchison (president of the Long Beach Harbor Commission), "Our Side of the COSCO Issue," press release, April 25, 1997.

35. The Port of Long Beach, "Fact Sheet About the Port of Long Beach" (February 1997); and Muller, *Intermodal Freight Transportation,* p. 110. See also Port of Long Beach, *Harbor Handbook* (1995 edition); "Ports Ready for 'Jumboships,'" *Intermodal Shipping* (July 1995), 29; *Port of Long Beach 1996 Annual Report;* "The National Economic Significance of the Alameda Corridor" (Alameda Corridor Transportation Authority, Long Beach, February 1994) 3.

36. *Port of Long Beach 1996 Annual Report,* pp. 4–5; on the deli counters in Wells, Maine, see *WSJ,* February 3, 1998, A1, A8.

37. Port of Long Beach, *Harbor Handbook* (1995 edition), p. 1; *Port of Long Beach 1996 Annual Report,* p. 15.

38. "As Economy Booms, Shipping Slows, Delaying Deliveries Across the Nation," *WSJ,* September 30, 1997, A2.

39. *WSJ,* February 27, 1998, 1. The full quote is: "Today the unthinkable has happened. Once unthinkable mergers, from aerospace and banking to health care and telecommunications, are leaving some markets with only a handful of major players."

40. *WSJ,* January 4, 1999, R8; see also *BusinessWeek,* December 8, 1997, 36; and *WSJ,* January 2, 1998, R6.

41. *WSJ,* May 11, 1998, A10; and *New York Times* (hereafter *NYT*) May 12, 1998, D1; for background of the NYNEX–Bell Atlantic merger, see *BusinessWeek,* January 8, 1996, 32 (though the merger itself took place in August 1997).

42. "High-Balling Toward Two Big Railroads," *BusinessWeek,* March 17, 1997, 32; "Rail Mergers Take Toll on Small Towns," *WSJ,* November 29, 1996, A2; "Transport Firms Increase Prices," *WSJ,* March 9, 1998, A6; and "U.S. Approves Plan to Divide Conrail in Two," *WSJ,* June 9, 1998, A3. These companies were CSX, Burlington Northern, Union Pacific, and Norfolk Southern.

43. "Delta and United Air Plan Huge Alliance," *WSJ,* April 25, 1998, A3–4; and "Delta's Alliance With United Is On Again," *NYT,* May 1, 1998, D2. The Salomon Brothers' quote appears in "Four

Airlines Set Two Alliances for Marketing," *NYT,* April 24, 1998, D1.

44. Miles, quoted in "Winds of Change," *Containerization International,* February 1998, 35; and Reeve, quoted in "Mergers Reshape Shipping," *Journal of Commerce,* January 5, 1998, 8.

45. *NYT,* January 21, 1998, D2; see also "Theater Consolidation Jolts Hollywood Power Structure," *WSJ,* January 21, 1998, B1; and "Attack of the Giant Theaters," *WSJ,* March 4, 1998, B8.

46. On hotels and gaming, see "ITT Accepts $9.8 Billion Bid, Forming the Biggest Hotel Chain," *NYT,* October 21, 1997, 1; "Hilton Makes $6.5 Billion Bid for ITT," *NYT,* January 28, 1997, D1; "Hilton Hotels to Buy Ball Entertainment for More Than $2 Billion," *NYT,* June 7, 1996, D1; on gold mines, "A New Breed of Wolf at the Corporate Door," *NYT,* March 19, 1997, D1; on department stores, see "Allen Questrom's Quest," *Business Week,* November 28, 1994, 116–17.

47. For quote, see *WSJ,* August 1, 1995, A2, A5. See also "Wave of Mergers Is Transforming American Banking," *WSJ,* August 21, 1995, A1; and *Business Week,* April 20, 1998, 40. On the $31.4 billion merger of Northwest and Wells Fargo, see *WSJ,* June 9, 1998, A2.

48. On the Gannett chain, see Richard McCord, *The Chain Gang: One Newspaper Versus the Gannett Empire* (Columbus: University of Missouri Press, 1996); and *NYT,* August 7, 1997, B1. On the subject of acquisitions by the New York Times Company, see *NYT,* June 12, 1993, 47; *NYT,* February 19, 1996, D1; October 13, 1998, p. C8.

49. "More Merger Mania," editorial, *NYT,* April 15, 1998, A24; "A Monster Merger," editorial, *NYT,* April 8, 1998, A18; and "A Big Bank Merger, Again," *NYT,* June 10, 1998, A28. In the last editorial, the paper said that "if mergers are well executed, they hold little threat to banking customers, who might even benefit from the combined institution being able to offer more services."

50. Among such REITs was Starwood Lodging (headed by Barry Sternlicht), which in 1997 operated the biggest chain of hotels in the world; another was Simon-DeBartolo, a 1993 merged firm worth $16 billion. Simon-DeBartolo specialized in building shopping malls and strips. In the mid-1990s it owned the Mall of

America (Bloomington, Ind.), the biggest mall in the country. For analysis of REITs and their history, see *National Real Estate Investor,* September 1993; S. L. Mintz, "Lukewarm Property," *CFO: The Magazine for Senior Financial Executives,* May 1996; "The New World of Real Estate," *Business Week,* September 22, 1997, 78–87; "REITs Come of Age," *Business Week,* December 29, 1997, 152; and John Holusha, "Trusts Are Making Strides as Investors in New York Buildings," *NYT,* January 21, 1998, B7.

51. Quoted in "Land of the Giants," *Business Week,* September 11, 1995, 34.

52. Quoted in *WSJ,* November 22, 1995, A1.

53. *Ibid.,* A1.

54. "Improved Distribution, Not Better Production Is Key Goal of Mergers," *WSJ,* August 29, 1995, A1, A2.

55. "Without today's permissive climate in Washington many of [the current] mergers would not have been possible," said *Business Week* in 1995 (September 11, 1995, p. 34). For a good survey of this governmental policy toward mergers from Reagan to Clinton, see series on "Amalgamated America," in *WSJ,* especially "Concentration," February 26, 1997, 1, 8; and "Trust in Markets," February 27, 1997, 1.

56. Muller, *Intermodal Freight Transportation,* p. 28. On airline deregulation, see Steven A. Morrison and Clifford Winston, *The Evolution of the Airline Industry* (Washington, D.C.: Brookings Institution, 1995).

57. U.S. Department of Transportation, *1997 Comprehensive Truck Size and Weight Study,* II-6, IV-7, 9.

58. U.S. Department of Transportation, *1997 Comprehensive Truck Size and Weight Study,* especially review of deregulatory laws, IV-3-9; phone interview with Bob Withuhn, curator of transportation, the Smithsonian Institution, Washington, D.C., December 16, 1996; Bob Gatty, "Why Railroads Are Making the Grade," *Nation's Business* 71 (May 1983), 42–44.

59. For summary account of this bill, see *The Congressional Record,* House of Representatives, August 4, 1998, pp. H7011–7019; and for the limitations of the bill, see especially opposition by Henry Hyde, p. H7017. See also "A Sea-Change in Shipping," *Journal of Commerce,* October 5, 1998, pp. 1A, 21B.

60. On surface freight transport, Clifford Winston, et al., *The Economic Effects of Surface Freight Deregulation* (Washington, D.C.: Brookings Institution, 1990).

61. For a description of CSX, see Muller, *Intermodal Freight Transportation,* p. 93; on Malcolm McLean, see "Containerization at 40," from a program given by the Container Industry in honor of McLean (courtesy *Fayetteville Observer-Times,* May 22, 1998); and, on the evolution of regulatory policy regarding cross-modal ownership, author phone interview with unnamed officer at the Office of Proceedings, Surface Transportation Board, Washington, D.C., June 1, 1998.

62. "Administration to Study Business Concentration," *WSJ,* May 13, 1998, A2. Clinton also said that the globalizing and nationalizing of industries placed "a premium on bigness, partly so you can afford to get into new market areas, partly so you can afford to handle bad years—you have more money."

63. "Embassies Pave Way for U.S. Executives," *Journal of Commerce,* August 12, 1998, 1C; "U.S. Embassies Give American Companies More Help Overseas," *WSJ,* January 21, 1997, A1, A12; "Daley to Barnstorm China, Pushing Contracts for U.S.," *WSJ,* October 3, 1997, A7; and "Yesterday's Diplomats Are Today's Entrepreneurs in Argentina," *WSJ,* January 8, 1998, A5.

64. Wolfgang Demisch, analyst for BT securities, quoted in James Sterngold, "A Swift Transformation," *NYT,* December 16, 1996, 1.

65. See speech by Secretary of Transportation Federico Pena, March 5, 1996, press release, DOT.

66. Editorial, "Let's Have Open Skies," *WSJ,* June 14, 1996, A14.

67. "Clearer Skies," *Journal of Commerce,* July 13, 1998, 6A; "Open Skies Pact with Peru Excludes Fine Air," *ibid.,* June 12, 1998, 11A; "Airline Pacts' Antitrust Question Sparks Controversy," *WSJ,* January 3, 1997; "A Megadeal in the Skies," *BusinessWeek,* June 3, 1996, 50–51; "U.S. Moves to Allow Two Airlines' Overseas Ties," *WSJ,* May 22, 1996, A2; and "How Maneuvering by Airlines Shaped U.S.-Japan Accord," *WSJ,* February 2, 1998, 1.

68. Quoted in *NYT,* January 20, 1998, D1.

69. "Past open-skies deals already are paying dividends," said the *Journal of Commerce* in July 1998. "U.S. Department of Transportation studies have shown much stronger traffic growth in open-skies

countries where alliances operate than in markets without alliances or open skies (July 13, 1998, 6A)."

70. The phrase belongs to Saskia Sassen, political economist; see her *Globalization and Its Discontents* (New York: New Press, 1998), p. xxviii. Sassen writes that "deregulation has . . . had the effect, particularly in the case of the leading economic sectors, of partly denationalizing national territory."

71. "Hope vs. Experience, the Rematch," *WSJ*, January 14, 1997, A21.

72. Muller, *Intermodal Freight Transportation*, pp. 1–5.

73. *Ibid.*, p. 2.

74. "Maxton Native Malcolm McLean, Shipping Innovator, Enters Hall," *Fayetteville* [N.C.] *Observer-Times*, March 21, 1982; and *BusinessWeek*, April 16, 1979, 80–90.

75. Quoted in "Malcolm McLean's $750 Million Gamble," *Business-Week*, April 16, 1979, 81.

76. Muller, *Intermodal Freight Transportation*, pp. 15–16; and Leah Robinson Rousmaniere, *Anchored Within the Vail* (New York: The Seaman's Church Institute of New York and New Jersey, 1995), p. 91.

77. See Jameson Doig, *Empire on the Hudson*, Epilogue.

78. "Building 'Cow-tainers,'" *Journal of Commerce*, May 29, 1998, 3B; and "Acknowledging the Roar of the Cargo," *ibid.*, 10C. On generalized use of containers by the nineties, see Muller, *Intermodal Freight Transportation*, p. 23.

79. Marvin Schwartz, *J. B. Hunt: The Long Haul to Success* (Fayetteville: University of Arkansas Press, 1992), pp. 52–53.

80. Muller, *Intermodal Freight Transportation*, pp. 55–56.

81. *WSJ*, February 3, 1998, A1; and telephone interview with Bob Withuhn, December 16, 1996.

82. Schwartz, *J. B. Hunt*, p. 59; and *WSJ*, February 26, 1997, p. A2.

83. Interview with Donal H. Lotz, intermodal manager, and Dimitri C. Rallis, principal shipping analyst, of the Port Authority of New York and New Jersey, April 20, 1998; Terry Brennan, "Eastern Ports' Fate Hangs on Dredging," *Journal of Commerce*, June 22, 1998, 1C–2C.

84. Interview with Lotz and Rallis, April 20, 1998; Joe Mysak with Judith Schiffer, *Perpetual Motion* (New York: General Publishing

Group, 1997), pp. 229–34; and Lillian Borrone, "Intermodal Transport—The Role of Ports," speech given at the International Symposium on Liner Shipping, Hamburg, Germany, June 15, 1993 (text courtesy of Don Lotz of the Port Authority of NY/NJ).

85. On the tropical fish, see "Aquarium Shop Worker Accused of Trafficking in Endangered Fish," *NYT,* April 17, 1998, B1; on the Seaman's Church Institute in Newark, see Rousmaniere, *Anchored Within the Vail,* pp. 91–93; on the decline in the number of port workers, see *NYT,* October 13, 1997, B1.

86. Statement by Rodney Slater, "The National Highway System: Commitment to America's Future," March 2, 1995, U.S. Department of Transportation, Federal Highway Administration.

87. For an account of this congestion, see Theodore Prince, "Intermodal Bottlenecks," *Journal of Commerce,* May 29, 1998, 7A; and "A Fragile System," *ibid.,* editorial, August 11, 1998, 6A.

88. *Ibid.,* August 11, 1998.

89. On this bill, see David Rogers, "Route of the New I-69 Follows a Trail Marked By Politics and Money," *WSJ,* May 22, 1998, A1, A9; Eric Planin and Charles Babcock, "Working the System," *Washington Post National Weekly Edition,* April 13, 1998, 6; Richard Berke, "Lawmaker Takes Highway to Power," *NYT,* September 25, 1997, A18; for a full account of the House bill, see "Highway and Transit Funding," *Congressional Quarterly,* House Action Reports (March 31, 1998).

90. "Small-Town Life Lures Young Professionals," *WSJ,* September 29, 1995, B8; on road building's boon for geology, see John McPhee, *Annals of the Former World* (New York: Farrar, Straus and Giroux, 1998), pp. 23–25.

91. These figures come from *Advertising Age,* September 14, 1981; May 12, 1986; May 6, 1991; May 12, 1997 (courtesy of Scott MacDonald, Information Center, *Advertising Age*).

92. Kenneth Jackson, "All the World's a Mall: Reflections on the Social and Economic Consequences of the American Shopping Center," *American Historical Review,* 101:4 (October 1996), 1111–21; for the 1972 figure, see, in the same *AHR* issue, Thomas W. Hanchett, "U.S. Tax Policy and the Shopping-Center Boom of the 1950s and 60s," 1106. For the relationship of highways and development,

see Owen D. Gutfreund's dissertation, "Twentieth-Century Sprawl: Accommodating the Automobile and the Decentralization of the U.S." (Dept. of History, Ph.D. diss., Columbia University, 1998).

93. "Power Shortage for 'Big Box' Retailers," *WSJ*, February 7, 1997, B12, and, for 1997 figure in shopping centers, see "The Scope of the Shopping Center Industry in the United States 1998" (New York: International Council of Shopping Centers, 1998), pp. 2–3. Thayer is quoted in the *WSJ* article. See also "Retail Building Surges Despite Store Glut," *WSJ*, January 17, 1996, A2; and "Retailers Keep Expanding Amid Glut of Stores," *WSJ*, May 28, 1996, A21, A26.

94. See Anita Raghavan, "Mall Rises, But Will Shoppers Come?" *WSJ* (July 29, 1998), B6.

95. Author's visit, September 1996.

2. THE LANDSCAPE OF THE TEMPORARY

1. "The Remembering Machines of Tomorrow," in W. S. Merwin, *Miner's Pale Children* (New York: Atheneum, 1970), pp. 127–31.

2. This account is based on a sketch by Dean Takahashi, "Road Warrior," *Wall Street Journal* (hereafter *WSJ*), November 18, 1996, R27.

3. Quoted in John Brinckerhoff Jackson, *Landscape in Sight: Looking at America,* edited by Helen Lefkowitz Horowitz (New Haven: Yale University Press, 1997), p. 246.

4. For this trend, see James Annable, "Insecure Executives Make the Economy Grow," *WSJ*, April 28, 1997, A18; see also Richard Lester (director of the Industrial Technology Center at MIT), *The Productive Edge* (New York: W.W. Norton, 1998), pp. 27–30, and part IV ("Living with Ambiguity: A Path to Faster Growth") pp. 261–331.

5. Morris R. Schechtman, *Working Without a Net* (Englewood Cliffs, N.J.: Prentice Hall, 1994), pp. 5–6. Newt Gingrich put this book on his reading list for incoming congressional freshmen.

6. Rosabeth Kanter, *World Class* (New York: Simon and Schuster, 1995), pp. 156–57; for another version of this position, see Lester, *The Productive Edge,* pp. 29–30, 320–27.

7. Carl Quintanilla, "More Top Executives Are Hitting the Road," *WSJ*, January 12, 1996, p. B1.

8. "Marriott to Buy Renaissance Hotel Group," *WSJ*, February 19, 1997, A3; "Marriott to Provide Long-Term Guests a New Economy-Priced Hotel Option," *WSJ*, February 13, 1996, B7; "No Room in the Inn," *WSJ*, December 13, 1996, B17; "Why Business Travel Is Such Hard Work," *WSJ*, December 30, 1996, B1; "Pace of Business Travel Abroad Is Beyond Breakneck," *WSJ*, May 31, 1996, B1.

9. "Global Managers Need Boundless Sensitivity, Rugged Conditions," *WSJ*, October 13, 1998, B6. Quintanilla, "More Top Executives Are Hitting the Road," *WSJ*, January 12, 1996, B1, B8; "An Overseas Stint Can Be Ticket to the Top," *WSJ*, January 1, 29, 1996, B1, B8.

10. Rachel Beck, "On the Road Again," *Putnam Courier Trader*, December 7, 1995, 8B.

11. Michael Lorelli and Drew Struzan, *Traveling Again, Dad?* (Traverse City, Mo., Publishers Design Service, 1996).

12. On Cowley, see Warren Susman, "Pilgrimage to Paris: The Backgrounds of American Expatriation, 1920–30," Ph.D. diss., Department of History, University of Wisconsin, 1957 (University Microfilm International, 1986), 22–23; on the general history of the early expatriate movement, see Susman and Mary McCarthy, "A Guide to Exiles, Expatriates, and Internal Emigrés," in Marc Robinson, ed., *Altogether Elsewhere* (New York: Harcourt Brace, 1994), pp. 49–58.

13. Darryl Pinckney, "How I Got Over," in Robinson, *Altogether Elsewhere*, p. 34. And on the increase in numbers of business-people abroad, see Windham International and National Foreign Trade Council, *Global Relocation Trends 1994 Survey Report* (New York: Windham International, 1994), p. 9; *Global Relocation Trends 1995 Survey Report*, 1–13; *Global Relocation 1998 Survey Report*, pp. 6–10.

14. Quoted by Michael Paterniti in his "Laptop Colonialists," *New York Times Magazine*, January 12, 1997, 24–29, 34.

15. Barry Newman, "The New Yank Abroad Is the 'Can-Do' Player in the Global Village," *WSJ*, December 12, 1995, p. A1.

16. Congress passed a 1996 tax law that attempted to penalize such

expatriates, but, as the *WSJ* reported in 1998, "If [that] law has dissuaded anyone from giving up U.S. citizenship, it doesn't show." *WSJ*, December 28, 1998, p. A2. For the Republican effort to discredit the reform that targeted the rich, see Joint Committee on Taxation, *Issues Presented by Proposals to Modify the Tax Treatment of Expatriation,* pursuant to Public Law 104-7 (Washington, D.C.: U.S. Government Printing Press, 1995).

17. *BusinessWeek,* July 10, 1995, 58–60; *BusinessWeek,* May 1, 1995, 140; *WSJ,* February 8, 1995, B1, *WSJ,* June 2, 1995, A3; *WSJ,* April 19, 1995, 1; *New York Times* (hereafter *NYT*), April 12, 1995.

18. "Top Dogs: U.S. Financial Firms Seize Dominant Role in the World Markets," *WSJ,* January 5, 1996, 1; James H. Johnson, "Realities of the Virtual Enterprise," unpaginated advertisement, *BusinessWeek,* December 4, 1995; "Developing World Gets More Investment," *WSJ,* December 15, 1995, A9A; "U.S. Companies Again Hold Wide Lead over Rivals in Direct Investing Abroad," *WSJ,* December 6, 1995, A2.

19. On this whole dilemma, see "Disappearing Taxes," *Economist,* May 31, 1997, 21–23. This magazine argued that if global companies persisted in eluding the taxpayer, the burden of taxation would fall more and more on labor: "In a world of mobile capital, labour is likely to bear a growing share of the tax burden—especially unskilled workers who are least mobile."

20. Quoted in Karen Curnow McCluskey, ed., *Notes from a Traveling Childhood: Readings for Internationally Mobile Parents and Children* (Washington, D.C.: Foreign Service Youth Foundation, 1994), p. 48.

21. On American unionization in the post–WWII period, see Edward Patterson, *Grand Expectations: The United States, 1945–74* (New York: Oxford University Press, 1996), pp. 40–60, 739–40; and Richard Barnet and John Cavanagh, *Global Dreams: Imperial Corporations and the New World Order* (New York: Simon and Schuster, 1994), pp. 310–13; and Lawrence Mishel, Jared Bernstein, and John Schmitt, *The State of Working America 1998–99* (Ithaca: Cornell University Press, 1999), prepared by the Economic Policy Institute, Washington, D.C., pp. 183–89.

22. The chicken and meatpacking businesses now produce at

unheard-of volumes for the world market, herding countless millions of animals and birds in pens for assembly-line slaughter and packaging; no work has become more ugly or demeaning, which explains why these companies have resorted so completely to immigrant labor (much of it illegal). On the demeaning side of it, see Tony Horwitz for his account of "blues on the chicken line," in "9 to Nowhere," *WSJ,* December 1, 1994, 1. The poultry-processing industry, he writes, "[has been] the second fastest growing factory job in America since 1980," and it "has consigned a large class of workers to a Dickensian time warp, laboring not just for meager wages but also under dehumanized and often dangerous conditions." In late 1998, conditions were unchanged; see Laurie P. Cohen, "With Help from INS, U.S. Meatpacker Taps Mexican Work Force," *WSJ,* October 15, 1998, A1, A8.

The literature on every facet of these new brigades is enormous, and countless articles on the "return of sweatshops" have been written in this decade, but see Peter Kwong, *The New China-town* (New York: Hill and Wang, 1992); "Despite Tough Laws, Sweatshops Flourish," *NYT,* February 6, 1995, 1; William Branigin, "Sweatshops Are Back," *Washington Post National Weekly Edition,* February 24, 1997, 6–7; "Government Links Retailers to Sweatshops," *WSJ,* December 15, 1997, B5A; "Garment Shops Found to Break Wage Laws," *NYT,* October 17, 1997, B1–3; and Roy Beck, *The Case Against Immigration* (New York: W.W. Norton, 1996).

23. Quoted in Alexander Keyssar, *Out of Work: The First Century of Unemployment in Massachusetts* (Cambridge, England: Cambridge University Press, 1986), p. 62.

24. Keyssar, *Out of Work,* pp. 74–75, 89–90. See also Timothy J. Hatton and Jeffrey G. Williamson, "International Migration, 1850–1939: An Economic Survey," in Hatton and Williamson, eds., *Migration and the International Labor Market, 1850–1939* (New York: Routledge, 1994), pp. 17, 20, 23.

25. They were also "structured" in different ways—numbering "men and women who were idle during slow seasons, employees who worked on short time, floaters who migrated from one place to another, casuals, and substitute spinners and printers who were

called up only when regular workers were absent or when the demand for labor was unusually great" (*ibid.,* p. 7).

26. The literature on temps has grown over the years, but see Kevin D. Henson, *Just a Temp* (Philadelphia: Temple University Press, 1996); Robert E. Parker, *Flesh Peddlers and Warm Bodies: The Temporary Help Industry and Its Workers* (New Brunswick, N.J.: Rutgers University Press, 1994).

27. Lawrence Mishel et al., *The State of Working America 1998–99,* pp. 8, 46–7, 242–52.

28. See "A Semi-Tough Policy on Illegal Workers," *Washington Post,* July 13, 1998, 22. And for increased figures, see "A Temporary Force to Be Reckoned With," *NYT,* May 20, 1996, D1; "Temp Firms Expected to Post Gains," October 14, 1996, B8; and Parker, *Flesh Peddlers,* p. 30.

29. Parker, *Flesh Peddlers,* p. 30.

30. "Temporary-Help Industry Now Features Battle of Giants," *WSJ,* November 6, 1997, B4.

31. "Big Companies Hire More Lawyer Temps," *WSJ,* September 23, 1994, B1; "The Newest Temps in Law Firms: Lawyers," *NYT,* February 24, 1998, B7; and, on biologists, chemists, and accountants, see "These Temps Don't Type But They're Handy in the Lab," *BusinessWeek,* May 24, 1993, 68; "Brains for Rent," *Forbes,* July 13, 1995, 99–100; and "Temp Tycoon Steers Jobseekers," *WSJ,* October 4, 1994, A19. On earlier use of temps, see Bennet Harrison, *Lean and Mean* (New York: Basic Books, 1994), pp. 201–9; and Richard Barnett, *Global Dreams* (New York: Simon and Schuster, 1994), p. 340.

32. Helene Cooper and Thomas Kamm, "Much of Europe Eases Its Rigid Labor Laws, and Temps Proliferate," *WSJ,* June 5, 1998, A1.

33. Among the corporations to draw on these foreign reserves were the fashion industry, which recruited well over 7,000 fashion models from around the world between 1990 and 1994, including the Italian male model Fabio, a definite rarity who recently obtained his green card under the H-1B program. Big accounting firms and related businesses reaped their bounty, too, for a total of 12,500 H-1B accountants and auditors; industrial and pharma-

ceuticals firms boasted a total of 14,000 foreign temps for the same period. Figures from "H-1B Progam—Survey Data—1992–1994—U.S. Department of Labor. On Fabio, see *WSJ,* September 3, 1996, 1.

34. For these features of the law, see the report of the Committee on the Judiciary, House of Representatives, "Workforce Improvement and Protection Act of 1998," 105–657, which accompanied H.R. 3736, July 29, 1998, pp. 10–11, 22.

35. "Forget the Huddled Masses: Send Nerds," *BusinessWeek,* July 21, 1997, 110–16.

36. Phone interview with Labor Ready staff, April 17, 1998; *Labor Ready Annual Report 1996,* courtesy Labor Ready, Tacoma, Washington, pp. 8–9; *Wall Street Corporate Reporter,* June 23–29, 1997, 1 (courtesy Labor Ready); and *New Tribune* (internet journal), February 23, 1997, 1 (courtesy Labor Ready).

37. Quoted in *Wall Street Corporate Reporter,* June 23–29, 1997, 1.

38. Phone interview with Labor Ready staff, April 15, 1998; "Company Provides Temporary Jobs to Blue-collar Workers," *Putnam Reporter Dispatch,* March 28, 1998, 5B; "Temp Firm Earns Niche in Manual Labor," *Chicago Tribune,* March 13, 1998; Charles Keenan, "Temp Agency Uses Diebold to Pay Daily in Cash," *American Banker,* March 3, 1998; and Julie Tamaki, "Hardware Chain Adds a Depot for Hiring Laborers," *Los Angeles Times,* December 11, 1997.

39. "Temp Tycoon Steers Jobseekers," *WSJ,* October 4, 1994, A19.

40. On high-tech "permatemps," see *NYT,* March 30, 1998, B1; and Mitchell Fromstein (CEO of Manpower), quoted in *Business Week,* June 10, 1996, 8. By the mid-nineties, moreover, upwards of 230 smaller temp firms had been created (well above the figure of forty in 1990) to serve these specialized markets, and sometimes making multimillion-dollar profits. See "A Temporary Force to Be Reckoned With," *NYT,* May 20, 1996, D1. On Silicon Valley as prototype for other workplaces, see "Full Time, Part Time, Temp—All See the Job in a Different Light," *WSJ,* March 18, 1997, A1, A10; and, for a subsequent development, see "Coopers and Lybrand Tackles Turnover By Letting Its Workers Have a Life," *WSJ,* September 19, 1997, R4: "About 900 of the [this] firm's 17,000 US employees . . . now work part time,

telecommute, or have other flexible schedules. Almost none did so six years ago."

41. Figures from "H-1B Program—Survey Data—1992–94" (Washington, D.C.: U.S. Department of Labor); and "A U.S. Recruiter Goes Far Afield to Bring in High-Tech Workers," *WSJ,* January 8, 1998, 1.

42. Even *Business Week* found serious fault with this position. See "Is There a Technie Shortage?," *Business Week,* June 29, 1998.

43. Testimony before the U.S. Commission on Immigration Reform, "Employment-Based Immigration Consultation," Washington, D.C., February 23, 1995, pp. 11–20; also January 18, 1995, p. 57 (for Motorola), and p. 66 (for 3M).

44. These corporate quotes come from Charles Keely, "Globalization and Human Resource Management: Nonimmigrant Visa Strategies and Behavior of U.S. Firms," 53. This report, heavily biased in favor of globalized firms, quotes abundantly from the firms themselves; it makes clear that they want, above all, "labor flexibility," which foreigners (not Americans) give them. "The problem would seem to be [for Americans] willingness to relocate and perhaps move into a new work environment." Keely is professor of international migration at Georgetown University.

45. See Keely, "Globalization and Human Resource Management," which speaks for seven major global firms but also pretends to represent the views of the majority of such firms. Among Keely's other listed companies are Deloitte and Touche, Ford, Procter and Gamble, and Eastman Chemical. All quotes in this discussion, once again, come from this seventy-five-page report.

46. *Ibid.,* p. 63.

47. The report of the House Committee on the Judiciary, "Workforce Improvement and Protection Act of 1998," pp. 10–11, 17–22. See also *Chronicle of Higher Education,* August 7, 1998, May 29, 1998, A33; "High-Tech Companies to Ask Congress for Easier Immigration for Workers," *WSJ,* February 24, 1998, A2; and *NYT,* October 16, 1998, p. A25.

48. Richard Chait, "Thawing the Cold War over Tenure," *Adjunct Advocate,* January–February 1998, 18; and Anne Matthews, *Bright College Years: Inside the Campus Today* (New York: Simon and Schuster, 1997), pp 177–91.

49. Some analysts put the figure even higher, at more than 50 percent (a figure that includes part-timers, temporary full-timers, and teaching and research assistants). If one included graduate assistants, the figure was possibly this high (phone interview with Ernest Benjamin, director of research, American Association of University Professors, July 21, 1998). See "For Some Adjunct Faculty Members, the Tenure Track Holds Little Appeal," *Chronicle of Higher Education,* July 24, 1998, A9; "Contracts Replace the Tenure Track for a Growing Number of Professors," *Chronicle of Higher Education,* June 12, 1998, A12; "Professors Are Working Part Time, and More Teach at 2-Year Colleges," *Chronicle of Higher Education,* March 13, 1998, A14. See also, for changes over time, Tony Horowitz, "Young Professors Find Life in Academia Isn't What It Used to Be," *WSJ,* February 15, 1994, 1; Seth Adams, "Part-Time College Teaching Rises," *NYT,* January 1, 1995, A17; Philip Altbach, "The Pros and Cons of Hiring 'Taxicab' Professors," *Chronicle of Higher Education,* January 6, 1995, B3; and Mary Elizabeth Perry, "The Invisible Majority: Myths, Realities, and a Call to Action," *Perspectives* (American Historical Association newsletter), May–June 1995, 33:5, 9–11; and P. D. Lesko, interview with Kali Tal, *Adjunct Advocate* (Nov./Dec. 1997), 17. On wage disparities, see P. D. Lesko, "What Scholarly Associations Should Do to Stop the Exploitation of Adjuncts," *Chronicle of Higher Education,* December 15, 1995, B3.

50. On the number of post-docs, see *Chronicle of Higher Education,* August 7, 1998, A60, and David North, *Soothing the Establishment* (New York: University Press of America, 1995), p. 98.

51. On community colleges, see Patricia M. Callan, "America's Public Community Colleges," *Daedalus* (Fall 1997) 126:4, 98.

52. Quoted in Judith Gappa and David W. Leslie, *The Invisible Faculty: Improving the Status of Part-timers in Higher Education* (San Francisco: Jossey-Bass Publishers, 1993), pp. 133. On recent attempts to organize on behalf of better conditions for adjuncts and temporaries, see, "Faculty Unions Move to Organize Growing Ranks of Part-Time Professors," *Chronicle of Higher Education,* February 27, 1998, A12–13.

53. Clark Kerr, *The Uses of the University* (Cambridge: Harvard University Press, 1963, 1982), p. 95.

54. The term "urban glamour zone" belongs to Saskia Sassen, who, more than any current urbanist, has stressed the formation of these two groups (the new immigrants and the new international elite) as they relate to one another. See her *Globalization and Its Discontents* (New York: The New Press, 1998), especially pp. xix–xxxvi. There is a huge literature on the informal economy, but on its spread and significance recently, in New York, see Louis Winnick, *New People in Old Neighborhoods* (New York: Russell Sage Foundation, 1990), pp. 123–71; and Peter Kwong, *The New Chinatown* (New York: Hill and Wang, 1997, rev. ed.), esp. chap. 10, "Unwelcome Newcomers: Chinatown in the 1990s," pp. 174–205; and Roger Sanjek, *The Future of Us All: Race and Neighborhood Politics in New York* (Ithaca: Cornell University Press, 1998), especially chapter 6, pp. 119–40.

55. *New York Post,* March 6, 1995, 2. In 1992, moreover, Governor Mario Cuomo's office published a handbook for immigrants, titled *Getting Started,* which includes an introduction by the governor (New York State, Office of the Governor, 1992). The handbook explained to "undocumented aliens" how they might get access to public housing, to schools and higher education, and to jobs; and it provided extensive information on how to protest discrimination.

On decriminalizing the informal economy, see the 1994 testimony on New York City's labor markets before the U.S. Commission on Immigration Reform by Emmanuel Tobier, professor at the Robert F. Wagner School of Public Service at NYU and a prominent city government adviser; Tobier told the commission that because "the workplace [is] changing tremendously," "you really have to decriminalize the underground economy" (November 3, 1994, typescript, p. 114). Another important shaper of New York City's policy has been the Regional Planning Association, which advised, in its third regional plan, that New York City "legalize activities that do not threaten health and safety; such as small, home-based businesses in areas zoned for residential use"; see Tony Hiss, *Region at Risk* (Washington, D.C.: Island Press, 1996), p. 192.

56. Kwong, *The New Chinatown,* p. 190.

57. On the implications of such cycles for place (or locality), see

Arjun Appadurai, *Modernity at Large: Cultural Dimensions of Globalization* (Minneapolis: University of Minnesota Press, 1996), p. 193. For an upbeat version of the pattern itself, see Winnick, *New People in Old Neighborhoods,* pp. 123–91.

58. "Home Run Athletes Build Mansions," *WSJ,* December 20, 1996, B14.

59. Drawbacks, of course, have always existed for this kind of temporary housing, never more so than today; such recyclable houses demand that owners *not* decorate, rebuild, or modify to suit their special tastes. As relocation consultant Tom Peiffer recently noted, "building [or occupying] a house too closely tailored to your personality or needs could make for a difficult sale, especially if it is out of sync with the rest of the neighborhoods." See "Executive Relocations—and Hassles—Increase," *WSJ,* April 5, 1996, B10.

60. "The Lure of Planned Suburbs," *WSJ,* October 7, 1998, p. B1.

61. "Young Americans Triumph in Paris," *NYT,* January 23, 1997, C1.

62. On "over-building blues," see *WSJ,* May 14, 1998, A2; on expansion of "extended stay hotels" and "temporary home hotels" over the past six years, see "Building a Brand," *Hotel and Motel Management,* April 20, 1998.

63. Limited-service budget hotels/motels have been the "fastest-growing sector of the lodging industry with the number of rooms rising 78% since 1980" (*Time,* July 15, 1986, 45). On Studio Plus, see *WSJ,* January 24, 1996, B1; "Room Service à l'Américain," *NYT,* October 3, 1997, D1; "Midlevel Hotels Look Abroad," *NYT,* September 28, 1995, D1; "Marriott to Buy Renaissance Hotel Group," *WSJ,* February 19, 1997, A3; "Marriott to Provide Long-Term Guests a New Economy-Priced Option," *WSJ,* February 13, 1996, B7; "No Room in the Inn," *WSJ,* December 13, 1996, B17; "Why Business Travel Is Such Hard Work," *WSJ,* December 30, 1996, B1; "Pace of Business Travel Abroad Is Beyond Breakneck," *WSJ,* May 31, 1996, B1; "Soon, Hotels Only a Boss Could Love," *WSJ,* February 2, 1996, B7; and "High-Tech Hotels Try Homier Touches," *WSJ,* March 29, 1996, B1.

64. See J. B. Jackson, 1952 and 1956 essays in *Landscape in Sight,* pp. 333–39.

65. For many, the dream of Charlotte Perkins Gilman, the late-nineteenth-century American feminist, has been realized—the emptying of the home of all those matters that inhibit the individual freedom and flexibility of both sexes. On the spread of the goliath suburban homes, see "Suburbs' Mass-Market Mansions," *NYT,* March 18, 1998, B1.

66. On the current European efforts to copy American "chain" hotel style and building, at the cost of abandoning older, more place-connected, traditions, see "Room Service *à l'Américain,*" *NYT,* October 3, 1997, D1, D4.

67. Dan Mercer, "The Market for Mobile Homes," *Housing Economics,* January 1995, 15.

68. Virginia Held, "Home Is Where You Park It," *The Reporter,* February 18, 1960, quoted in George S. Pierson, *The Moving American* (New York: Alfred A. Knopf, 1972), pp. 113–14; and Steinbeck, *Travels with Charley,* p. 97.

69. Steinbeck, *Travels with Charley,* pp. 95–106.

70. Dan Mercer, "The Market for Mobile Homes," *Housing Economics,* January 1995, 17.

71. Michael J. Ybarra, "Real Estate: Mobile Homes Zip Past Sales of Houses," *WSJ,* August 29, 1994, B1; U.S. Department of Commerce, "Mobile Homes," Bureau of Census statistical brief, May 1994; Mercer, "The Market for Mobile Homes," 17, 1; and phone interview with Robert Bonnette, author of Department of Commerce's "Mobile Homes," July 20, 1995.

72. See "Mobile Mansions Offer RV Market a Lift," *WSJ,* January 8, 1998, B2; and "Six Days in a Rolling Home," *BusinessWeek,* April 27, 1998, E2–4.

73. John Brinckerhoff Jackson, *A Sense of Place, a Sense of Time* (New Haven: Yale University Press, 1994), p. 62.

74. *Ibid.,* pp. 60–62.

75. John Brinckerhoff Jackson, *Discovering the Vernacular Landscape* (New Haven: Yale University Press, 1984), p. 156.

76. Jackson, *A Sense of Place,* p. 167.

77. Quoted in D. W. Meinig, ed., *The Interpretation of Ordinary Landscapes* (New York: Oxford University Press, 1979), pp. 232–33.

78. Jackson, *Landscape in Sight,* pp. 201–5.

79. Compare with Foucault's "limit-experiences" (see James Miller,

The Passion of Michel Foucault [New York: Simon and Schuster, 1993], pp. 30–35, 273–75).

80. Quoted in Meinig, *The Interpretation of Ordinary Landscapes,* p. 94.
81. Jackson, *Landscape in Sight,* pp. 175–82.
82. Jackson, *A Sense of Place, a Sense of Time,* p. 10; see also Jackson, *Discovering the Vernacular Landscape* for similar comments, pp. 155–56.
83. Quoted in Meinig, *The Interpretation of Ordinary Landscapes,* p. 222.
84. *Ibid.*
85. Jackson, *The Necessity for Ruins* (Amherst: University of Massachusetts Press, 1980), pp. 125–26.
86. Jackson, *Discovering the Vernacular Landscape,* pp. 100–101.
87. Jackson, *Landscapes* (Amherst: University of Massachusetts Press, 1970), pp. 152, 160.
88. *Ibid.*, p. 154.
89. Jackson, *Discovering the Vernacular Landscape,* pp. 13–15.
90. Jackson, *Landscapes,* p. 158.
91. *Ibid.,* 158; *Discovering the Vernacular Landscapes,* pp. 110–12, 151–52.
92. *Ibid.,* pp. 133–35.
93. *Ibid.,* pp. 135–37.
94. Jackson, *The Necessity for Ruins,* pp. 16–17.
95. *Ibid.,* pp. 16–17.
96. For a different sense of what peasant villages were like, see Richard Critchfield, *The Villagers* (New York: Anchor Books, 1994), pp. 18–39.
97. James Brooke, "Cry of Wealthy in Vail: Not in Our Playground," *NYT,* November 5, 1998, A-20; Joseph Pereira, "Low-Cost Trailer Parks Are Shutting Down, Stranding the Poor," *WSJ,* November 15, 1995, 1; Michael Shear, "Trailer Park in Transit," *Washington Post,* February 10, 1994.

3. "A WONDERFUL SENSE OF PLACE": TOURISM AND GAMBLING TO THE RESCUE

1. White House Conference on Travel and Tourism, at the Sheraton Washington Hotel (Washington, D.C.), October 28–30, 1995.
2. Author's visit, August 19–20, 1995; Meredith L. Oakley, *On the*

Make: The Rise of Bill Clinton (Washington, D.C.: Regnery Publishing, 1994), pp. 26–27; Virginia Kelley, *Leading with My Heart* (New York: Simon and Schuster, 1994), pp. 72–77, 91, 107–8.

3. Speech by Greg Farmer, White House Conference on Travel and Tourism, October 29, 1995.

4. "The White House Conference on Travel and Tourism," advertising supplement, *Washington Post,* October 30, 1995, C1. On Brown's years living in the Hotel Theresa, see Tracey L. Brown, *The Life and Times of Ron Brown* (New York: William Morrow, 1998), pp. 40–46.

5. On tourism workforce and overall tourism growth, see "Tourism's Role Rises, Creating Some Risks," *Wall Street Journal* (hereafter *WSJ*), October 7, 1996, 1; and special supplement, "Travel and Tourism," *The Economist,* January 10, 1998, 1–16. For histories of tourism, see Daniel Boorstin, *The Image* (New York: Vintage, 1992); John Brinckerhoff Jackson, *The Necessity for Ruins* (Amherst: University of Massachusetts Press, 1980), pp. 1–19; Neil Harris, "Urban Tourism and the Commercial City," in William Taylor, ed., *Inventing Times Square* (New York: Russell Sage Foundation, 1991), pp. 66–83; and James Gilbert, "Imagining the City," in James Gilbert, et al., eds., *The Mythmaking Frame of Mind* (Belmont, Calif: Wadsworth Publishing, 1992), pp. 135–55.

6. Quoted in "Regional Marketing Effort Hunts the Tourist Dollar," *Putnam Reporter Dispatch,* May 3, 1997, 1. By summer 1997 this switch in New York to tourism as the new "economic development tool" climaxed with the influx of nearly $150 million from the federal government to help exploit the "rich" tourist potential throughout the state. "Once [towns and cities] move out of manufacturing, what do they do?" asked Andrew Cuomo, secretary of HUD and mastermind of the project. "The answer for the nation has been tourism" (*New York Times* [hereafter *NYT*], August 15, 1997, B4).

7. "Expelled in 1877, Indian Tribe Is Now Wanted as a Resource," *NYT,* July 22, 1996; James Brooke, "Boom Times Hit Utah, and Sticker Shock Follows," *NYT,* January 31, 1996, A10; "Impact of Travel and Tourism on Arizona," preliminary estimates, USTTA and the U.S. Travel Data Center, Travel Industry Association, Washington, D.C., March 1995. On the nineteenth-century

treatment of this tribe, see Angie Debo, *A History of the Indians* (Norman: University of Oklahoma Press, 1970), pp. 261–64; and Richard White, *"It's Your Misfortune and None of My Own": A New History of the American West* (Norman: University of Oklahoma Press, 1991), pp. 107–8.

8. Peter Nabokov, ed., *Native American Testimony* (New York: Penguin Books, 1992), p. 387.

9. *Indian Country Today,* December 16–23, 1996, A7; on international tourists, see "Culture Camp Attracts Many International Tourists," *Indian Country Today,* 1996 Tourism and Gaming Edition, Summer 1996, 3–4; and "At One with Indians: Tribes of Foreigners Visit Reservations," *WSJ,* August 6, 1996, 1.

10. Arthur Rubenstein, *My Young Years* (New York: Alfred A. Knopf, 1973), p. 143; and George W. Herald and Edward D. Radin, *The Big Wheel: Monte Carlo's Opulent Century* (New York: William Morrow, 1963). For other gambling histories, see Ann Fabian, *Card Sharps, Dream Books, and Bucket Shops* (Ithaca: Cornell University Press, 1990); George Sternlieb and James W. Hughes, *The Atlantic Gamble* (Cambridge: Harvard University Press, 1983); David Johnston, *Temples of Chance* (New York: Doubleday, 1992); John M. Findlay, *People of Chance* (New York: Oxford University Press, 1986); and Robert Goodman, *The Luck Business* (New York: Free Press, 1995).

11. Herald and Radin, *The Big Wheel,* pp. 124–25.

12. I. Nelson Rose, "Trends," *Indian Gaming,* June 1998, p. 6.

13. Michael M. Phillips, "As Economy Thrives, So Do Many Workers Accustomed to Poverty," *WSJ,* March 4, 1998, 1. See also *NYT,* December 13, 1997, 1.

14. On the "cruise to nowhere," see Kirk Johnson, "For Gamblers, Shortest Route to High Seas," *NYT,* December 14, 1996, 27; and Jonathan Rabinowitz, "Partners Plan Night Cruises for Gamblers," *NYT,* November 13, 1997, B1.

15. New York City, for instance, had only a little over 60,000 rooms in 1998 (source: PKF Consulting, Inc., hotel and real estate consulting firm, New York City). See also promotional material, Bellagio, courtesy of Jennifer D. Michaels, director of public relations, July 10, 1998; "Las Vegas: Are There No Limits?," *Washington Post National Weekly Edition,* February 10, 1997, p. 30;

and "Las Vegas Sees Its Growth Bubble Burst," *WSJ*, September 26, 1995, p. A2.

16. The phrase "islands of Indianness" appears in Charles F. Wilkinson, *American Indians, Time, and the Law* (New Haven: Yale University Press, 1987), p. 101; see also Frederick E. Hoxie, "From Prison to Homeland: The Cheyenne River Indian Reservation Before World War I," *South Dakota History* 10 (winter 1979), 1–24.

17. On big growth before 1990, see Bruce Johansen, *Life and Death in Mohawk Country* (Golden, Col.: North American Press, 1993), pp. xxviii–xxix: "by early 1985, approx. 80 of the nearly 300 recognized American Indian tribes in the US were conducting some sort of game of chance. By the fall of 1988, more than 100 tribes participated in some form of gambling, which grossed as much as $255 million yearly."

18. *Indian Country Today*, January 20–27, 1997, B2; on the Kotenai, *Indian Country Today*, Jan. 27–Feb. 3, 1997, B1; on the Grande Ronde, *Indian Country Today*, Jan. 27–Feb. 3, 1997, A1; on the Puyallup, *Indian Gaming*, May 5, 1997, 8–9, and August 1997, 20; on Foxwoods and Mohegan Sun, *Indian Gaming Business* (supplement to *International Gaming and Wagering Business*, spring 1998, 1–10.

19. Author's visit, May 1996.

20. Quoted in *International and Wagering Gaming Business*, September 1, 1995, 16:9, 12.

21. See David Melmar's columns in *Indian Country Today*, May 4, 1995, and October 5, 1995.

22. Author's visit to Spearfish Canyon, May 19–21, 1996; interview with Craig Lundsdorf, Forest Service ranger, Spearfish Canyon, U.S. Park Service headquarters, South Dakota, May 20, 1996; interview with David Melmar, columnist for *Indian Country Today*, Rapid City, South Dakota, May 21, 1996; U.S. Forest Service, "Environmental Assessment, the Dunbar/U.S. Forest Service Proposed Land Exchange," Black Hills National Forest, Lawrence County, South Dakota; and "Decision Notice and Findings of No Significant Impact, the Dunbar, Inc., Land Exchange," September 28, 1995, USDA Forest Service (courtesy of C. Lundsdorf). Tourism was often on the minds of Forest Ser-

vice officials, which explains why the Service saw much merit in Costner's dreams. Not only did they believe that the "current non-federal tract in Spearfish would contribute to sightseeing and dispersed recreation in the Canyon," but they also were certain that the Dunbar would aid even more in reinforcing and expanding "the tourism/recreation industry in Lawrence County."

23. "The Dunbar," brochure (courtesy, office of the Dunbar, Deadwood, South Dakota), p. 1.

24. *Ibid.*, p. 4; phone interview with Dunbar management, February 26, 1997; and author's visit to site, May 21–22, 1996.

25. Phone interview with Larry Weiers, executive editor of *The Black Hills Pioneer* (Deadwood, South Dakota), September 1, 1998, March 6, 1997.

26. Phone interview with Paul Biederman, March 1, 1996.

27. For data on commercial airline growth, see Bureau of Transportation Statistics, *Transportation in Statistics Annual Report 1997* (Washington, D.C.: 1997), pp. 176–77; and Steven A. Morrison and Clifford Winston, *The Evolution of the Airline Industry* (Washington, D.C.: Brookings Institution, 1995), p. 7.

28. Between 1990 and 1995, according to government studies, there was a 17.7 percent rise in the number of people employed in this industry, while manufacturing *declined* by 4.5 percent, construction by 6.3 percent, and mining by 15.7 percent. See "Industry Facts," media kit, October 30–31, 1995, distributed by the USTTA, Washington, D.C.

29. South Dakota Labor Department, quoted in "Environmental Assessment. The Dunbar/U.S. Forest Service Proposed Land Exchange," Black Hills National Forest, July–Aug. 1995; January 31, 1996; and Craig Johnson (secretary of labor) to Elizabeth Estill (regional manager, U.S. Forest Service), June 13, 1995, correspondence. "Dunbar," wrote Johnson to Estill, "will . . . attract more year-round visitors," with the "net effect of reducing the seasonality of our visitor industry" (U.S. Forest Service Records, Spearfish Canyon).

30. The term "measured separatism" comes from Charles Wilkinson, *American Indians, Time, and the Law* (New Haven: Yale University, 1987), pp. 120–22. The whole movement toward renewed tribalism has been documented by Wilkinson, as well as by Edward

Lazarus, *Black Hills Justice* (New York: HarperCollins, 1991); and Fergus M. Bordewich, *Killing the White Man's Indian* (New York: Doubleday, 1996).

31. Richard White, "The Return of the Native," *New Republic,* July 8, 1996, 37.

32. Bordewich, *Killing the White Man's Indian,* p. 12. This order was followed by a remarkable body of state and federal laws, most noteworthy of which were: Nixon's 1972 restaffing of the Bureau of Indian Affairs entirely with Indians; Nixon's 1973 signing of the Menominee Restoration Act, which formally ended the termination policy of the government; the passage by Congress in 1975 of the Indian Self-Determination Act, which handed over many federal programs to the control of the tribes; and the 1978 Supreme Court decision *U.S. v. Wheeler,* which insisted that the "inherent sovereignty" of the tribes, forged hundreds of years ago, was an outcome of tribal history and never dependent on the states or on "grants from the U.S." In its own right, the *Wheeler* decision, by reviving the concept of the *inherent* sovereignty of the tribes, liberated a whole series of other court decisions that recognized, among other matters, tribal civil jurisdiction over non-Indians; the right of tribes to make their own laws and to be ruled by them; the right to tax, as sovereigns, anyone on their reservations; and the right not to be taxed or regulated by the states or federal government. See Wilkinson, *American Indians,* pp. 61–63; Bordewich, *Killing the White Man's Indian,* pp. 56–57; Nabokov, *Native American Testimony,* p. 75; and Laurence M. Hauptman and James D. Wherry, eds., *The Pequots of Southern New England* (Norman: University of Oklahoma Press, 1993).

33. Wilkinson, *American Indians,* p. 75.

34. For instance, Congress reestablished the "Cherokee Nation" in 1971; in 1983, Connecticut recognized the Pequots; and in March 1994, the California Legislature "acknowledged" all California's Indian nations as sovereign entities. On the Californian "nations," see Judy Zelio, "The Fat New Buffalo," *State Legislatures,* June 1994, 38; on the Cherokees, see Bordewich, 56; on the Pequots, see Hauptman and Wherry, 222.

35. Lazarus puts this well in *Black Hills Justice:* Beginning in the period 1967–70, "millions of Americans (mostly liberal) reindicted

themselves for the nation's old imperialism, its often brutal conquest of the Indians. They read of the poetry and beauty of the
old Indian ways, reproached themselves for what their ancestors
had destroyed, and warmly embraced the new Indians, the Indian
of Alcatraz, who defiantly promised a rebirth of native heritages
that many whites had feared extinct" (p. 293). This romance lived
in New Age cults, in white obsessions with sweat lodges and
Indian spirituality, and in white acceptance of practices by Indians, from race-based citizenship to extreme forms of body-
piercing, which most whites refused to tolerate in their own
behavior (at least up until very recently).

36. Nabokov, *Native American Testimony,* p. 383.
37. This discussion draws on Bordewich's excellent analysis (*Killing
the White Man's Indian,* pp. 170–71).
38. "Collectively, these actions," Bordewich has argued, "along with
similar legislation in many states, some of them requiring reburial
of any Indian remains in museum collections, represented the
clearest extension yet of the principle of tribal sovereignty into
the realm of American culture" (*Ibid.,* p. 171).
39. Johansen, *Life and Death in Mohawk Country,* p. xxiii.
40. On water and fishing rights, see Timothy Egan, "Indians of Puget
Sound Get Rights to Shellfish," *NYT,* January 1, 1995, A12.
41. National Indian Policy, "Reservation-Based Gambling," pp. 35–
38; and Lynn Montante, "An Imposition on Tribal Sovereignty:
The Indian Gaming Regulatory Act," *Daybreak Magazine* (winter,
1994), 18–22.
42. IGRA, however, may have been unnecessary as a spur to economic sovereignty, although many today argue that it was; as
Charles Wilkinson has indicated, long before 1986 "the tribes"
had "begun to take back their reservations." See his essay "Paradise Revised," in William E. Riebsame, general editor, *Atlas of
the New West* (New York: W.W. Norton, 1997), p. 33. Today a
huge advocacy system exists to plead for all "the Indian nations"
as one voice. This system has a national magazine called *Indian
Gaming;* it boasts full-time Washington lawyers; and it has lobbyists and organizations such as the National Indian Gaming Organization.
43. "A Battle Topped With Felt, Casino Mogul Helps Mohegans

Renew an Old Rivalry," *NYT,* August 5, 1996, B1; "Not the Last of This Tribe," *NYT,* March 24, 1994, B4; "Place Your Bets: A New Casino," *NYT,* December 11, 1996, B1; *International Gaming and Wagering News,* December 5, 1994, 53. On Lyle Berman, see "You Gotta Know When to Hold 'Em," *Business Week,* September 9, 1996, 69; "Roller-Coaster Ride of Stratosphere Corporation Is a Tale of Las Vegas," *WSJ,* October 29, 1996, 1, A10.

44. An essay could be written comparing the South African approach to tribal homelands with the American approach. Obviously the biggest difference was that Pretoria used tribalism to weaken the tribes and to strengthen the government, while in America, the government sought to revitalize tribalism as a way of strengthening the tribes. But there were obvious similarities. Both governments exploited or manipulated or bought into phony ideas about place—about culture, inheritance, the past—to achieve their ends, thus opening up opportunities, of course, for unscrupulous developers and other place-exploiters.

45. On the South African government's approach to the "tribal homelands," see Brian Lapping, *Apartheid: A History* (London: Grafton, 1986), pp. 106–8, 128–47; and George Fredrickson, *White Supremacy* (New York: Oxford University Press, 1981), pp. 240–46.

46. For an account of this history, see "Report of the Division of Gaming Enforcement to Casino Control Commission in the Matter of the Application of Sun International Hotels Limited For Plenary Qualification as a Holding Company of Casino Licensee Resorts International Hotel, Inc." (Trenton: New Jersey Casino Control Commission, September 2, 1997), 123–76. This document provides much information on Kerzner's casino dealings in South Africa.

47. "Let the Games Begin," *International Gaming and Wagering Business,* June 1998, S6. This restriction, however, did not mean that the new South Africa had turned away from gambling; on the contrary, by 1998 the country was awash in it, with the government granting licenses for forty new large casinos in that year alone. This country of 60 million people already had many casinos, plus a national lottery, slot operations, and many horse racing tracks.

48. *NYT,* March 24, 1994, B4; and *NYT,* August 5, 1996, B1–2, and December 11, 1996, B1.

49. "Report of the Division of Gaming Enforcement . . . ," 25–26, 45–46.

50. Quoted in Jonathan Rabinowitz, "South African Gets Approval for a Casino in New Jersey," *NYT,* October 23, 1997, B7.

51. Daniel Boorstin, *The Image: A Guide to Pseudo-Events in America* (New York: Vintage, 1987), pp. 91–93.

52. Lee Lescaze, "Strangers in Strange Lands" (book review), *WSJ,* March 27, 1996, A20.

53. Wallace Stegner, *Where the Bluebird Sings to the Lemonade Springs* (New York: Penguin Books, 1993), p. 81.

54. "Preserving A Heritage Via Beds and Barns," *NYT,* August 13, 1998, D1.

55. Indeed, most residents began to move out after 1970, when Las Vegas growth hit new levels; they sought to insulate themselves within a "culture of privacy"; and even as they depended on Las Vegas for their livelihoods, they turned their backs on it as a "community" worthy of their respect or care, looked with contempt on those who remained, and refused to pay taxes to maintain the schools, the roads, or the city infrastructure. See John Findlay, *People of Chance,* pp. 173–208.

56. Geoff Schumacher, "Urban Decay," *Las Vegas Sun,* May 24, 1997, p. 143.

57. Hunter Thompson, *Fear and Loathing in Las Vegas* (New York: Popular Library Edition, 1971).

58. Author's visit, May 23–24, 1997.

59. Author's visit, May 1997; and "Steve Wynn's Big Gamble," *The American Way,* November 15, 1997.

60. Author's visit, May 1997; and on the casinos' change in strategies (once they became publicly traded corporations), see Johnston, *Temples of Chance,* pp. 9–22; and John Mohawk, Review of *Temples of Chance, Daybreak* (spring 1993), 22.

61. Author's visit, November 24, 1995.

62. "Viejas Casino and Turf Club," *Indian Gaming,* September 1996, 4; "Economics Brings Rebirth for Native Americans," *Indian Gaming,* April 1997, 4; and *BusinessWeek,* September 9, 1996, 47.

63. Herbert Muschamp, "A Primal Phantasmogoria," *NYT,* October 21, 1996, C13, C15.

64. John Mohawk, "Last Words," *Akwe-kon's Journal of Indigenous Issues* (summer 1995), 64.

65. Tim Giago, "Notes from Indian Country," *Indian Country Today,* December 2–9, 1996, A4.

66. Letter to editor, *Indian Country Today,* August 10, 1995, A4. Doug George-Kenatiio, Mohawk leader and journalist, has repeatedly argued in his columns in the *Syracuse Herald American* that "commercial gambling runs contrary to the ancestral Iroquois laws," and its spread has "eclipsed [our] cultural survival and the effort to retain language and our indigenous spiritual rituals. Some [Indians] no longer cite our longstanding relationship with the earth or the valiant fight for religious freedom. . . . Our Iroquoian 'seventh generation' commandment has been swept aside by an entirely American attitude of 'get while the getting is good.' We never were a material people [and] we must return to the circle of our clans and families" (*Syracuse Herald American,* February 19, 1995, and May 14, 1995).

67. Transcript of interview, quoted in Robert W. Venables, ed., *The Six Nations of New York: The 1892 United States Extra Census Bulletin* (Ithaca: Cornell University Press, 1995), p. xix.

68. For an excellent account of this recent development and of the problems resulting from it, see "Sprawling Toward the Millennium," a six-part series published by *The New Day* (a newspaper serving the southeastern Connecticut towns of North Stonington, New London, and Norwich), May 18–23, 1997.

69. Phone interview with Charles Elias, selectman from North Stonington, August 18, 1997.

70. "Trains Proposed to Link to Foxwoods," *The New Day,* June 12, 1997, A1, A7.

71. Phone interview with Charles Elias.

72. See Wilkinson (*American Indians,* pp. 186–87), on the role anthropology has played in arming these kinds of "Indians" with philosophical material to justify these positions. "We shouldn't reject everything," said William Belvado, a Sioux leader who urged his tribe to embrace tourism as well new technologies, scientific

advances, and new business methods (Bordewich), *Killing the White Man's Indian,* pp. 237–38. Men like Belvado might have agreed with Terry L. Anderson, free-market thinker and journalist, who insisted in an influential essay in *Reason Magazine* that Indians, far from being communalists and nature "mystics," have historically been more capitalist than most Americans. Indians, Anderson said, have always defended "private property rights" against government intervention; and they have "encouraged investment and production in personal property as well." In the context of these arguments, then, gambling and tourism did not stand against but emerged out of Indian life, just as they did in the case of non-Indians (Anderson, "Dances with Myths," *Reason Magazine,* February 1997, 48–50).

73. Mark Marvel, "Gambling on the Reservations: What's Really at Stake," *Interview,* May 1994, 114; *Minnesota Gaming Directory,* 1994 edition; and David Segal, "Dances with Sharks," *Daybreak* (winter 1993), 21.

74. Julie Nicklin, "Casinos Bring Riches to Some Tribal Colleges, but Windfalls Are Rare," *Chronicle of Higher Education,* September 8, 1995, A54; and Angie Debo, *A History of the Indians of the United States* (Norman: University of Oklahoma Press, 1970), p. 373.

Jo Ann Jones, president of the Ho-Chunk Indians in Black River Falls, Wisconsin, echoed these themes in her testimony in defense of Indian gambling before the U.S. Senate. Thanks to gambling, she argued, we "have increased employment by 2,000 people in three years, and it is able to pay a good living wage" (see Segal, "Dances with Sharks," 21).

Such leaders, in fact, were confident that they could separate the cultural life of the tribes from economic life; in the classic American manner, they believed that the private spiritual world could flourish in a public setting that threatened to destroy it. Their aim, as Christopher Jocks, professor of Native American culture at Dartmouth, argues, has been to "put tourist and gambling operations somewhere on the margins and not at the heart of things" (phone interview, April 2, 1996). "We have made an attempt not to mix tribal culture with the business," insisted Keller George, spokesman for the Oneidas in upstate New York. (Keller

George quoted in Melissa Gedachian, "Oneida Nation: Keeping an Eye on the Sparrow," *Indian Gaming,* February 1996, 28.)

75. Quoted in Tim Johnson, "The Dealer's Edge," *Akwe-kon's Journal of Indigenous Issues* (summer 1995), 20.

76. Kathryn Harrison, chairperson of the Grand Ronde Indian tribe near Portland, Oregon, on the tribe's Spiritual Mountain casino, which has the distinction of having introduced high-stakes gambling to Oregon (quoted in *Indian Country Today,* Jan. 27–Feb. 3, 1997, B2).

77. Doug George-Kanetiio, columns for the *Syracuse Herald American,* February 19, 1995, and May 14, 1995.

78. On the Seneca referendum, see *Putnam Reporter Dispatch,* May 3, 1998, B1.

79. Interview with Elaine Quiver (Grey Eagle), Pine Ridge Reservation, May 21, 1997. This testimony can be found on pre-printed postcards mailed in May 1995 and used by many tribes to get their members to communicate their convictions to the Forest Service. See Archives of the U.S. Forest Service, Spearfish Canyon, South Dakota. The quote from Jesse Taken Alive was recorded by Forest Ranger Craig Lunsdorff, May 16, 1995, Lunsdorff's notes, U.S. Forest Service, Spearfish Canyon, South Dakota.

80. Wendell Berry, *Unsettling of America* (San Francisco: Sierra Club Books, 1977), pp. 3–4; John Collier, *From Every Zenith: A Memoir and Some Essays on Life and Thought* (Denver: Sage Books, 1963), pp. 15, 137; and Thoreau, "Walking," in Robert Finch and John Elder, eds., *The Norton Book of Nature Writing* (New York: W.W. Norton, 1990), p. 183.

81. See Bill Bradley, *Time Present, Time Past* (New York: Alfred A. Knopf, 1996), pp. 314–16; Lazarus, *Black Hills Justice,* pp. 319–20; and Bordewich, *Killing the White Man's Indian,* pp. 232–33.

82. Armstrong Wiggins, "Indian Rights and Environment," *Daybreak* (spring 1993), 3; Oren Lyons, "The Faith Keeper," interview with Bill Moyers, video (Public Affairs Television, 1991); N. Scott Momaday, *The Man Made of Words* (New York: St. Martin's Press, 1997), pp. 49–51, 111, 124.

83. For a fine analysis written in this spirit, see Donald Worster, "The Black Hills: Sacred or Profane?" in Worster, *Under Western Skies* (New York: Oxford University Press, 1992), pp. 106–53.

84. Edward Shils, *Tradition* (Chicago: University of Chicago Press, 1981), p. 326.

85. Anonymous speaker, circa 1990, quoted in Nabokov, *Native American Testimony*, p. 412.

4. EDUCATING FOR THE ROAD:
AMERICAN UNIVERSITIES IN A GLOBAL AGE

1. Clark Kerr, *The Uses of the University* (Cambridge: Harvard University Press, 1963, 1982), p. 86; Susan M. Fitzpatrick (program officer for the James S. McDonnell Foundation) and John T. Bruer (president of the McDonnell Foundation), "Science Funding and Private Philanthropy," editorial, *Science,* August 1997, 621.

2. Vance Packard, *A Nation of Strangers* (New York: David McKay and Co., 1972), p. 85.

3. Even universities in the South, hitherto immune, felt the impact of this trend; in 1970, the University of Georgia boasted an unprecedented 17 percent out-of-state enrollment. These figures come from *ibid.,* pp. 85–88.

4. Packard wrote in 1972 that "one unsettling result of this trend has been that hundreds of U.S. towns and villages are stripped of about half of all their young people in the 18–22 age bracket" (*ibid.,* p. 83).

5. *Ibid.,* pp. 88–90. Packard drew here on a study by David G. Brown, *The Mobile Professors,* commissioned in 1967 by the American Council on Education.

6. The South African writer Es'kia Mphahlele, who taught in the United States in the 1960s and early seventies before returning to his country in 1977, expressed dismay at this way of organizing academic life. "I got to learn, when I was in the United States," he observed, "that an academic can, if he likes, lose himself in intellectual pursuits, move only in the university community, and be insulated from the rest of the larger community out there. . . . I didn't want that to happen to me, so that my self-respect hung on the thin thread of long-distance commitment." See Mphahlele, "Africa in Exile," in Marc Robinson, ed., *Altogether Elsewhere* (New York: Harvest, 1994), p. 127.

7. Bill Bray, chief executive officer of a tribal corporation, quoted in *Chronicle of Higher Education,* July 11, 1997, B9.

8. On this diversity of schools, see Anne Matthews, *Bright College Years: Inside the American Campus Today* (New York: Simon and Schuster, 1997), pp. 63–65; Patrick Callan, "Stewards of Opportunity: America's Public Community Colleges," *Daedalus* (fall 1997), 95–112.

9. Sheldon Rothblatt, "The 'Place' of Knowledge in the American Academic Profession," *Daedalus* (fall 1997), 259, 245–65; see also Rothblatt, *The Modern University and Its Discontents* (Cambridge: Cambridge University Press, 1997), pp. 79–84.

10. "Every U.S. research university," said Rodney Nichols, CEO of the New York Academy of Sciences in 1993, "is a powerhouse, and more such campuses exist than a generation ago. For this growth Uncle Sam deserves much credit." See Nichols, "Federal Science Policy and Universities, in Jonathan Cole, ed., *The Research University in a Time of Discontent* (Baltimore: Johns Hopkins University Press, 1994), p. 273. By 1995 the government was supporting more than 60 percent of all research, a percentage leap that occurred principally during the Reagan years (see *Science,* vol. 270, October 6, 1995, 136). In 1973, funding was about $2 billion; in 1983, $5 billion; in 1988, $8 billion; and in 1993, more than $12 billion.

11. "For both NYU and Greenwich Village," NYU's president, L. Jay Oliva, said in 1993, "the days of working as isolated satellites are over." Quoted in Craig Smith, "Jay Oliva: Optimism Born of Experience," *Stern Business* (winter 1993), 12. For a thumbnail sketch of NYU, see Nathan Glazer's essay in Thomas Bender, ed., *The University and the City: From Medieval Origins to the Present* (New York: Oxford University Press, 1988).

12. Interview with Don Lotz, Port Authority of New York and New Jersey, March 27, 1998. On the value of an "ordinary" Las Vegas casino, see *Wall Street Journal* (hereafter *WSJ*), March 13, 1998, A3; and on the size of university endowments in 1997, see "Bullish Stock Market Pushes Endowments Up 21.9% in 1997, to More Than $150 Billion," *Chronicle of Higher Education,* February 20, 1998, A48. (For example, Harvard has a $10 billion endowment;

University of Texas, $6.7 billion; Yale, $5.7 billion; Princeton, $5 billion; Columbia, $3 billion; and so forth.)

13. Quoted in Matthews, *Bright College Years,* p. 106.

14. Eugene B. Skolnikoff, "Knowledge Without Boundaries," in Cole, *The Research University,* pp. 339–40.

15. "Columbia University in the City of New York," *The President's Report,* 1994–95, 40–42; and *ibid.,* 1995–96, 45–53.

16. *New York Times* (hereafter *NYT*), November 6, 1994, 4A, and March 1, 1994, B1; also "Experience Summer at the First Truly Global University," document distributed to the NYU Summer School, 1996, in author's possession.

17. Quoted in Karen Arenson, "At N.Y.U. a Global Strategy to Encourage Foreign Study and Travel," *NYT,* March 26, 1997, B11. In the 1982 postscript to his book, *The Uses of the University,* Clark Kerr argued that the research universities of today have changed little from those in the past. "The Harvard of 1982," he wrote, "is not all that different from the Harvard of 1963, or the Berkeley of 1982 from that of 1963" (p. 152). This can no longer be said, for, as this chapter shows, these universities have entered a new age.

18. The University of Phoenix is the best known of these institutions, but others have been mandated into existence by state legislatures. See Thomas Mitchell (vice chancellor, UCLA), "Border Crossings: Organizational Boundaries and Challenges to the American Professoriate," *Daedalus* (fall 1997), 265–92; Mitchell, "For Profit Higher Education Sees Booming Enrollments and Revenues," *Chronicle of Higher Education,* January 23, 1998, A36.

19. The bigger endowments, too, have in some fashion contributed to the breakdown of the walls separating universities from the market (and from the priorities set by the market). For the past five years, academic investment offices have invested in not only developed but also *emerging* global markets, thus linking their schools more than ever to the global economy. On investments in emerging markets, see "Universities Weigh the Risk and Rewards of Investing in 'Emerging Markets,'" *Chronicle of Higher Education,* March 13, 1998, A45. "Investing in emerging markets," the *Chronicle* reported, "was virtually unheard of just 15 years ago." In

another article, the same journal indicated that college investments in foreign markets had grown from 1.5 percent of the value
of endowments in 1988 to 9.5 percent of that value in 1996
("Ten Years after 'Black Monday,' Colleges Run with the Bulls,"
Chronicle of Higher Education, October 17, 1997, A44).

20. "Advanced Technology Program Proposal Preparation Kit" (U.S.
Department of Commerce, Technology Administration, November 1996), 1. This program has not gotten the public (or historical) scrutiny it deserves. On the long history of this relation, Paul
Gray, former president of MIT, has written that "no other country has had that capacity or linkage" (quoted in Norman Bowie,
ed., *The University-Business Partnerships* [Lanham, Md.: Rowman
and Littlefield, 1994], pp. 122–23). On the different patterns in
Germany, France, and so on, see Robert R. Locke, "Business
Education in Germany: Past Systems and Current Practice," *Busi-
ness History Review* 59 (summer 1985), 232–53; Locke, *End of the
Practical Man, Entrepreneurship and Higher Education* in *Germany,
France, and Great Britain, 1880–1942* (Greenwich, Conn.: JAI
Press, 1984). On the business phaseout of research labs, see Walter
Massey, "Uncertainties in the Changing Academic Profession,"
Daedalus (fall 1997), 77; on the federal role, see David Noble,
"Technology Transfer at MIT: A Critical View," in Bowie, *The
University-Business Partnerships,* pp. 130–31; on state enthusiasm,
"States Compete to Recruit Top Scientists," *WSJ,* April 23,
1997, A2.

21. Rothblatt, "The 'Place' of Knowledge," p. 262. See also Rothblatt, *The Modern University and Its Discontents,* pp. 43–48.

22. Michael I. Luger and Harvey A. Goldstein, *Technology in the Garden: Research Parks and Regional Economic Development* (Chapel Hill:
University of North Carolina, 1991), pp. xv–xvii; Roger Geiger,
*Research and Relevant Knowledge, American Research Universities Since
World War II* (New York: Oxford, 1993), pp. 316–17; and, for
1997 numbers, see Peter Schmidt, "Engineering Complex at Virginia Commonwealth University Helps Lure Motorola," *Chronicle
of Higher Education,* June 6, 1997, p. A30.

23. On the character of this park, see Luger and Goldstein, *Technology
in the Garden,* pp 76–99; "A Staid Research Park Finds New Life

as a Cultivator of High-Tech Start-Ups," *WSJ,* August 16, 1996, B1; Therese R. Welter, "Pooling in the Park," *Industry Week,* April 4, 1988, 26, 28.

24. *Chronicle of Higher Education,* October 3, 1998, A41; "Engineering Complex at Virginia Commonwealth University Helps Lure Motorola," *Chronicle of Higher Education;* on the University of Connecticut, see *Hartford Courant,* March 6, 1998 (courtesy of Mark Prisloe, economist, Department of Economic and Community Development State of Connecticut); and on the University of Massachusetts, see *NYT,* January 21, 1998, A14.

25. Paul Selvin, "The Future University: Leaner and Meaner?" *Science,* October 6, 1995, 136. Recent articles on Monsanto include: "American Home, Monsanto Accord Won't Fill a Void," *WSJ,* June 4, 1998, B10; "Monsanto Tackles a Sceptical Public," *Marketing Week,* Sept. 4, 1997, 19–20.

26. It had the further outcome of inspiring the reinvention of that university in a way that suited the cost-effective passions of Monsanto. In the late 1990s, Richard Mahoney, former CEO of the firm, chaired the Finance Committee of the Board of Trustees of the Washington University School of Medicine. Under his leadership, the medical school slashed administrative expenses by many millions of dollars; it did this, in Mahoney's words, by "consolidating units" and by contracting "with outside companies to handle such things as purchasing, payroll, billing, and collection." "We are now making comparable changes in several of the academic departments," Mahoney wrote in a 1997 article for the *Chronicle of Higher Education* in which he also urged other universities to follow the Wash. U. model. "Hire outside contractors," he advised, not just in restaurants or bookstores (schools were already doing that) but in "any activity that is not at the heart of an institution's mission." Why not "buy out or phase out unproductive faculty members?" "Just think about the cost of 10 or 15 years of salary and support services for unproductive people." "Although a university is not a corporation," Mahoney also said, "I firmly believe that academic institutions can derive enormous benefit by applying lessons from the experience of Monsanto and other companies that have 'reinvented' themselves during the past decade" (Richard J. Mahoney, " 'Reinventing' the University:

Object Lessons from Big Business," *Chronicle of Higher Education,* October 17, 1997, B4–5).

27. *Chronicle of Higher Education,* December 19, 1997, A38; and Theodore Mitchell, "Border Crossings," *Daedalus* (fall 1997), 283–84. On Stanford's early history, see Luger and Goldstein, *Technology in the Garden,* pp. 122–53; Kerr, *The Uses of the University,* p. 89; and James Alley, "The Heart of Silicon Valley," *Fortune,* July 7, 1997, 66–74. For other university-business partnerships, see Bowie, *The University-Business Partnerships,* pp. 23–31, 107–42; Edwin Artzt, "Developing the Next Generation of Quality Leaders," *Quality Program,* October 1992, 25–27; and *Chronicle of Higher Education,* November 3, 1993, A27.

28. "How Stanford and Yamaha Cut an Unusual Technology Deal," *Chronicle of Higher Education,* August 7, 1998, pp. A36–38.

29. Stewart Brand, *The Media Lab: Inventing the Future at MIT* (New York: Viking, 1987), p. 6.

30. See Charle M. Vest, "Research Universities: Overextended, Underfocused, Overstressed, Underfunded," in Ronald G. Ehrenberg, ed., *The American University: National Treasure or Endangered Species?* (Ithaca: Cornell University Press, 1997), pp. 43, 46, 55. Just as Vest was making his charge about the decline in the "national will to excel," Peter V. Domenici, senator from New Mexico and expert on the budget, urged, in an editorial letter to *Science,* that "scientists" should "take note that total federal R&D spending increased by 1% (from $71.0 to $71.7 billion)." "Congress wrote these increases into law," he reported "while decreasing overall discretionary spending by 2.4%. Contrary to claims that Congress is threatening to turn the clock backward with the largest cuts in 15 years, Congress sets a high priority on science and backs it up with research dollars" (September 6, 1996, 1319). A month later, *Science* itself conceded that "the drastic cuts in federal R&D . . . failed to materialize" (October 18, 1996, 332). In May of 1997, moreover, the House of Representatives voted to increase 1998 spending for the National Science Foundation by 7.2 percent over what it spent the previous year (*Chronicle of Higher Education,* May 2, 1997, A38).

Finally, in 1998, the Clinton administration requested in its 1999 federal budget that Congress invest $14.47 billion in *academic* research and development, an increase of $838 million, or nearly 6 percent. The congressional leadership—above all, Newt Gingrich—backed this up. On the increase, see *Chronicle of Higher Education,* February 13, 1998, A38. See also, "New Budget Provides Life for Science," *Science News,* February 7, 1998, 87. ("Presidential adviser John H. Gibbons," *Science News* reported, "notes that the 1999 budget emphasizes the research component of R&D—welcome news to universities whose faculty pursue fundamental questions in science. Indeed, funding for basic research, both civilian and military, would increase 5.5 percent after inflation.")

31. Quoted in Mark Slouka, *War of the Worlds: Cyberspace and the High-Tech Assault on Reality* (New York: Basic Books, 1995), pp. 68–69.
32. Quoted in "MIT Media Lab Plans New Effort for Children," *Chronicle of Higher Education,* October 31, 1997, A39.
33. Michael Dertouzos, *What Will Be* (New York: Harper Edge, 1997), pp. 239–41, 282–83.
34. Paul Gray, quoted in Bowie, *The University-Business Partnerships,* pp. 122–23.
35. Bowie, *The University-Business Partnerships,* p. 132; and Brand, *The Media Lab,* p. 167.
36. Quoted in *Chronicle of Higher Education,* October 9, 1998, A56.
37. Rhoads Murphy, professor of history at the University of Michigan, in response to a 1995 curriculum retrenchment at U. of M. (in particular, the elimination of the geography department), in Selvin, "The Future University: Leaner and Meaner?" 135. For accounts of the growing relationship between business and the academy in its many incarnations, see "Louisiana Plans to Meld 50 Campuses into a Coherent 2-Year College System" (. . . "with business leaders given extraordinary influence to guide the effort") *Chronicle of Higher Education,* May 1, 1998, A40; "Increase in Number of Chairs Endowed by Corporations Prompts New Concerns," May 1, 1998, A51, A53; "Pacts Between Universities and Companies Worry Federal Officials," May 15, 1998; "Conflict-of-Interest Fears Rise as Universities Chase Industry Support," May 22, 1998, A41.

38. "Freshman Class Adds a New Meaning to the Term 'Diversity,'" *NYU Today,* January 20, 1992, 1.

39. Asian representation in freshman classes after 1995 was especially very high, although their number in the overall population was small (3 percent)—35 to 40 percent at Berkeley, nearly 50 percent at UCLA, 60 percent at Irvine, 20 percent at Harvard, 27 percent at Stanford, 25 percent at Columbia. See Chan-Liu Tien, "The Role of Asian Americans in Higher Education," speech delivered at City University of New York, May 5, 1995, excerpted in *Migration World* 23 (1995) 4: 14, 23–25; *Chronicle of Higher Education,* March 17, 1995, A26, December 14, 1994, A33; *Rochester Review,* Spring–Summer 1993, 9.

40. *NYT,* July 22, 1996, D7. On the assumed economic rewards of going to the best schools, see Gene Katz, "Sheepskins to Show Off," *Business Week,* April 25, 1996. On immigrant characteristics generally, see David S. North, *Soothing the Establishment: The Impact of Foreign-Born Scientists and Engineers on America* (New York: University Press of America, 1995).

41. Quoted in Matthews, *Bright College Years,* p. 33.

42. Officials quoted in *Chronicle of Higher Education,* October 9, 1998, A45; Richard Krasno (president of the Institute for International Education), quoted in *Chronicle of Higher Education,* December 6, 1996, A64; and Todd Davis (director of research for same institution and associate professor of "higher-education administration" [*sic*] at the University of North Texas), quoted in *Chronicle of Higher Education,* November 23, 1994, A38.

43. On declining enrollments, see David Riesman, *On Higher Education: The Academic Enterprise in an Era of Student Consumerism* (San Francisco: Jossey-Bass Publishers, 1980); Geiger, *Research and Relevant Knowledge,* pp. 309–11; and *NYT,* January 4, 1995, A17.

44. *Chronicle of Higher Education,* July 7, 1995, A41.

45. On recruitment, see *Chronicle of Higher Education,* September 25, 1998, A55; also *Open Doors, 1994–95: Report on International Educational Exchange* (New York: Institute of International Education, 1995), p. viii; and *Chronicle of Higher Education,* November 23, 1994, A38–39; and *ibid.,* Almanac Issue, August 28, 1998, 24.

46. At Harvard, in 1996, more than 400 foreign students got aid; see

Chronicle of Higher Education, June 13, 1997, A37. This article also mentions that Yale, Stanford, and Williams College, among others, did not give financial aid to foreigners. Nevertheless, the article also makes clear *how many institutions* offered such aid, not merely Harvard and MIT, but also many less prestigious colleges and universities.

47. North, *Soothing the Establishment,* pp. 12–14. On educated (East) Indians, Joel Kotkin (*Tribes* [New York: Random House, 1992]) has written that many left India because, among other things, they loathed the increasing Indian reliance on "special preferences for lower castes" as a means of righting historic wrongs (p. 106).

48. On growth overall, see *Chronicle of Higher Education,* November 21, 1997, A10–11; and December 12, 1997, A42.

49. For foreign nationals in the life sciences, see National Research Council, *Trends in th Early Careers of Life Scientists* (Washington, D.C.: National Academy Press, 1998), pp. 21–23, 31.

50. "There can be no argument," North has written in *Soothing the Establishment,* "that the foreign-born graduate students of science and engineering secure their graduate education largely at American expense" (p. 84). According to the testimony of Joel Snyder (professor at Polytechnic University in Brooklyn, New York, and a licensed professional engineer) before the U.S. Commission on Immigration Reform in 1995, both the foreigners and the universities benefited from this situation. The students got "a free tuition [between $7,500 and $12,000 yearly], which is something they could not normally afford." For its part, the university got "low-cost labor and an actual cash outlay that is nominal and an in-house book transfer, if you will, of the tuition, which is fairly substantial. So from the university standpoint, to have students willing to live at substandard conditions for free tuition is a tremendous boon because it gives them people to teach courses, to work with students at the lower levels, to teach laboratories and so forth." See "Report of the U.S. Commission on Immigration Reform," vol. II, transcript, 120.

51. Foreign students, fully aware of Uncle Sam's generosity, "go where they can get the most assistance," observed Hyaeweol Choi, in her study of Asian scholars, *An International Scientific Community: Asian Scholars in the United States* (Westport, Conn.:

Praeger, 1995). "From the early 1970s," an Indian-born scientist told Choi, "the U.S. opened up its doors to foreign students . . . [and for most Indian students] economic reasons" were the "particular reasons" for coming; "80.2 percent of all Indian students study abroad in the U.S." "In England," another Indian-born scientist explained to Choi, "they provided financial aid only to British citizens. I thought the United States was the most easily accessible country in getting a student visa and getting financial assistance." A Taiwanese-born full professor of science effused to Choi that "even when I was graduate student, my fellowship was so good" that "I saved money and sent some to my family in Taiwan" (pp. 16–43).

52. *Chronicle of Higher Education,* December 11, 1998, A18. Choi, *An International Scientific Community,* p. 131; David North, *Soothing the Establishment,* p. 70.

53. On the Association of American Universities, see Steven Muller (former president of Johns Hopkins University), "Presidential Leadership," in Cole, *The Research University in a Time of Discontent,* pp. 115–30. "The Association of American Universities," Muller said, "brings the presidents of major research universities together twice a year, and has been transformed from an organization whose primary activity consisted of free-wheeling discussion of common problems into a tightly organized, well-staffed, and relentlessly active lobbying organization."

54. *Chronicle of Higher Education,* December 11, 1998, A69. Madden, quoted in *Chronicle of Higher Education,* November 23, 1994, A40. On number of foreign faculty recruited, see, "Math Ph.D.s Add to Anti-Foreigner Wave," *WSJ,* September 4, 1996 A2; and Eric Weinstein (founder of the Pandora Science Policy Project), letter to *WSJ,* September 24, 1996.

55. Daniel Greenberg, quoted in North, *Soothing the Establishment,* p. 98.

56. The Commission on Professionals in Science and Technology, "Postdocs and Career Prospects: A Status Report" (printed and funded by the Alfred P. Sloan Foundation, June 1997), 5.

57. Lena Sun, "A High Price Tag on Foreign Professionals," *Washington Post,* July 10–16, 1995; "59,981 Scholars from Abroad Teach and Study in the U.S.," *Chronicle of Higher Education,* November

23, 1994, A40; "Number of Foreign Scholars in U.S. Continues to Drop," *Chronicle of Higher Education,* November 10, 1995, A38. This last article, however, indicated only a slight decline, with numbers actually "going up in California."

58. Phone interview, July 12, 1996. (Another group of native-born American scientists to emerge in this period was Boston's Pandora Science Policy Project, founded by Eric Weinstein, a math postdoc.)

59. For the percentage of American workers without college degrees, see Lawrence Mishel, Jared Bernstein, and John Schmitt, *The State of Working America 1998–99* (Ithaca: Cornell University Press, 1999), prepared by the Economic Policy Institute, Washington, D.C., p. 120.

60. Quoted in *Chronicle of Higher Education,* March 16, 1996. A52; for the Harvard quote, see *Chronicle of Higher Education,* June 13, 1997, A37.

61. *Chronicle of Higher Education,* November 23, 1994, A38.

62. See Lucie Cheng and Philip Q. Yang, "Global Interaction, Global Inequality, and Migration of the Highly Trained to the United States," *International Migration Review* 3 (Fall 1998): pp. 626–53. "The flow of professional, technical, and kindred workers (PTKS) to developed countries," these authors argue, "is an integral component of . . . the global restructuring process" (p. 626); the authors' article is built on this contention. Hyaeweol Choi writes in her *An International Scientific Community* that "a scholar's decision to migrate goes beyond an individual's choice for his or her well-being. It reflects factors embedded in the global economic and political systems, and patterns of migration change as the global economy changes" (p. 46).

63. William E. Kirwan, testimony before the Immigration Task Force and the Subcommittee on Immigration, Refugees, and International Law, Committee of the Judiciary, the House of Representatives, March 1, 1990. For similar statements made five years later, also in response to pending immigration reform, see Lena Sun, "A High Price Tag on Foreign Researchers"; and "Proposals Strike Fear at Universities," *Chronicle of Higher Education,* April 12, 1996.

64. In the life sciences over the last ten years, for instance, doctorates have been produced at a rate 2.5 times "the number of Ph.D.s needed to fill jobs that are currently available in academe," according to the National Research Council in a 1998 report. See National Research Council, *Trends in the Early Careers of Life Scientists,* p. 78. See also Alejandro Portes, "Introduction: Immigration and Its Aftermath," *International Migration Review* (winter 1994), pp. 632–61; North, *Soothing the Establishment,* pp. 121–59; "Foreign Influx in Science Found to Cut Americans' Participation," *Chronicle of Higher Education,* July 14, 1995, A33.

65. *Ibid.,* pp. 67–68. On the 60 percent of foreign nationals who stay in the country, see p. 24.

66. Paul Douglas, in preface to Walter Adams, ed., *The Brain Drain* (New York: Macmillan, 1968), pp. xii–xiii; Paul Douglas, *In the Fullness of Time* (New York: Harcourt Brace Jovanovich, Inc., 1971), pp. 66–84, 274–308.

67. *NYT,* May 24, 1991, in file, Office of Public Relations, Columbia University; also vita, same office. In the early nineties, Bhagwati worked as a key economic policy adviser to the General Agreement on Tariffs and Trade (GATT) in Geneva, striving to shape trade policy at the highest levels; in his words, he attempted to "insert scientific arguments for free trade" into the "economic analysis." For data on immigrant professionals, see Roger Sanjek, *The Future of Us All* (Ithaca: Cornell University Press, 1998), pp. 80–81.

68. Quoted by V. M. Dandekar in his essay, "India," in Adams, *The Brain Drain,* p. 225.

69. Jagdish Bhagwati and John Douglas Wilson, eds., *Income Taxation and International Mobility* (Cambridge; MIT Press, 1989), p. xiv; Jagdish Bhagwati and Martin Parrington, eds., *Taxing the Brain Drain* (New York: North-Holland Publishing Co., 1976), pp. 4–5.

70. Co-authored with Milind Rao, this piece appeared as "Foreign Students Spur U.S. Brain Gain," in *WSJ,* August 31, 1994, A12. Bhagwati republished it in his *Stream of Windows: Unsettling Reflections on Trade, Immigration, and Democracy* (Cambridge: MIT Press, 1998), pp. 353–72.

71. On the way India's relatively small elite still systematically exploits

the poor, see Peter Waldman, "For the Lowest Caste, Cleaning Toilets Remains Life's Work," *WSJ,* June 20, 1996, 1.

72. Adams, *The Brain Drain,* p. 227.

73. Professor Kumar (assistant professor of social science), quoted in Choi, *An International Scientific Community,* pp. 128–29. Universities have been unmatched in their sophistication regarding the laws, so much so that they have enlisted immigration lawyers to get the foreign faculty they desire. In 1996, for instance, the University of Chicago School of Business actually hired an immigration lawyer to "argue that the newly hired junior finance professor, Nicholas Barberis, a native of Britain, was a certified 'genius' who deserved a special visa from the U.S. government. The school won its case" (*BusinessWeek,* October 21, 1996, 126). Universities have also helped foreigners negotiate the thicket of regulations to become, in all due speed, American citizens. It is thanks to this expertise, so generously bestowed, that the U.S. Immigration and Naturalization Service has approved almost all applications for green cards from foreign scholars and faculty (see North, *Soothing the Establishment,* p. 65).

74. For an account of this growth, see "New Marketing Magnets: Student Unions," *WSJ,* March 3, 1997, B1.

75. Academia has, in recent years, become the country's biggest laboratory for the study of "prejudice" and "bigotry." Some scholars, of course, have grappled with these subjects with care and intelligence. But others have approached them as "viruses," invisible and lurking, or as things "intrinsic" to small-town life or to the very nature of all "backwater communities." An exemplary figure, who combines the lurking-virus approach with the small-town angle, is Raphael S. Ezekiel, senior research scientist at Harvard's School of Public Health (see his *The Racist Mind* [New York: Viking, 1995]). On campus "prejudice professionals," see "Breaking the Prejudice Habit; or, Can the Habit of Prejudice Be Broken?" *Chronicle of Higher Education,* October 27, 1995, A12; "A Tour of Prejudice," *Chronicle of Higher Education,* February 23, 1996, A41.

76. Recently, Michael Young, vice chancellor of student affairs at the University of California, Santa Barbara, officiated at that school's sixth annual "Queer Wedding," a public same-sex marriage cere-

mony that was held on campus and was attended by more than 200 people. "Gays and lesbians," he said, "they don't have their rights as heterosexuals. That's wrong, and as an ally I am a part of an effort to change that" (quoted in *Daily Nexus,* the student newspaper, April 28, 1997), 1. Andre McKenzie, student affairs officials at St. John's University, in New York, observed at a 1993 "diversity event" that "without residence halls," students will only "go back to the worlds they came from—where all the faces are the same" (author's notes, NYU Diversity Event, May 1993). According to David Finney, NYU's chief of admissions, NYU aimed to get Americans out of the "cornfield" into the wide-open spaces of the urban university. New York City, Finney said in 1997, "is a place where people go about living. You can't come out of quiet reflection in a cornfield for your years and know how to live a life" (quoted in *Chronicle of Higher Education,* September 26, 1997, A46). "If you can't have groups on the margin here, where can you have them?" said Roger W. Bowen, president of the State University of New York at New Paltz, who in the fall of 1997 had helped organize a conference at his university on such subjects as "Sex Toys for Women" and "Safe, Sane, and Consensual S&M: An Alternate Way of Loving" (quoted by Karen W. Arenson, "At SUNY, A Conference About Sex Is Criticized," *NYT,* November 7, 1997, B5).

77. Author's campus tour, May 1997.
78. Author's interview with Juergensmeyer, May 23, 1997, Santa Barbara, California.
79. See 1998 brochure, "Project on Cities and Urban Knowledges," NYU, International Center for Advanced Studies and 1998 fellowship announcement; Liz McMillen, "A New Cadre at Chicago," *Chronicle of Higher Education,* March 22, 1996, A10–11; and phone interview with Rashid Khalidi, director of the Center for International Studies, the University of Chicago, September 12, 1996.
80. John Cardinal Newman, *The Idea of a University* (1853, 1858; New York: Doubleday and Co., 1962), p. 149.
81. John Lukacs, *Confessions of an Original Sinner* (Boston: Ticknor and Fields, 1990), p. 149–50; for the quote from the Japanese and

Indian scholars, see Choi, *An International Scientific Community*, p. 50.

5. COSMOPOLITANISM AND THE ART OF MOPPING UP

1. Walter Capps, C–Span (coverage of Democratic National Convention, Chicago), August 24, 1996.
2. Robert Jay Lifton, *The Protean Self* (New York: Basic Books, 1993), pp. 230–32.
3. For literature on cosmopolitanism, see Friedrich Meinecke, *Cosmopolitanism and the National State* (Princeton: Princeton University Press, 1970; orig. pub. 1907); William H. McNeill, *The Rise of the West* (Chicago: University of Chicago Press, 1963, 1990); Thomas J. Schelereth, *The Cosmopolitan Ideal in Enlightenment Thought* (Notre Dame: University of Notre Dame Press, 1977); William Leach, *True Love and Perfect Union: The Feminist Reform of Sex and Society* (Basic Books, 1980, Wesleyan University Press, 1989), pp. 13–15, 337–46; Christopher Lasch, *True and Only Heaven* (New York: Norton, 1991), pp. 120–26; and Peter Riesenberg, *Citizenship in the Western Tradition* (Chapel Hill: University of North Carolina Press, 1992), pp. 52–55. For a more recent discussion of the subject, see Joshua Cohen, ed., *For Love of Country: Debating the Limits of Patriotism* (Boston: Beacon Press, 1996); and Pheng Cheah and Bruce Robbins, *Cosmopolitics: Thinking and Feeling Beyond the Nation* (Minneapolis: University of Minnesota Press, 1998).
4. William H. McNeill, *The Rise of the West*. See especially pp. xvi–xx and chapter 8, "The Rise of the West: Cosmopolitanism on a Global Scale 1850–1950 A.D.," pp. 726–92.
5. Daryl Pinckney, in Marc Robinson, ed., *Altogether Elsewhere* (San Diego: Harcourt Brace and Company, 1994), p. 28.
6. On the decline of Western dominance, see Samuel Huntington, *The Clash of Civilizations* (New York: Touchstone, 1997), pp. 51–53, 66–68.
7. Judith Lichtenberg, "National Boundaries and Moral Boundaries," in Peter G. Brown and Henry Shue, eds., *Boundaries: National Autonomy and Its Limits* (Totowa, N.J.: Rowman and Littlefield, 1981), pp. 79–100.

8. For these quotes, see Martha Nussbaum, in Cohen, *For Love of Country,* pp 3–17, 131–44; and Nussbaum, "Patriotism and Cosmopolitanism," *The Boston Review,* October–November 1994, 5, 3–6, 14.

9. For good critical discussions of multiculturalism, see James W. Ceaser, *Reconstructing America* (New Haven: Yale University Press, 1997), esp. chapter 5, "From Ethnology to Multiculturalism," pp. 106–35; and Stanley Fish, "Boutique Multiculturalism, or Why Liberals Are Incapable of Thinking About Hate Speech," *Critical Inquiry* (winter 1996), 378–95.

10. On early multiculturalism the best account is still Milton Gordon, *Assimilation in American Life* (New York: Oxford University Press, 1964). On the countercultural enthusiasm, see Charles Reich, *The Greening of America* (New York: Random House, 1970), a popular countercultural manifesto coming out of the sixties; in page after page, Reich praises all outsiders, insisting that youth link arms with them and suspend all "judgment" in regard to them. "Because there are no governing standards," he said, "no one is rejected" (210). "An individual cannot hope," moreover, "to achieve an independent consciousness unless he cultivates . . . the feeling of being an outsider. Only a person who feels himself to be an outsider is genuinely free of the rules and temptations of the Corporate State (210). . . . So the generation struggles to feel itself as outsiders, and it identifies with the blacks, with the poor, with Bonnie and Clyde, and with the losers of the world" (221).

11. In the early 1980s, Walzer was not so multicultural (indeed few people were in those days). See, for example, his informative "The Distribution of Membership," in Brown and Shue, *Boundaries,* pp. 7–9.

12. Michael Walzer, *What It Means to Be an American* (New York: Marsillio Press, 1992), pp. 13–15.

13. Here Walzer made arguments resembling those developed by the conservative multiculturalist Michael Novak who, in 1972, in *The Rise of the Unmeltable Ethnics,* claimed that "the new ethnic politics . . . asserts that *groups (sic)* can structure the rules and goals of procedures of American life. It asserts that individuals, if they do not wish to, do not have to 'melt.' They do not have to submit themselves to atomization" (New York: Macmillan, 1972), p. 318.

14. Walzer, *On Toleration,* p. 110.

15. Walzer, *What It Means to Be an American,* pp. 17–18.

16. Gary Gerstle, "Liberty, Coercion, and the Making of Americans," *Journal of American History,* September 1997, pp. 527–58.

17. To quote George Orwell in "Looking Back on the Spanish War," in his *Such, Such Were the Joys* (New York: Harcourt, Brace, and Company, 1945), pp. 141–42.

18. For a good exponent of these views, see Ishmael Reed, introduction, in Ishmael Reed, ed., *MultiAmerica: Essays on Cultural Wars and Cultural Peace* (New York: Viking, 1997), pp. xv–xxviii. All the quotes here come from Reed's essay. See also Gerstle, "Liberty, Coercion, and the Making of Americans," who also argues that immigrants were "coerced" into assimilation.

19. Quoted in *Chronicle of Higher Education,* February 9, 1994, B2.

20. As philosopher Philip Selznick has noted critically, for years the "fluid" watchword has been "contingency." See Selznick's insightful *The Moral Commonwealth* (Berkeley: University of California Press, 1992), p. 15.

21. On the Jewish contribution to modern academic cosmopolitanism, see David Hollinger, *Science, Jews, and Secular Culture* (Princeton: Princeton University Press, 1996), esp. chapter 2, "Jewish Intellectuals and the De-Christianization of American Public Culture in the Twentieth Century," pp. 17–42. For the liberal Protestant contribution to academic cosmopolitanism, see George M. Marsden, *The Soul of the American University: From Protestant Establishment to Established Nonbelief* (New York: Oxford University Press, 1994). Marsden demonstrates (brilliantly) that at nearly all the major universities, liberal Protestants, with their secular, pro-science point of view, had managed, after 1920, to marginalize competing religious adversaries as backward, bringing to the fore a non-Christian cosmopolitan point of view. By the 1950s most university managers came from this group. And, on social science's position on "place," see economic geographer John Agnew ("The Devaluation of Place in Social Science," in J. A. Agnew and James S. Duncan, eds., *The Power of Place: Bringing Together Geographical and Sociological Imaginations* [Boston: Unwin Hyman, 1989]), who has shown that most social scientists today still look at all place-rooted societies as provincial and backward,

while approaching larger "place-transcending" entities, such as national "communities" or states, as more civilized and enlightened. "Thus, has orthodox social science effectively and systematically devalued place as a concept relevant to our time," Agnew writes. "The association [of place] in the academic mind with localism and parochialism has become so rooted that the idea of place as a structuring . . . context for social relations seems strange and out of temper with the national-society focus of most contemporary social science" (pp. 9–11). On the same pattern, see Michael Sandel, *Liberalism and Its Critics* (New York: New York University Press, 1984), pp. 142–43.

22. To see the connection between the countercultural age and this one, one need only read Robert Jay Lifton's *Boundaries* (New York: Vintage, 1970) written when he was forty-five, which in almost every way resembles the book he was to write twenty-five years later, *The Protean Man*. Here, too, Lifton invokes the "Protean man" as the wonderful new figure, the man "who breaks down boundaries, the walls" (p. xii). In the late sixties, Lifton sees a big trend toward "fluidity . . . emerging everywhere" (pp. 39, 99–100). "What this means is that more and more people are at last blurring perceptions of where self begins and ends." A new "polymorphous style" now stands poised against the "anti-Protean fixities," "the simple purities," "the absolutized boundaries of 'law and order,'" the "narrow nationalism" and "personal rectitude" of the past (pp. 112–13). *Boundaries* not only prefigured *Protean Man,* but it *is* that book in almost all essential respects.

Out of the 1960s, moreover, came hybrids of fluidity, major thinkers such as Harvey Cox, liberal Protestant theologian at the Harvard Divinity School whose widely read 1965 book, *The Secular City* (New York: Collier Books, 1965, 1996), blended countercultural thought with secular religiosity. Writing at a time of race riots, when many whites were fleeing the major cities, Cox stated—sincerely—that "mobility is always the weapon of the underdog. The desire to combat mobility, to encourage residential and occupational *im*mobility, is a romantic distortion which springs from a reactionary mentality." Self-inventing "people on the move spatially," he said, "are usually on the move intellectually, financially, or psychologically." Cox also claimed that place-based thinking was not even religious; he argued instead that Christianity was indebted to "rootlessness," that "Yahweh was a nomad," and that Jesus was "mobile" and "despatialized." "An advanced industrial society," he also said, "strangles without mobility. People must be ready to move. Only during the miserable Middle Ages did Christianity undergo a 'fatal respatialization'" (pp. 45–51).

23. David Thelen, *Chronicle of Higher Education,* July 28, 1993, A44.

24. José David Saldívar, *Border Matters, Remapping American Cultural Studies* (Berkeley: University of California Press, 1997), p. 9.

25. Mary Ellen Wolf, "Out of Frame: Border(line) Images," *Critical Inquiry* (winter 1997), 494–508.

26. Richard Sennett, *The Corrosion of Character* (New York: W. W. Norton, 1998). This book, whose arguments I mostly share, appeared too late (in October 1998) for me to incorporate completely into my own analysis.

27. *Ibid.,* pp. 30–31, 47, 85–87, 122, 133, 146–47.

28. Sennett does nothing in *The Corrosion of Character* to reconcile these opposing approaches to the same kind of behavior.

29. Richard Sennett, *The Conscience of the Eye* (New York: Alfred A. Knopf, 1990), pp. 28–30, 127–29, 136–37, 200–202, 225.

30. *Ibid.,* p. 197.

31. It should be noted that the notion that pond or wood edges are more intense, active, or social contradicts the modern ecological approach to edges and centers, which argues that ecosystems with weak (or destroyed) centers and active edges (where weeds, opportunist interlopers, and predators congregate) are destined to decline or die out. Today, scientists define the "edge effect" as "the *negative* influence of the habitat edge on interior conditions of habitat or on the species that use the interior habitat." It is the big central systems that contain the core of the rarest species; these species, in turn, abhor any disturbance; all edges disturb them. Moreover, while it is true that centers and edges often function fruitfully together, it is never true that edges are more "socially active," more "diverse," or more critical to the life of an eco-system than centers. See, for quotations, Gary Meffe and Ronald Carroll, *Principles of Conservation Biology* (Sunderland,

Mass.: Sinauer Associates Inc., 1994), chapter 9, "Habitat Fragmentation," pp. 237–64; and see also, John Terborgh, *Where Have All the Birds Gone: Essays on the Biology and Ecology of Birds* (Princeton: Princeton University Press, 1989). I would like to thank Alison Beall, curator of the Marshlands Conservancy, Westchester County, New York, for directing me to these sources.

32. Richard Sennett, *The Conscience of the Eye,* pp. 198–202. Other exponents of this position include Werner Sollors and Marjorie Garber. Sollors, Harvard professor of comparative literature who has written a history of "the mulatto," claims that "race" and "ethnicity" have no meaning any more, because they are fixed, inflexible categories; what does have meaning, he argues, is the "transethnic" and the "international": "The mulatto is the wave of the future" because he/she "reaches across national and racial boundaries." In the same vein, Marjorie Garber, also of Harvard, writing on gender, insists that the ideal model for gender behavior is the "transvestite" because he/she rejects "binary thinking," "violates boundaries," and experiments with the "space of possibility." See Werner Sollors, introduction to Sollors, ed., *The Invention of Ethnicity* (New York: Oxford University Press, 1989), pp. x–xx; and Marjorie Garber, *Vested Interests: Cross-Dressing and Cultural Anxiety* (New York: Harper Perennial, 1992), pp. 9–11.

33. David Hollinger, *Postethnic America* (New York: Basic Books, 1995), pp. 4–5. Hollinger, however, is concerned about the direction of this kind of thinking; his views are more complex than those presented by Sennett, Gerstle, and even Walzer. In a piece in the *Journal of American History* (actually a response to an essay by Gerstle) he recognized the necessity of nation-building, warned of the excesses in the multicultural argument, and insisted that "Americans had a shared history." Hollinger encouraged some kind of immigration restriction and—as he did in *Postethnic America*—condemned "ethnoracial" groupism; he also pointed to irresponsible "global capitalism" and "diasporic consciousness" as the key threats to "national community." Still, it seems to me, Hollinger does not do enough justice to the concept of place.

34. For similar views, see Maurizio Viroli (associate professor of politics at Princeton), *For Love of Country: An Essay on Patriotism and*

Nationalism (Oxford: Clarendon Press, 1995), pp. 2–9, 13, 164–79; and Kwame Anthony Appiah, "Cosmopolitan Patriots," *Critical Inquiry* (spring 1997), 316–39.

35. Richard Sennett, "Something in the City: The Spectre of Uselessness and the Search for a Place in the World," *Times Literary Supplement* (London), September 22, 1995, 15.

36. Richard Sennett, *Boston Review of Books,* Oct.–Nov. 1994, 13.

37. Appiah, "Cosmopolitan Patriots," 624.

38. Quoted in Santayana, "The Philosophy of Travel," in Robinson, *Altogether Elsewhere,* p. 44.

39. Orlando Patterson, "Migration in Caribbean Societies: Socioeconomic and Symbolic Resource," in William H. McNeill and Ruth S. Adams, eds., *Human Migration* (Bloomington: Indiana University Press, 1978), pp. 106–45.

40. W. G. Sebald, *The Emigrants* (New York: New Directions, 1993), pp. 224, 116.

41. The modern "diaspora" is "celebrated," because "it flows from the free decision of individuals or of groups," Harvard professor Kwame Anthony Appiah has written (see his "Cosmopolitan Patriots").

42. Roger Cohen, authority on "diasporas," writes that "all scholars recognize that the Jewish tradition is at the heart of any definition of the concept. Yet if it is necessary to take full account of this tradition, it is also necessary to transcend it." One reason "is that the word diaspora is now being used, whether purists like it or not, in a variety of new, but interesting and suggestive contexts" (Cohen, *Global Diasporas* [Seattle: University of Washington Press, 1997], p. 21). Even as the Jewish diaspora itself has shrunk in size (or perhaps *because* it has shrunk), more and more groups who had little or no right to it as a defining event, now claim that right. For an account of the shrinking of the European Jewish diaspora, see Bernard Wasserstein, *Vanishing Diaspora* (Cambridge: Harvard University Press, 1996), pp. 285–86.

The new approach to diaspora, with focus on virtually every human group "in motion," is immensely fashionable in the academy, so much so that the Ford Foundation has funnelled millions of dollars into studying it. According to the foundation, its program,

"Crossing Borders," supports efforts to understand "processes that are at once 'local' and 'global,' such as diaspora and migration. . . ." See *Chronicle of Higher Education,* May 2, 1997, A40; August 15, 1997, A29; and *Business* Week, May 12, 1997, 39.

43. People from many groups have described themselves as "diasporic," among them Haitians, Chinese, French-Canadians, West Indians, and Filipinos; even many Irish in this country dare to call themselves "diasporic." The Pequot Indians, who operate the Foxwoods Casino in Connecticut, describe themselves as "diasporic." See Laurence M. Hauptman and James D. Wherry, eds., *The Pequots in Southern New England* (Norman: University of Oklahoma Press, 1990), p. 78. The journal *Diaspora,* published at the University of Toronto (earlier at Wesleyan University in Middletown, Connecticut), has also contributed to the currency of this term. For more on the commonplace use of "diaspora" in a variety of literatures, see Gabriel Sheffer, "Ethnic Diasporas: A Threat to Their Hosts?" in Myron Weiner, ed., *International Migration and Security* (Boulder, Colo.: Westview Press, 1993), pp. 264–84. On the "Filipino diaspora," see Keith Richburg, "Becoming a 'Nation of Gypsies,'" *Washington Post National Weekly Edition,* November 13–19, 1995, 14; on the "French-Canadian diaspora," William Grimes, "A Quiet Power at the Library," *New York Times* (hereafter NYT), May 16, 1995, C1; on the "American diaspora" of American "senior executives" working abroad, Barry Newman, "The New Yank Abroad Is the 'Can-Do' Player in the Global Village," *Wall Street Journal* (hereafter WSJ), December 12, 1995, A1; on the "black diaspora," Erol Lewis, "To Turn on a Pivot: Writing African Americans into a History of Overlapping Diasporas," *American Historical Review,* June 1995, 765–81; on the "Chinese diaspora," see *Migration World* 23:4 (1995), 25; Aihwa Ong, "On the Edges of Empire: Flexible Citizenship Among Chinese in Diaspora," *Positions* 1:3, 745–78; and R. Waldinger and Y.-E. Tseng, "Divergent Diasporas: The Chinese Communities of New York and Los Angeles," in *Revue Européene Des Migrations Internationales* 8:3 (1992), 91–116. On the "Cuban diaspora," see Bishop Augustin A. Roman, "Cuban Ecclesial Reflection Communities in the Diaspora," *Migration World* 21:5 (1993), 27.

44. Arjun Appadurai, *Modernity at Large: Cultural Dimensions of Globalization* (Minneapolis: University of Minnesota Press, 1996), p. 158.

45. Other advocates include immigrants from the Caribbean and Africa. At NYU, for instance, a whole group of Third World scholars have come together at a new Africana Institute to examine the "thought and culture of the African diaspora." A Caribbean poet, Kamau Brathwaite, and a Kenyan novelist, Ngugi wa Thiong'o belong to this group; Manthia Diawara, a French-educated native of Mali with a doctorate from Indiana University, leads it. Diawara believes that "New York is fast replacing Paris as the center of the African diaspora." He wants to develop a "whole-world cultural, analysis approach," with the "diaspora" at the core, "revolving around black culture and black cosmopolitanism." See Manthia Diawara, "Building Africana Studies," *University* (NYU publication, winter 1996), 11–13; and Craig Smith, "Africana Studies Program, Afro-American Institute Establish Formal Collaboration," *NYU Today*, November 13, 1995, 1.

46. On these Indian scholars as "pacesetters" in the American academy, see Arif Dirlik, "The Postcolonial Aura: Third World Criticism in the Age of Global Capitalism" *Critical Inquiry* (winter 1994).

47. Dipesh Charakbarty, "Postcoloniality and the Artifice History," in Bill Ashcroft et al., eds. *The Postcolonial Studies Reader* (London and New York: Routledge, 1995), pp. 383–88.

   In *Rescuing History from the Nation,* Prasenjit Duara, professor of Asian history at the University of Chicago, presents a similarly grim critique of the "nation as the subject of History," which is, he argues, fashioned out of racist theories and determined by false conceptions of development. He sympathizes and identifies with the "subaltern" voices now struggling everywhere to "negotiate" the nation. "Nationalism," he writes, "is rarely the nationalism of the nation, but rather marks the site where different representations of the nation contest and negotiate with each other" (Duara, *Rescuing History from the Nation* [Chicago: University of Chicago Press, 1995], pp. 8–10).

48. See Appadurai, *Modernity at Large,* pp. 158–78; and, for back-

ground on Appadurai's antinationalism, see Bidyut Chakrabarty, *Subhas Chandra Bose and Middle-Class Radicalism: A Study in Indian Nationalism, 1928–1940* (New York and London: I.B. Tauris and Co., 1990), pp. 38, 21–37.

49. Phone interview with author, September 12, 1996.

50. Appadurai, "Patriotism and Its Futures," in his *Modernity at Large*. All the quotes in this discussion come from this essay.

51. This perspective has been adopted by urbanist Saskia Sassen in her *Globalization and Its Discontents* (New York: New Press, 1998). Sassen refers to the "unmooring of identities from what have been traditional sources of identity, such as the nation or the village. This unmooring in the process of identity formation engenders new notions of community, of membership, and of entitlement" (p. xxxii).

52. "A New Cadre at Chicago," *Chronicle of Higher Education,* March 22, 1996, pp. A10–A11.

53. *Ibid.,* 11.

54. Homi Bhabha, *The Location of Culture* (London: Routledge, 1994). The citations in this discussion come from this book. For a recent, updated (but essentially similar) analysis by Bhabha, see his "Editor's Introduction: Minority Maneuvers and Unsettled Negotiations," *Critical Inquiry* (spring 1997), 33. This essay reaches a level of abstract-theory-speak unrivaled, perhaps, by anyone in the academy.

55. Bhabha himself embraces the tragic status of the "migrant," thus offering himself as voice and architect of transnational culture. "I have lived the scattering of people," he reports, "that in other times and other places, in the nations of others, becomes a time of gathering." Bhabha has been influenced by kindred postcolonial writers such as Paul Gilroy and Stuart Hall, who have argued that "the future belongs to the impure" or that "all cultures are hybrid." Stuart Hall, quoted by Karen Winkler, "The Significance of Race," *Chronicle of Higher Education,* May 11, 1994, A10; see also Stuart Hall et al., eds., *Modernity and Its Futures* (London: Open University, 1992).

56. David Ricci, *The Transformation of American Politics, The New Washington, and the Rise of Think Tanks* (New Haven: Yale University, 1993), pp. 233–34.

57. Author's visit, August 1996. On Cato, see James A. Smith, *The Idea Brokers. Think Tanks and the Rise of the New Policy Elite* (New York: Free Press, 1991), pp. 206–21, 275–76; E. J. Dionne, *Why Americans Hate Politics* (New York: Simon and Schuster, 1991); and David Boaz (executive vice president, Cato Institute), *Libertarianism* (New York: Free Press, 1997). For the libertarian impact on Republican leadership, see Stephen Moore (Cato expert), ed., *Restoring the Dream: The Bold New Plan by House Republicans*, with foreword by Rep. Dick Armey (New York: Times Book, 1995); and Dick Armey, *The Freedom Revolution* (Washington, D.C.: Regnery Press, 1995). "The free market alone," says Armey, "entrusts each one of us with a leading role" (p. 63). The exemplary cosmopolitan libertarian magazine, published out of Los Angeles, is *Reason Magazine;* and see Virginia Postrel (editor), "Laissez Fear," April 1997, for standard line, pp. 4–5.

58. In a fall 1997 editorial, the *Wall Street Journal* attacked "universities and government" for having embraced multicultural "group" thinking and for "having been successfully intimidated by the diversity movement"; but no mention whatever was made of businesses, which have been at the forefront of the multicultural-diversity movement since the late 1980s, and have acted as its most influential advocates. For years, firms such as American Express and The St. Paul Companies have practiced diversity management for their workforce and multicultural marketing for their customers, aiming for complete "inclusiveness" and for bringing the "outsider inside." In the last three years, American Express has established more than fifteen "Diversity Learning Labs" throughout the company, to ensure that it "focuses on diverse segments in the African-American, Gay and Lesbian, Hispanic, and women's market." (Quoted in "Diversity—Making the Business Case," unpaginated advertising supplement, *BusinessWeek*, December 9, 1996.)

But this practice had become so common by 1995 as to excite little surprise: what was surprising was the extent and sophistication of it. In the fall of 1996, for instance, corporations from coast to coast organized to carry their "in-house" diversity agenda into the "community." In October, the CEOs of New Jersey's major corporations, retailers, and banks joined together, under the auspices of The Partnership for New Jersey, in the publication of a major full-page document in the *Wall Street Journal* called the "Declaration of Diversity." In its appearance it resembled the Declaration of Independence, bearing the same bold opening caption, the same sweeping phrases, and the same grouping of signatures at the bottom. Since 1987, these firms had practiced "in-house" diversity management; now, according to Richmond Rabinowitz, head of The Partnership for New Jersey, they had decided to carry their efforts into the community, realizing that "only there" would "real change" and a new mentality emerge.

"We the undersigned," it began, "believe" that everyone must "appreciate and celebrate the state's growing diversity." New Jerseyans, it said, must embrace the following *key* items: "acknowledge and respect differences"; "be sensitive to the many cultures in and beyond the workforces"; "avoid conduct that disadvantages any group"; and "encourage policies and practices that are truly inclusive." "When we strive in the workplace to reduce bigotry and prejudice, the effort to recognize the full potential of an increasingly diverse workforce begins to succeed." Richmond Rabinowitz, who wrote the document, culled the prose from the "in-house" diversity procedures of the firms themselves. The principal signers were the CEOs of Bell Atlantic, Kings Super Markets, Deloitte and Touche, Prudential Insurance Company, Johnson and Johnson, Merck and Co., and Poppe Tyson Advertising and Public Relations.

59. By the mid-1990s, American financial firms dominated world markets; seven out of the ten major "merger advisers" in 1996 were American, and "the top global underwriters" were American ("U.S. Financial Firms' Dominant Role in the World Markets," *WSJ*, January 5, 1996, 1).

60. Quoted in William C. Taylor and Alan M. Webber, *Going Global* (New York: Viking, 1996), p. 93; and, for biographical material, see Jason Zengerle, "Silicon Smoothies," *New Republic,* June 8, 1998, 21; and "The 'New Economy' and Its Biggest Fan," *BusinessWeek,* March 16, 1998, 29.

61. Walter Wriston, *The Twilight of Sovereignty: How the Information Revolution Is Transforming Our World* (New York: Charles Scrib-

ner's Sons, 1992), pp. 100, 61–62. For recent data on Citibank, see *WSJ,* December 29, 1997, A6, A8.

62. Quoted in "Diversity—Making the Business Case."

63. Quoted in Taylor and Webber, *Going Global,* p. 22. On Whirlpool's global expansion, see Chris Adams, "Hot Metal," *WSJ,* August 26, 1997, 1.

64. "Bellagio Fact Sheet," press release and promotional literature, Mirage Resorts public relations; Robert Goodman, *The Luck Business* (New York: Free Press, 1995), p. 58; and Sturges, quoted in *NYT,* March 24, 1994, B4.

65. George Murchinson, introduction, *Port of Long Beach 1996 Annual Report,* 1.

66. On the antiprovincialism of the Port Authority of New York and New Jersey, see Jameson Doig, "Regional Conflict in the New York Metropolis: The Legend of Robert Moses and the Power of the Port Authority," *Urban Studies* 27:2 (April 1990), 201–32.

67. The quote regarding these companies is from "Workers of the World," *The Economist,* November 1, 1997, 82.

68. From jacket blurb for Rosabeth Kanter's *World Class* (New York: Simon and Schuster, 1995).

69. Barde, quoted in "Diversity—Making the Business Case"; the Childs quote appears in "Global Diversity," unpaginated advertising supplement, *Business Week,* December 1, 1997.

70. "Celebrate Today, But Era Curbs Politicians' Sway," *WSJ,* November 11, 1996, A18; "Bob Dole and the Philistines," *WSJ,* June 15, 1996, A12; and "'No Guardrails': Values Debate a Tectonic Clash," April 15, 1993.

71. In 1997, Dow Jones ceased publishing *American Demographics;* the Cowell Company now publishes it.

72. Chip Walker and Elissa Moses, "The Age of Self-Navigation," *American Demographics,* September 1996, 36.

73. "Matters of Culture," *American Demographics,* September 1997, 24–29.

74. "The New Democrats Need to Sever Ties with Clinton," *WSJ,* December 7, 1994, editorial; "A Union's War on Workers," *WSJ,* December 9, 1997, A22, editorial; and "Catching the Third Wave," *Washington Post National Weekly Edition,* February 6–12, 1995.

75. Joel Kotkin, *Tribes: How Race, Religion, and Identity Determine Suc-*

cess in the New Global Economy (New York: Random House, 1993), pp. 3–4.

76. Kotkin, *Tribes,* pp. 5–13.

77. Kotkin, *Tribes,* p. 20.

78. "The Post-Mall World," *Los Angeles Times,* June 1, 1997, M1.

79. Rosabeth Kanter, *World Class: Thriving Locally in the Global Economy* (New York: Simon and Schuster, 1995); all quotes come from this book. For a more recent statement by Kanter along the same lines, see her "Good for Them and Us," NYT, May 12, 1998, A19.

80. John Lukacs, *Confessions of an Original Sinner* (New York: Ticknor and Fields, 1990), p. 195. Lukacs, in turn, was influenced by George Orwell's 1945 essay, "Notes on Nationalism" in Orwell, *Such, Such Were the Joys* (New York: Harcourt, Brace, and Company), pp. 71–97.

81. Arguments opposing this position abound, but see especially Michael Novak, *The Catholic Ethic and the Spirit of Capitalism* (New York: Free Press, 1993), and Tyler Cowen, *In Praise of Commercial Culture* (Cambridge: Harvard University Press, 1998). Both books are animated by a powerful, almost unquestioning faith in commercial capitalism.

82. Milton Gordon, *Assimilation in American Life* (New York: Oxford University Press, 1964), pp. 1–11.

CONCLUSION: VEBLEN REVISITED

1. For a defense of this position, see David Rothenberg, associate professor of philosophy at New Jersey Institute of Technology, "The Sounds of Global Change: Different Beats, New Ideas," *Chronicle of Higher Education,* June 5, 1998, B8. "Indian, African, Greek, Lebanese, Korean, Japanese—I've got my whole class hearing and singing songs from cultures that somehow fit together," says Rothenberg. "Sure, the world's developing, and no tradition will stay the same. But diverse musical strains need not fade away into one global monotone. If there is such a thing as development, it will include a joyful and chaotic mix of many sounds, as music plays on while no one knows how it's going to end."

2. William Trevor, *Excursions in the Real World* (New York: Penguin Books, 1993), p. xi; Alice James in Anna Robeson Burr, ed., *Alice James, Her Brothers, Her Journal* (New York: Dodd, Mead, and Company, 1934), p. 179.

3. Quoted in Madeleine David and David Wallbridge, eds., *Boundary and Space: An Introduction to the Work of D. W. Winnicott* (New York: Brunner/Mazel Publishers, 1990), p. 151. The term "indestructibility" is Winnicott's.

4. J. B. Jackson, *The Necessity for Ruins* (Amherst: University of Massachusetts Press, 1980), p. 115.

5. Josiah Royce, *Philosophy of Loyalty* (Nashville, Tenn.: Vanderbilt University Press, 1908, 1995), pp. 115–16.

6. The biographical material that follows here is taken from Joseph Dorfman's *Thorstein Veblen and His America* (New York: Viking Press, 1934), pp. 3–10. I have interpreted this material, however, in my own way.

7. Al. M. Bartel, "Thorstein B. Veblen, Homestead No Longer a Mystery," *Manitowac County Historical Society Newsletter* (March 1980), pp. 6–8.

Index

About the Author

William Leach is the author of two previous books, *True Love and Perfect Union: The Feminist Reform of Sex and Society* and *Land of Desire: Merchants, Power, and the Rise of a New American Culture,* which was a finalist for the National Book Award and won the 1993 Hoover Prize awarded by the Hoover Presidential Library. He has received fellowships from the Guggenheim Foundation, the National Endowment for the Humanities, and the Woodrow Wilson International Center for Scholars in Washington, D.C. He is currently at work on a study of butterflies. He lives in Carmel, New York.